Communications
in Computer and Information Science 1310

More information about this series at http://www.springer.com/series/7899

Schahram Dustdar (Ed.)

Service-Oriented Computing

14th Symposium and Summer School
on Service-Oriented Computing, SummerSOC 2020
Crete, Greece, September 13–19, 2020

 Springer

Editor
Schahram Dustdar ⓘ
Distributed Systems Group
Technische Universität Wien
Vienna, Austria

ISSN 1865-0929   ISSN 1865-0937   (electronic)
Communications in Computer and Information Science
ISBN 978-3-030-64845-9   ISBN 978-3-030-64846-6   (eBook)
https://doi.org/10.1007/978-3-030-64846-6

This Springer imprint is published by the registered company Springer Nature Switzerland AG
The registered company address is: Gewerbestrasse 11, 6330 Cham, Switzerland

Preface

The 14th advanced Summer School on Service Oriented Computing (SummerSoC 2020) continued a successful series of summer schools that started in 2007. As the COVID-19 pandemic did not allow traveling, the symposium of SummerSoC 2020 unfortunately had to be turned into a virtual event. SummerSoC is regularly attracting world-class experts in Service Oriented Computing (SOC) to present state-of-the-art research during a week-long program organized in several thematic tracks: IoT, formal methods for SOC, Cloud Computing, Data Science, Advanced Manufacturing, Software Architecture, Digital Humanities, Quantum Computing, and emerging topics. The advanced summer school is regularly attended by top researchers from academia and industry as well as by PhD and graduate students.

During the SummerSoC symposium original research contributions in the areas mentioned above were presented. All accepted contributions were submitted in advance and have been peer-reviewed in a single-blind review process. Most papers where reviewed by three reviews per paper, with an absolute minimum of two reviews per paper. Based on the reviews the program chairs accepted or rejected contributions. Out of 23 submitted contributions, only 11 were accepted with an acceptance rate of less than 50%. In addition, the contributions were extensively discussed after their presentation during the paper session. In addition to the reviewers comments, the feedback from this discussion was folded into the final version published in this special issue.

The volume is structured into four parts focusing on (i) IoT and cyber-physical systems, (ii) advanced application areas, (iii) cloud and edge, and (iv) service-based applications. The first article in the section IoT and cyber-physical systems provides an approach towards personalized recommendations in an IoT-driven tour guide platform. The next article introduces situation-aware updates for cyber-physical systems, followed by a vision, method, and architecture for an IoT beehive network for monitoring urban biodiversity. The section on advanced application areas provides three articles introducing data science approaches to quality control in manufacturing, a NISQ analyzer for automating the selection of quantum computers for quantum algorithms, as well as a concept and tooling for pattern views for interconnected pattern languages. The following section on cloud and edge investigates possibilities for protecting and hardening installable FaaS platforms, followed by a quantitative evaluation approach for edge orchestration strategies. Finally, the section on service-based applications provides a qualitative literature review on microservices identification approaches and introduces navigational support for non HATEOAS-compliant web-based APIs. The section, and journal, is concluded with an article on domain-driven service design; this last contribution received the SummerSoC Young Researcher Award sponsored by ICSOC.

October 2020

Schahram Dustdar

Organization

General Chairs

Schahram Dustdar	Technische Universität Wien, Austria
Frank Leymann	Universität Stuttgart, Germany

Organization Committee

Johanna Barzen	Universität Stuttgart, Germany
George Koutras	OpenIT, Greece
Themis Kutsuras	OpenIT, Greece

Steering Committee

Marco Aiello	Universität Stuttgart, Germany
Schahram Dustdar	Technische Universität Wien, Austria
Christoph Gröger	Bosch, Germany
Frank Hentschel	Universität zu Köln, Germany
Willem-Jan van Heuvel	Eindhoven University of Technology, The Netherlands
Rania Khalaf	IBM, Germany
Frank Leymann	Universität Stuttgart, Germany
Kostas Magoutis	University of Crete, Greece
Bernhard Mitschang	Universität Stuttgart, Germany
Dimitris Plexousakis	University of Crete, Greece
Wolfgang Reisig	Humboldt-Universität, Germany
Norbert Ritter	Universität Hamburg, Germany
Jakka Sairamesh	CapsicoHealth Inc., USA
Sanjiva Weerawarana	WSO2, Sri Lanka
Guido Wirtz	Universität Bamberg, Germany
Alfred Zimmermann	Hochschule Reutlingen, Germany

Program Committee

Marco Aiello	Universität Stuttgart, Germany
Johanna Barzen	Universität Stuttgart, Germany
Steffen Becker	Universität Stuttgart, Germany
Wolfgang Blochinger	Hochschule Reutlingen, Germany
Uwe Breitenbücher	Universität Stuttgart, Germany
Gerd Breiter	IBM, Germany
Antonio Brogi	Università di Pisa, Italy
Florian Daniel	Politecnico di Milano, Italy
Christian Decker	Hochschule Reutlingen, Germany

Stefan Dessloch	Technische Universität Kaiserslautern, Germany
Schahram Dustdar	Technische Universität Wien, Austria
Christoph Freytag	Humboldt-Universität, Germany
Frank Hentschel	Universität zu Köln, Germany
Melanie Herschel	Universität Stuttgart, Germany
Willem-Jan van Heuvel	Eindhoven University of Technology, The Netherlands
Dimka Karastoyanova	Rijksuniversiteit Groningen, The Netherlands
Christian Kohls	Technische Hochschule Köln, Germany
Eva Kühn	Technische Universität Wien, Austria
Ralf Küsters	Universität Stuttgart, Germany
Winfried Lamersdorf	Universität Hamburg, Germany
Frank Leymann	Universität Stuttgart, Germany
Kostas Magoutis	University of Crete, Greece
Bernhard Mitschang	Universität Stuttgart, Germany
Daniela Nicklas	Universität Bamberg, Germany
Florian Niedermann	McKinsey, Germany
Maria Papadopouli	University of Crete, Greece
Adrian Paschke	Freie Universität Berlin, Germany
Cesare Pautasso	University of Lugano, Switzerland
Ilia Petrov	Hochschule Reutlingen, Germany
René Reiners	Fraunhofer FIT, Germany
Wolfgang Reisig	Humboldt-Universität, Germany
Norbert Ritter	Universität Hamburg, Germany
Jakka Sairamesh	CapsicoHealth Inc., USA
Heiko Schuldt	Universität Basel, Switzerland
Holger Schwarz	Universität Stuttgart, Germany
Stefan Schulte	Technische Universität Wien, Austria
Ulf Schreier	Hochschule Furtwangen, Germany
Craig Sheridan	The University of Edinburgh, UK
Albrecht Stäbler	BigData4Biz, Germany
Damian Tamburri	Eindhoven University of Technology, The Netherlands
Massimo Villari	Università degli Studi di Messina, Italy
Stefan Wagner	Universität Stuttgart, Germany
Sanjiva Weerawarana	WSO2, Sri Lanka
Guido Wirtz	Universität Bamberg, Germany
Uwe Zdun	Universität Wien, Austria
Alfred Zimmermann	Hochschule Reutlingen, Germany
Olaf Zimmermann	Hochschule für Technik Rapperswil, Switzerland

Additional Reviewers

Martin Garriga	Michael Wurster
Pascal Hirmer	Tim Würtele
Indika Kumara	Daniel Vietz

Contents

IoT and Cyber-Physical Systems

Towards Personalized Recommendations in an IoT-Driven Tour
Guide Platform 3
*Margianna Arvaniti-Bofili, Stelios Gkouskos, Konstantinos Kalampokis,
Gerasimos Papaioannou, Georgios Gogolos, Ilias Chaldeakis, Konstantinos Petridis, and Kostas Magoutis*

Situation-Aware Updates for Cyber-Physical Systems 12
Kálmán Képes, Frank Leymann, and Michael Zimmermann

An IoT Beehive Network for Monitoring Urban Biodiversity:
Vision, Method, and Architecture 33
Mirella Sangiovanni, Gerard Schouten, and Willem-Jan van den Heuvel

Advanced Application Areas

Data Science Approaches to Quality Control in Manufacturing:
A Review of Problems, Challenges and Architecture 45
*Yannick Wilhelm, Ulf Schreier, Peter Reimann, Bernhard Mitschang,
and Holger Ziekow*

The NISQ Analyzer: Automating the Selection of Quantum Computers
for Quantum Algorithms 66
*Marie Salm, Johanna Barzen, Uwe Breitenbücher, Frank Leymann,
Benjamin Weder, and Karoline Wild*

Pattern Views: Concept and Tooling for Interconnected Pattern Languages. . . 86
*Manuela Weigold, Johanna Barzen, Uwe Breitenbücher,
Michael Falkenthal, Frank Leymann, and Karoline Wild*

Cloud and Edge

Investigating Possibilites for Protecting and Hardening Installable
FaaS Platforms 107
Mike Prechtl, Robin Lichtenthäler, and Guido Wirtz

A Quantitative Evaluation Approach for Edge Orchestration Strategies 127
Sebastian Böhm and Guido Wirtz

Service-Based Applications

A Qualitative Literature Review on Microservices
Identification Approaches. 151
    Christoph Schröer, Felix Kruse, and Jorge Marx Gómez

Navigational Support for Non HATEOAS-Compliant Web-Based APIs 169
    Sebastian Kotstein and Christian Decker

Domain-Driven Service Design. 189
    Stefan Kapferer and Olaf Zimmermann

Author Index 209

IoT and Cyber-Physical Systems

Towards Personalized Recommendations in an IoT-Driven Tour Guide Platform

Margianna Arvaniti-Bofili[1,2]([⊠]), Stelios Gkouskos[3],
Konstantinos Kalampokis[3], Gerasimos Papaioannou[3], Georgios Gogolos[3],
Ilias Chaldeakis[3], Konstantinos Petridis[3], and Kostas Magoutis[1,2]

[1] Computer Science Department, University of Crete, Heraklion, Greece
{margianna,magoutis}@csd.uoc.gr
[2] FORTH-ICS, Heraklion, Greece
[3] Terracom Informatics Ltd, Ioannina, Greece
{sgous,kokalabo}@terracom.gr

Abstract. In this paper we describe a system for personalized recommendations as part of a smart IoT-driven tour guide platform. The system builds user profiles out of historical localization information (movement of users in space within a museum) and indications of their interests, inferred through interaction with digital content, and time spent around exhibits. Users with similar movement style and interests are clustered together in order to provide useful personalized recommendations. The presented system leverages data-streaming technologies for online training and interactive response in coordination with a commercial IoT platform and mobile application. Our evaluation focuses on validating the profile-building and clustering parts of the platform using an experimental testbed that allows for testing under controlled conditions.

Keywords: Internet of Things · Personalized recommendations · Data stream processing

1 Introduction

We all visit museums or archaeological sites from time to time to appreciate culture, to learn, and to overall have a pleasant experience. However museums are usually large spaces that are hard to navigate, with the volume of exhibits and information available being overwhelming to the visitor. For this reason most museums today provide guided tours, traditionally via licensed staff, and more recently by offering electronic tour guides that help visitors navigate the space, often providing additional information about the exhibits. These tools are undoubtedly helpful to many visitors, but they are typically generic.

Supported by the Greek Research Technology Development and Innovation Action "RESEARCH - CREATE - INNOVATE", Operational Programme on Competitiveness, Entrepreneurship and Innovation (ΕΠΑνΕΚ) 2014–2020, Grant T1EΔK-04819.

S. Dustdar (Ed.): SummerSOC 2020, CCIS 1310, pp. 3–11, 2020.
https://doi.org/10.1007/978-3-030-64846-6_1

ProxiTour [3] is an IoT-driven platform for digital tours, whose aim is to create a more custom-made experience for the visitors. By collecting information produced in real time, such as the visitor's interaction with the space and the exhibits, ProxiTour aims to create on the fly a custom-made profile for each user. Based on that profile, which is updated during the visit, the platform can suggest exhibits and sights likely to interest the user, improving their experience.

ProxiTour relies on Bluetooth beacons embedded within places of interest (e.g. museums, historical sites) for localization and for correlating visitor location with exhibits. Visitors are tracked from the point they enter the space with their mobile device. Every time they come within range of a beacon, they receive recommended information (audio and visual) based on their position, nearby exhibits, and their movement pattern so far. In outdoor spaces, the GPS on mobile devices can also be used to track visitor location. The interaction of visitors with the provided digital content and their movements in space can be interpreted as indirect feedback for the recommendations, enabling adaption.

In this paper, we present a novel system for providing personalized recommendations within the context of a smart IoT-driven tour guide platform [3]. Our contributions in this paper are:

- Creation of user profiles, based on data collected in real time from a Bluetooth beacon-based localization service and from interaction with digital content through an end-user mobile application.
- Creating groups of user profiles with similar interests aiming to use such groups for recommendation purposes.
- An implementation, drawing information from state-of-the-art IoT technologies, for localization and data collection.
- Online analysis, using Spark Structured Streaming, to perform data analysis live (online), in a scalable manner.
- Experimental validation of the profile-building and clustering parts using a deployment of ProxiTour in a controlled physical environment.

The system aims to advance over standard approaches for e-guides that are either unaware of the history of users' movement in space and in relation to exhibits, or have very basic information about it, often requiring significant user involvement (such as manually browsing through digital content or scanning an NFC tag next to exhibits).

The paper is structured as follows. In Sect. 2 we discuss related work. In Sect. 3 we present the architecture and current implementation of the ProxiTour platform, including user and exhibit profiling, key drivers of recommendations. In Sect. 4 we present the evaluation and in Sect. 5 we conclude.

2   Related Work

The first approaches to e-guides were heavily based on user interaction, by having users either select exhibits from a provided list or scan NFC codes associated with specific exhibits. In both cases the user receives information about an exhibit, but at the expense of having to closely interact with the device for input. Such guides are usually based on generic pre-programmed tours that are stored in the device and are not fitted to the individual interests or touring style of the visitor.

More recent systems provide the ability to track visitors via Bluetooth beacons or video cameras. There has been significant work in the field of user tracking in museums [2], focusing on either providing information to the museum curators [7] or on providing recommendations to visitors by requiring them to provide extensive profile information or answer questions [6]. In our work, we take inspiration from techniques of the first approach [7], to build visitor profiles and leverage and extend work on recommendations [6] to improve the quality of the tours with implicit profile characteristics. ProxiTour, the personalized touring platform evaluated in this paper, was recently introduced by Chronarakis *et al.* [3]. Real-time processing of localization streams tracking museum visitors through video cameras was described by Stamatakis *et al.* [9]. Our work extends this previous research by applying profile building and analytics on historical information, creating the basis for personalized recommendations.

Recommendation systems are a broad and interesting field of study and the goal is to figure out the best subset of options for some particular user, based on their profile. They can help reduce "buyer's anxiety" when faced with overwhelming choices; in our case they can contribute to a more personalized experience for visitors. The three main approaches to this task are: collaborative filtering, content-based filtering, and hybrid filtering [1]. Collaborative filtering, the most commonly used and mature approach, groups users with similar tastes to make recommendations. The system constructs tables of similar items offline and then uses those tables to make online suggestions, based on the user's history. Content-based filtering predicts the user's interests, based solely on the current user and ignoring information collected from other users. Hybrid filtering combines two or more filtering techniques to increase the accuracy and performance of the system and overcome some of the issues inherent in each approach.

ProxiTour takes a hybrid approach combining collaborative and content-based filtering. It defines a level of similarity between exhibits based on user feedback, profiles, and expert input and uses that to compile a list of proposed exhibits. It then ranks the items in the list using our visitor's profile as a guide. The list is presented via the application, using direct and indirect feedback to evaluate the recommendations and fine-tune user models.

3   Architecture and Implementation

3.1   Proxitour Platform and Testbed Setup

Figure 1 shows the architecture and basic workflow of the ProxiTour platform evaluated in this paper. The platform supports a variety of mobile devices (phones, tablets, etc.) by which users interact with the beacons in the museum and the digital content. The devices communicate events over a RabbitMQ service to a commercial IoT platform, Zastel, whose main functions are the management of location services (beacons, GPS), dynamic data sharing and decision making, managing/monitoring beacons and administrative users and connecting with third party systems and applications through an API.

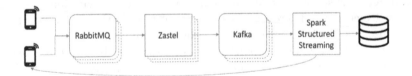

Fig. 1. Architecture and basic workflow

Relaying events between the IoT platform and a stream-processing service is Apache Kafka, a distributed messaging and streaming platform, used here for interoperability purposes. Spark Structured Streaming is a scalable and fault-tolerant stream processing engine, built on the Spark SQL engine [8] that we use to implement our applications (analytics on the messages produced by the mobile devices and recommendation lists for the tours). The results of the analysis sessions are stored (with the users' consent) in a MongoDB database, to be used in the future for training models or to help us initialize the profile of a visitor who used the app in the past. During a user's visit, the application will send recommendations, as push notifications to their device, through Zastel.

Figure 2 depicts the test space where we run our controlled experiments. Beacons have been set up in various locations/rooms and associated with certain thematic areas, exhibits, or people. In our evaluation, we examine test scenarios by having users emulate certain behavioral patterns. For more details regarding the architecture of the platform and the beacons used, we refer the reader to [3].

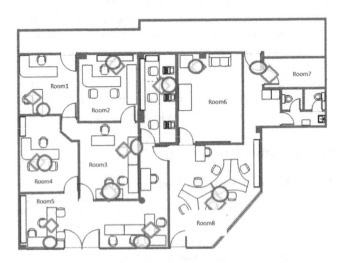

Fig. 2. Overview of experimental space used for controlled testing. Circles indicate the location of BLE beacons and diamonds the associated exhibits.

Next we describe the concepts and implementation underlying our recommendations system. In this paper, we focus on techniques to construct visitor and exhibit profiles based on the location tracking history of visitors.

3.2 Support for a Recommendations System

The first step towards any recommendation system is building a **profile for its users**. Initially, that profile is based solely on the general information provided by the user[1] (e.g. gender, age) and historical information known for the studied population (e.g. most popular exhibits). As specific users interact with the system and we see how they respond to the digital content and to the recommendations (they seem to follow them or not), the profile can be updated to enrich knowledge of their preferences (preferred exhibits, recommendations taken, etc.), which can lead to more customized suggestions.

In the beginning of the tour, we assume that the initial information about a user is a userID and their age category (e.g., 5–12 (primary school), 13–17 (high school), 18+ (adults), etc.) entered during registration. Users will be asked to enable Bluetooth and Location services on their mobile devices and be informed that without those features, users cannot be tracked and therefore recommendations will have to be based only on basic information and the general historical information collected from previous visitors. It is our expectation that the anticipation of richer content and better targeted (personalized) services, in conjunction with minimal privacy implications, will entice most users to enable the required support, as has been the case for online shopping and search services.

From the historical information, ProxiTour can create a list with the most popular exhibits based on direct and indirect feedback from the users. This leads to the creation of **profiles for exhibits** as well.

Assuming that a user allows location tracking, the tracked characteristics of the current tour can enrich the default content (e.g., the *top-K exhibits list*, typically the well-known exhibits in a museum's collection), with a list of the most interesting exhibits based on their profile (past visits and current tour track). The list of featured exhibits can be dynamically adapted based on the users' current location (e.g. room) and their interaction with the information on the application and the time they spent on each exhibit. If they spent a long time at an exhibit, they most likely found it intriguing, especially if they also interacted with the digital content that was served to them about the same exhibit. If the user visits some exhibits more than once that can also indicate increased interest in this category.

User Profiling: Our first objective is to create user profiles by processing localization information. We split the incoming stream of events into user-sessions, by userID.

Creation of user sessions works as follows: If a session is already open for this user it updates the information of the session. If a session for the user

---

[1] We assume GDPR-compliant processes involving explicit user consent.

does not exist, the application will look in the (stored) history to see if it has historical information for the user to initialize and link this session to, otherwise it will create a new clean session. Every new user profile contains only basic information, given at registration (e.g., ageCategory, language, gender, etc.). While the user moves through each room, we store information like the average time he spent near each exhibit, the categories of the exhibits he spent the most time on and the total amount of time spent in the room, current session duration and more.

There has been a lot of work in defining the best set of characteristics that define a museum visitor [4,5]. In addition to the more common ones described above, we chose to include the visitor's movement pattern. We were motivated by earlier work by Veron and Levasseur [10] who identified associations of the movement style of visitors moving through an art gallery space with general characteristics of the movement style of specific species, in particular ants, fish, grasshoppers, and butterflies: Visitors in the "ant" category tend to move close to the walls and the exhibits, follow the suggested route and study each exhibit carefully. "Fish" tend to move mostly in the empty space, in the center of the room and do not come very close to the exhibits, spending a short time on some. "Grasshoppers" tend to also move in the empty space, but approach the exhibits that interest them and spend more time studying them. "Butterflies" tend to move in and out of the empty space, not following the suggested route, observing almost all exhibits with varying time spent on each one.

These different types of movements can be good indicators of different visitor personality traits and levels of interest. For example, an "ant" is likely to visit most of the exhibits, so a guide should focus more on the type of digital information they enjoy. "Ants" are also more likely to give feedback. On the other hand, "grasshoppers" have clearer preferences, so we can give them more targeted content or direct them to more obscure exhibits matching their interests. "Fish" can have varying degrees of engagement, as can "butterflies", so we will need to handle them accordingly.

In ProxiTour, the movement pattern of each visitor is continuously analyzed to categorize them accordingly. Each user is eventually represented by a vector, containing the information summary of their profile.

Exhibit Profiling: Every exhibit is defined by an ID and is associated with a room. For every room and exhibit we have a list of keywords that are closely associated with them, as well as a list of information and audio-visual sources that are available to the visitors through their mobile device. We can use direct and indirect feedback from the user to "rate" the exhibits and get a sense of which of the additional information provided they find interesting.

Direct feedback can be as simple as having the user rate each item (e.g., on a scale of 1–5), but that can be annoying for users who will likely ignore it after a while. The indirect approach is less intrusive to the visitor's experience and they can focus solely on the tour; however, it requires them to have enabled the location tracking option on the mobile device (Bluetooth or GPS). We can store information about how long the user spent on each exhibit and use that as a metric of how interesting they found it, based on their overall attention span (avgExhibitVisit) and the time spent on it by other users. If the user chooses not to enable that option, we can still get some feedback, by checking which of the additional sources the visitor chose to open and for how long he kept them open. We assume that the longer they looked at an exhibit the more engaged they were with it.

4 Evaluation

In this work we use experimental data from the testbed depicted in Fig. 2 to validate the interoperability of the various components of the system, and to demonstrate that the created profiles can be used to differentiate the behavior of different users who move in the monitored space. The setup of Fig. 2 features 11 (hypothetical) exhibits and 11 beacons laid out in distances that would be typical of a museum environment. Users (project members) moving around the museum space test the beacons' functionalities and perform controlled experiments by emulating users with specific behavior patterns. The events of the resulting streams contain key-value pairs of collected information (e.g. longitude, latitude, timestamp, etc.).

Our preliminary tests demonstrate that the setup is functional and that ProxiTour can successfully track users moving about the experimental site. Thanks to the localization and exhibit information included in the messages, we can calculate for example, how long each user spends on each exhibit. The information we produce is used to enrich the profile of the user that evolves, as more information is collected.

The experiment involves 40 users (project members), moving about the test space and interacting with the exhibits in a predefined manner. Each user moves emulating one of the species-inspired behaviors we described in Sect. 3.2. If distinction of the patterns is possible, then recommendations should be customized to fit the pattern of behavior detected within each group. Our evaluation in this work focuses on the former aspect (detecting pattern of behavior and profile building); testing of the recommendation system itself is planned for an upcoming pilot with real users.

As discussed in Sect. 3.2, detecting a new user requires matching him/her to a category based on the basic initial information to start creating their personalized tour. Initially, basic categories are primarily split by age group. Each group will receive an initial recommendations list that consists of the top K exhibits for users in that age group (determined from historical data). This is a general choice that will likely be adapted during the visit.

The users are split equally, based on movements patterns, into four groups (ants, fish, grasshoppers, butterflies). During the visitor's tour we note how they move about the space. We create movement vectors for the users from one exhibit to the next and try to classify those in one of the four categories. We test, with an autoML approach, the performance of some very well known machine

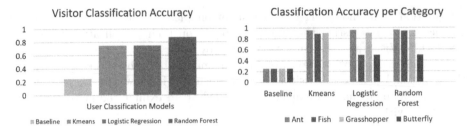

Fig. 3. (a) Visitor categories representation based on movement patterns (b) Accuracy of visitor's movement classification. (c) Breakdown of classification accuracy per category.

learning models (Logistic Regression, Random Forest, KMeans), using different configurations for each, in an effort to define the best classifier.

We compare the three best performing model configurations, with the random classifier that acts as our baseline. Each visitor, when entering the museum, has equal chance of belonging in each group (not entirely accurate, but for the purposes of this experiment we assume equal representation of each class). In Fig. 3-(b) we see that we can actually separate the users in the test space with high confidence. All three of the models perform much better than the baseline, with random forest performing the best.

However, we want to see which visitors troubled the models the most, in order to see if we can use other metrics to classify them. In Fig. 3-(c) we have a breakdown of performance of each model in correctly identifying each category. Baseline is trivial (25%). All three models have trouble identifying butterflies, since they can resemble either grasshoppers or more commonly fish. Their random movement in space can sometimes resemble other patterns, which confuses the models. KMeans does not recognise them at all, matching them to other cluster as extreme cases. Logistic Regression mixes them with fish, which makes sense if they moved in the empty space mostly. Random Forest performs the best, by only missing 50% of butterflies and classifying them as fish or grasshoppers, based on how close to the exhibits they went. We will reevaluate the classifiers when we run the pilot, but so far Random Forest seems to be performing the best.

Aside from the visitor's pattern of movement, we take into account other information as well. We calculate various statistics about the visitor's interests and their interaction with the content (preferred exhibit categories, etc.). In our recommendation system design we use the movement patterns and some other metrics to match the visitor with similar ones and then we create a list of possible exhibits they might like, based on the similar visitors and we filter that list down further using a vector describing the user's preferences.

As more historical data are available to train statistical models, it becomes possible to make more accurate decisions and to provide more meaningful suggestions. As the user moves from room to room we can detect how satisfied they are with our recommendations, by seeing if they follow them and if they are engaged with the additional materials. If recommendations are ignored or users appear to be very interested in other exhibit categories we can try to run the user through the model again and see if we can classify them better. This can be done periodically, on exiting a room or when we see that the user's interests deviate significantly from the recommendations. We have not evaluated this approach yet, since it requires real users to give feedback. However this is planned in an upcoming pilot experiment in a museum environment.

5 Conclusions

This paper describes current support for building user profiles and exhibit profiles via processing of localization and activity information/events collected by the ProxiTour IoT-enabled platform. Our experimental evaluation in a controlled testbed demonstrated that classification of users (key to effective personalized recommendations) is possible through an online stream-processing platform using ML libraries.

Future work on a larger scale pilot will study the effectiveness of recommendations and further investigate the potential of other ML techniques such as reinforcement learning to more aggressively explore the space of possible recommendations.

References

1. Bobadilla, J., Ortega, F., Hernando, A., Gutiérrez, A.: Recommender systems survey. J. Knowl.-Based Syst. (Elsevier) **46**, 109–132 (2013)
2. Cheverst, K., Davies, N., Mitchell, K., Friday, A., Efstratiou, C.: Developing a context-aware electronic tourist guide: some issues and experiences. In: Proceedings of ACM SIGCHI Human Factors in Computing Systems (CHI 2000), pp. 17–24 (2000)
3. Chronarakis, A., et al.: ProxiTour: a smart platform for personalized touring. In: Proceedings of 13th Symposium and Summer School on Service-Oriented Computing (SummerSOC'19); also IBM Technical Report RC25685. Hersonissos, Crete, Greece, 17–23 June 2019 (2019)
4. Dean, D.: Museum Exhibition Theory and Practice. Routledge, London (1994)
5. Hatala, M., Wakkary, R.: Ontology-based user modeling in an augmented audio reality system for museums. User Model. User-Adap. Inter. **15**, 339–380 (2005)
6. Huang, Y.M., Liu, C.H., Lee, C.Y.: Designing a personalized guide recommendation system to mitigate information overload in museum learning. Educ. Technol. Soc. **15**, 150–166 (2012)
7. Lanir, J., et al.: Visualizing museum visitors' behavior: where do they go and what do they do there? Pers. Ubiquit. Comput. **21**, 313–326 (2017)
8. Spark Structured Streaming. https://spark.apache.org/docs/latest/structured-streaming-programming-guide.html
9. Stamatakis, D., Grammenos, D., Magoutis, K.: Real-time analysis of localization data streams for ambient intelligence environments. In: Keyson, D.V., et al. (eds.) AmI 2011. LNCS, vol. 7040, pp. 92–97. Springer, Heidelberg (2011). https://doi.org/10.1007/978-3-642-25167-2_10
10. Veron, E., Levasseur, M.: Ethnographie de l'exposition, Paris, Bibliothèque Publique d'Information. Centre Georges Pompidou (1983)

Situation-Aware Updates
for Cyber-Physical Systems

Kálmán Képes$^{(\boxtimes)}$, Frank Leymann, and Michael Zimmermann

Institute of Architecture of Application Systems, University of Stuttgart,
Stuttgart, Germany
{kepes,leymann,zimmermann}@iaas.uni-stuttgart.de

Abstract. The growing trend of integrating software processes and
the physical world created new paradigms, such as, the Internet of
Things and Cyber-Physical Systems. However, as applications of these
paradigms are rolled out, the management of their software and hardware
components becomes a challenge, e.g., an update of a mobile system must
not only consider the software but also the surrounding context, such as,
internet connection, current position and speed, or users activities, and
therefore must be aware of their current context and situations when
executed. The timing of executing management tasks is crucial as the
surrounding state of the system and its context must hold long enough
to enable robust execution of management tasks. We propose an approach to model software updates in a Situation-Aware manner, enabling
to observe context, such as, time, environment, application state and
people, hence, enabling to execute update tasks at the right time and
in the right time-frame. We implemented our approach based on a train
scenario within the OpenTOSCA Ecosystem.

Keywords: Cyber-Physical Systems · Context-Aware Systems ·
TOSCA

1 Introduction

The trend of integrating the physical world with the so-called cyber world builds
upon integration of software and hardware components creating new paradigms,
such as the Internet of Things (IoT) [2] and the more general paradigm of Cyber-
Physical Systems (CPS) [17]. The wide range of applicable domains, such as
health care [19], mobility [18] and energy [1], enable the seamless integration
of digital and physical processes with our everyday life. These systems must
combine different types of components, starting from commodity hardware to
embedded devices, from off-the-shelve software components to specialized real-
time functions, e.g., embedded devices that control motors sending data to local
databases hosted on edge cloud resources, which are used to aggregate the data
before sending it further to the cloud. Maintenance of these heterogeneous components is a complex task, e.g., the exchange of complete components at runtime

S. Dustdar (Ed.): SummerSOC 2020, CCIS 1310, pp. 12–32, 2020.
https://doi.org/10.1007/978-3-030-64846-6_2

to achieve a system update. As every system can have its bugs it is crucial to enable updates in CPS, as errors that lead to faults within such a system can have severe safety issues in the real world possibly harming people or resources.

However, management processes that use or configure components must also consider the surrounding environment, i.e., its overall context must be regarded. For example, applying runtime updates of components effect their functional availability and may create severe safety issues in case of errors that can be caused by external environmental changes, such as, changing network connections or actions by people affecting the update process. Additionally, if a CPS should be as autonomous as possible the execution of updates should be started without the explicit affirmation by users every time an update is available. This autonomy can only be achieved if the management system of a CPS is aware of its context, and further, to enable a robust execution of updates, it is important to observe the current state in the context and apply these at the right time. Hence, such systems must be Context-Aware in nature [32]. To enable such an execution it is not only important to know how long a situation will be active in the application context, e.g., are all users absent from the CPS and don't use it, but also how long it takes to execute an update, e.g., how long applying a new firmware takes or how long it takes to restart a database. In summary, it is important to combine both views, how much time does an update have and how long does it take to enable the robust execution of an update.

Therefore, we propose an approach to enable the modeling and execution of management processes based on awareness of the context and worst-case execution time of the needed management tasks, enabling to determine when a system has a proper state and enough time to execute management processes. The main idea of our approach is to model the desired update with addition of specifying which components must be updated only when certain situations are active for enough time to update. Our approach builds on previous work within the DiStOpt project (successor of SitOPT) [23] that enabled to model Situation-Aware workflows, but did not consider the timing of Situation-Aware tasks, and therefore, was only reactive in nature, hence may turn applications not to be available at the right time again. One of the project goals of DiStOpt is decoupling high level knowledge from low level data and queries on top of the received data, and therefore, enable easier modeling of Situation-Aware workflows. The concept of Situation-Aware workflows is used in this paper and applied to updating CPS in a situation-aware manner to enable desired properties of safe and autonomous execution of management processes. Another work we build upon is to enable the generation of workflows from so-called declarative deployment models that only specify what should be deployed and not how. The generated processes from these models are able to install, configure and start software components in an fully automated manner [7], but not under given time constraints such as those given by the current context of a CPS. We extended and combined concepts of both previous works enabling the observation of time in context and execution, therefore, enabling proactive management of CPS.

This paper is structured as follows: In Sect. 2 we describe a motivating scenario and background information, in Sect. 3 we describe our approach, in Sect. 4 we describe our prototypical implementation and related work in Sect. 5, followed by a conclusion and future work in Sect. 6.

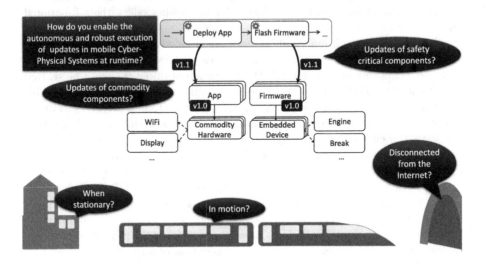

Fig. 1. Motivating example for Timing and Situation-Aware execution of updates.

2   Motivation and Background

In this section we describe a motivating scenario based on autonomous trains (see Subsect. 2.1) and give brief background information on CPS (see Subsect. 2.2), worst-case execution time (see Subsect. 2.3) and timed situations based on the DiStOPT project, successor of the SitOPT project (see Subsect. 2.4).

2.1   Motivating Scenario

Think about a mobile CPS such as trains consisting of heterogeneous components (see middle in Fig. 1), e.g., embedded devices that read sensor data and control actuators to enable safety-critical functions (see firmware hosted on embedded device in the middle of Fig. 1). On the other side, software for passengers, such as, multimedia services are running on commodity hardware (see app hosted on commodity hardware in the middle of Fig. 1). Each of the component types have different requirements when regarding updates. Updating such commodity components doesn't affect the availability of safety-relevant functions and updating these components could be done at any time when the needed update files are locally available. However, updating all of these components while passengers may want to use them, the availability of those services can be reduced and therefore reduce customer satisfaction. This issue is much more severe when regarding availability of safety-critical components running on embedded devices of the autonomous train. A failure when updating these components, such as a firmware that enables control of brakes and motors, has severe impact on the safety of CPS systems. To enable the automated and robust execution of runtime updates in such a scenario two challenges arise: (i) when do you start and (ii) how much time is left to execute updates before the system has to be available again. For example, in our scenario updating the end-user components should be achieved when those are not needed, i.e., are not actively used by passengers. In case of safety-critical components, the train should be in state where it is safe to execute the update, such as when the autonomous train has stopped at a station, i.e., the train is not in motion. Therefore the update system must know when components are not used and know how much time is left before the components are in use again. Depending on the components to be updated it is not sufficient to only determine the state of the software and hardware components to find a suitable time for update execution. As it is done in research for dynamic software updating [26] it is observing the so-called quiescence of components and executing updates only when the necessary components are not in use. In this field of research the quiescence of components was only observed in the context of applications itself without regarding the physical environment. To determine the perfect time to start an update the overall environment of the system must be observed as well, e.g., whether the train is stopped at a train station or somewhere outside on the tracks, or whether passengers are connected to the wireless network of a train wagon (see lower part of Fig. 1). In our train scenario the execution of software updates would be most sufficient when the train is at halt at a station and passengers are disconnected from the network components. Enabling a robust execution of an update in our scenario of autonomous trains means that updates should not disrupt the availability of the system when it is actually needed and be started without the need of human interaction. An update should be execute in a way that it is run at a time slot where the update can take place completely and successfully, e.g., when an update takes five minutes and the train is at a train station for at least the same time, it is safe to update.

2.2   CPS

In research and industry the trend of integrating the physical world and software emerged to paradigms such as the Internet of Things [2] or the more general paradigm of CPS[17]. The wide-range of application scenarios for CPS, such as, energy [34], health care [19] and mobility [18] implies the growing integration within our everyday lives. These applications build on heterogeneous hardware and software components such as embedded devices to commodity hardware or from off-the-shelve components to specialized software. As these components may be deployed and run within physical environments and interacting with users in a physical manner, CPS in cases can be seen as real-time systems executing (near-)real-time tasks that have deadlines on the execution of their functions to enable properties such as safety. These properties are crucial for CPS as missing deadlines may put people into danger, e.g., when an airbag of a car reacts to late. Therefore it is crucial that CPS are highly resilient to errors and do not create severe faults, hence, it is crucial to immediately apply (critical) updates of the heterogeneous CPS components to make the system more resilient over their lifetime. This also must be regarded when executing management tasks such as updates, as the execution of as such may have severe side effects as well.

2.3   Tasks and Their Worst-Case Execution Time

The timing of the update operations does not only depend on the duration a situation is active, but, the execution time of the operations as well, especially their worst-case execution time (WCET) [40]. This enables our approach to proactively decide whether to execute operations based on the currently active situations. However, determining the WCET of an operation is not trivial and in general not possible to calculate an exact value in modern systems, i.e., it is only possible to get approximations of the WCET [40]. But especially, in the case of CPS calculating the WCET is crucial, e.g., airbag control in cars or emergency braking in trains. The precision of a so-called WCET upper bound that specifies how long an operation will take at most depends on the underlying hardware. The closer the software is to the hardware the more precise a WCET bound can be calculated, which can be done by so-called static analysis or measurement-based approaches. While the static approaches calculate a WCET bound based on the source code and target hardware, the measurement-based approaches calculates upper bounds on previous executions of operations [40]. This problem of calculating upper WCET bounds gets more complicated in modern Cloud or Edge Computing scenarios, as the underlying hardware is visualized and heterogeneous, further complicating the problem getting proper WCET values. In our example, the most sensitive part to update is the firmware on the embedded device, as flashing the system disables safety-critical functionality and must not be aborted while executing. However, as firmware is the first software layer on top of embedded devices the WCET of flashing can be practically determined. Hence, the WCET of tasks that are sensitive and close to the hardware is easier to determine, and therefore, usable within our approach.

2.4   Timed Situations

The overall goal of our approach is to execute activities of a process at the right time, e.g., in our motivating scenario updates on safety-critical components should only be executed when the train is at a train station, while other software components may only be updated when passengers don't use them. Another important aspect is that the execution should be aborted as less as possible, in case of hardware, such as ECUs in trains or cars, retries of the flashing process reduces lifetime and may even make the hardware unusable when the flashing process fails [20]. Therefore, we extends our previous approaches on modeling situations within the SitOPT project [8,39], where a situation was defined as a state in the context of an object. To observe situations, context data from objects, such as, machines, software components or users are processed to calculate a particular situations state. We extended situations to give a guarantee on how long they are active, enabling to use the timing-aspect of situations directly while executing situation-aware tasks. These specify at runtime for how long a situation will be either active or inactive, hence, enable to proactively manage the execution of tasks. For example, if we know that the necessary situations are available for enough time, e.g., the train is stopped at a station and passengers don't use specific components for at least a minute, we can execute an update.

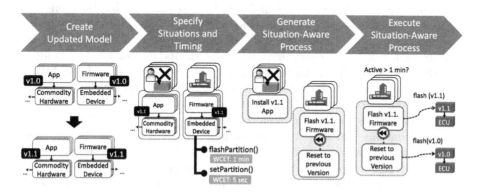

Fig. 2. Overview of the UPTIME method.

3 UPTIME - Update Management for Things in Motion and Environments

In this section we describe our concept to enable the situation-aware modeling and execution of software updates, based on our method called UPTIME (see Fig. 2) which is based on a so-called *Situation-Aware Deployment Metamodel* and *Time-Aware Situational Scopes* (see Subsect. 3.2). The first is used to model an update while the second is used to for situation-aware execution.

3.1 Overview

The main idea of the UPTIME method is to specify components and their exposed operations with the situations that must be active long enough in the current context of the application to execute such operations properly. The first step in the UPTIME method is to model the desired update from a source to a target deployment model, i.e., model the components and relations which shall be installed and configured in the running systems via deployment models (see first step in Fig. 2). In the second step the target deployment model is annotated with situations (see Subsect. 2.4) and the worst-case execution time (WCET, see Subsect. 2.3) of the available operations and their compensation operations. For example, in our scenario an operation to flash embedded devices, and also to compensate previously executed flash operations, is annotated with a WCET of one minute and the situation that a train shall be at a station, indicating that the update of a firmware should only be executed when the train is at a station for at least a minute at runtime (see on the right side in Fig. 2). In case of components used by passengers, we only specify the situation that no passenger is using these components. Both steps are based on the Situation-Aware Deployment Metamodel described in Subsect. 3.2 in detail. After specifying situations and execution times, in step three we generate an imperative deployment model, i.e., a process from the given source and target deployment models that contains activities using the operations of modeled components in an order to update the system (see Subsect. 3.3). The order of generated processes are derived by determining which components must be removed, updated or newly installed, and using the available management operations to achieve this. In addition, each annotated operation from the original declarative models which are needed within the generated process is added to a so-called Time-Aware Situational Scope. These scopes control the execution of these operations by observing the specified situations and therefore can calculate whether there is enough time to execute an operation according to its annotated WCET. The execution of operations in such scopes is only started when the proper situations are active for a duration that is enough to execute management tasks and possibly their compensation, i.e., revert already executed operations. This strategy enables to keep a system in a consistent state even if the execution of operations fail as a scope will start to compensate already executed update operations in time.

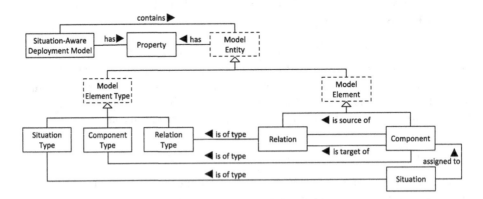

Fig. 3. Metamodel of Situation-Aware Deployment Models (SADM).

3.2   Situation-Aware Deployment and Process Metamodels

The Situation-Aware Deployment Metamodel (SADMM) enables to model the deployment of an application by specifying components, relations and situations. In our method the current state and updated state of an applications' configuration is modeled within two models of a SADMM. Fig. 3 gives an overview of the metamodel with our extension for situations, which will be presented in the following. An instance of a SADMM, a SADM, is a directed and weighted multigraph that represents structural configuration of an application under a set of situations, i.e., it represents components and relations that can be started and configured at runtime, however, only when the specified situations are active their exposed operations can be used. Let $\mathcal{M}$ be the set of all SADMs, then $d \in \mathcal{M}$ is defined as a tuple:

$$d = (C, R, S, CT, RT, ST, type, operation, sits, active)$$

The elements of the tuple d are defined as follows:

- C: The set of components in d. Each $c_i \in C$ represents an application component that should be configured and started.
- $R \subseteq C \times C$: The set of relations, whereby each $r_i = (c_i, c_j) \in R$ represents a relationship between two components: c_i is the source and c_j the target.
- S: The set of situations in d, whereby each $s_i \in S$ specifies a certain situation in the context of an application.
- CT: The set of component types whereby each $ct_i \in CT$ describes the semantics of components, e.g., it specifies that a component is firmware.
- RT: The set of relation types whereby each $rt_i \in RT$ describes the semantics of relations, e.g., it specifies whether a relation is used to model that a component is hosted on or connected to another.
- ST: The set of situation types whereby each $st_i \in ST$ describes the semantics of situations, e.g., it specifies that a situation is used to determine whether a train is moving.
- $type$: The mapping function, which assigns the component type, relation type and situation type to each component, relation and situation.
- $operation$: The mapping function, which assign operations to components via their type, therefore, the mapping $operation$ maps each $ct \in CT$ to a set of tuples $(id, wcet)$ where $id \in \Sigma^+$, with Σ being an alphabet and Σ^+ denoting all strings over Σ, and $wcet \in \mathbb{R}_{>0}$, specifying the available operations and their WCET.
- $sits$: The mapping function, which assigns each component in d its set of situations under which it is valid to be deployed. Therefore, $sits$ maps to each $c_i \in C$ a set $s_i \subseteq S \cup \epsilon$ where ϵ denotes that any situation is feasible, allowing that a component is always valid to be deployed.
- $active : S \times \mathbb{R}_{>0} \to \{true, false\}$, where $active(s, t) = true$ if and only if the situation s is active for the duration t.

To achieve the adaptation needed within our method, i.e., update from the current configuration to target configuration, different methods can be applied to determine an abstract process of needed activities to be used in executable languages. In the following we will define a meta model for such processes and so-called Time-Aware Situational Scopes (TASS).

Let a process G with a set of TASS be a directed and labeled graph represented by the tuple $G = (A, L, c, scopes)$.

- A is the set of activities. We separate A into $A_B \cup A_C = A$ where A_B is the set of activities implementing the desired deployment logic and A_C is the set of compensation activities.
- L defines the order of the control flow of process G and a control connector $l \in L$ is defined as a pair (s, t) where $s, t \in A_B$ specifies to execute the activity s before t.
- c is the mapping of activities to their compensation activities via $c : A_B \to A_C \cup \{NOP\}$, allowing activities to not have a compensation activity by using NOP.
- $scopes$ is the set of TASS in G (Fig. 4).

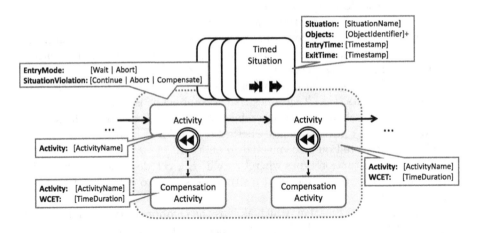

Fig. 4. Time-Aware Situational Scope.

We define a TASS $scope \in scopes$ to be an acyclic subgraph of G defined as $scope = (A_{scope}, L_{scope}, S, situations, active, guarantee, wcet_{duration})$ with the elements defined as the following:

- A_{scope}, L_{scope} is the subgraph of G spanned by A_{scope}
- S is the set of situations, whereby each $s_i \in S$ specifies a certain situation in the context of an application.
- $situations : A \to \mathcal{P}(S)$ is the mapping from A to S to indicate that activities may only be executed when all annotated situations are active.
- $active$ is the mapping $active : S \times \mathbb{R}_{>0} \to \{true, false\}$, where $active(s, d) = true$ if and only if the situation s is active for the duration d, analogous to those in a SADM.

- *guarantee* is the function to determine the minimal duration of a scope to be safely executed. We define it as $guarantee(A_{scope}) := min(\{d | a \in A_{scope} \land s \in situations(a) \land active(s, d) = true\})$, i.e., we search for the minimal duration all relevant situations are active.
- $wcet_{duration}$ is the mapping of activities to their WCET with $wcet_{duration} : A \rightarrow \mathbb{R}_{\geq 0} \cup \{\bot\}$ denoting the duration it takes for an activity to finish with its execution, or $wcet_{duration}(a) = \bot$ means that it has no duration defined.

In addition, a TASS must hold that $\forall a \in A_{scope} : wcet_{duration}(c(a)) \neq \bot$, i.e., all activities in a scope have a compensation activity with a WCET defined and $\exists a \in A_{scope} : situations(a) \neq \emptyset$ meaning that at least one activity of *scope* defines which situations of S must be regarded at runtime. From these definitions the WCET time of a *scope* can be calculated by finding a path $p = a_1 \rightsquigarrow .. \rightsquigarrow a_i \rightsquigarrow .. \rightsquigarrow a_n, a_i \in scope$ for which $\sum_1^n wcet_{duration}(a_i)$ is maximal, as the graph in *scope* is acyclic by definition. We define the set p^{max} to be the set of paths with the maximal WCET for a TASS. However, to enable the robust execution the most important aspect is that, even in case of errors, compensating already executed tasks must be achieved before the currently active situations are changing their state. Therefore it is important to know how much time the overall compensation can take, we need to calculate how much time the longest path of compensation activities takes to finish. In our model the compensation of activities is in reverse order of the actual tasks and therefore we must find a path $p_c = b_1 \rightsquigarrow .. \rightsquigarrow b_i \rightsquigarrow .. \rightsquigarrow b_m, b_i = c(a_i)$ for which $\sum_1^m wcet_{duration}(b_i)$ is maximal, analogous to the WCET for a set of activities in a *scope*. We define the set p_c^{max} to be the set of paths with the maximal WCET for the compensation activities of *scope*. Calculating how long a *scope* has time to execute the tasks or compensation is based on the time situations are active. After, finding the longest paths p^{max} and p_c^{max} inside a *scope* we take all situations $s_i \in situations(a), a \in A_{scope}$ and take the minimum guaranteed duration that the situations s_i are active, via $guarantee(A_{scope})$. The $guarantee(A_{scope})$ becomes the deadline for the execution of *scope*, which means to properly enter such a scope at runtime the compensation path $p_c \in p_c^{max}$ of scope must take less time to compensate as the situations have time to change their state, therefore, $\sum_{b \in p_c} wcet_{duration}(b) < guarantee(A_{scope})$. However, this just guarantees, that when the tasks themselves take to long they can be compensated in time, in addition, to give a better assurance that the task will actually be executed, we can check that $\sum_{a \in p} wcet_{duration}(a) + \sum_{b \in p_c} wcet_{duration}(b) < guarantee(A_{scope})$, stating that we have enough time to execute the provisioning tasks and are still able to compensate if any error may occur.

3.3 Generating Situation-Aware Processes

In Algorithm 1 we describe a simple method to generate such processes as directed and labeled graphs. It starts by first calculating the maximum common and deployable subgraph *mcs* between the current configuration *currentConf* and the target configuration *targetConf* (see line 2 in Algorithm 1). The set

---

Algorithm 1. createProcess($currentConf, targetConf \in \mathcal{M}$)

1: // Get maximum set of common components and ensure that it is deployable
2: $mcs := maxCommonAndDeployableSubgraph(currentConf, targetConf)$
3: // Find with mcs the components that have to be started or terminated
4: $toTerminate := currentConf \setminus mcs$
5: $toStart := targetConf \setminus mcs$
6: $A_B := \{\}, A_C := \{\}, L := \{\}, scopes := \{\}$
7: // For each component that will be terminated or started add a *terminate* or *start*
8: // task that will use its operations to terminate or start an instance
9: **for all** $c \in toTerminate$ **do**
10:     $A_B \leftarrow A_B \cup (c, terminate)$
11:     $A_C \leftarrow A_C \cup (c, start)$
12: **end for**
13: **for all** $c \in toStart$ **do**
14:     $A_B \leftarrow A_B \cup (c, start)$
15:     $A_C \leftarrow A_C \cup (c, terminate)$
16: **end for**
17: // Add control link based on relations between components
18: **for all** $r \in \{e|e \in \pi_2(currentConf)\} : \pi_1(r), \pi_2(r) \in toTerminate$ **do**
19:     $L \leftarrow L \cup ((\pi_1(r), terminate), (\pi_2(r), terminate))$
20: **end for**
21: **for all** $r \in \{e|e \in \pi_2(targetConf)\} : \pi_1(r), \pi_2(r) \in toStart$ **do**
22:     $L \leftarrow L \cup ((\pi_2(r), start), (\pi_1(r), start))$
23: **end for**
24: $termSinks := \{t \mid t \in A_B : \pi_2(t) = terminate \wedge \nexists e \in L : \pi_1(e) = t\}$
25: $startSources := \{t \mid t \in A_B : \pi_2(t) = start \wedge \nexists e \in L : \pi_2(e) = t\}$
26: // Connect the sinks and sources, termination tasks before start tasks
27: $L \leftarrow L \cup (e, r) : \forall t_1 \in termSinks, \forall t_2 \in startSources$
28: // For paths of activities with annotated compensation activities create a TASS
29: **for all** $p = a_1 \rightsquigarrow .. \rightsquigarrow a_i \rightsquigarrow .. \rightsquigarrow a_n, a_i \in A_B, c(a_i) \neq NOP, sits(c(a_i)) \neq \epsilon$ **do**
30:     $scopes \leftarrow scopes \cup (\{a_1, .., a_n\}, \{(a_1, a_2), .., (a_{n-1}, a_n)\},$
31:     $sits(a_1) \cup sits(c(a_1)) \cup sits(a_2) \cup sits(c(a_2))..,..)$
32: **end for**
33: **return** graph $(A_B \cup A_C, L, c, scopes)$

---

mcs contains all components between the two configurations which hold the following: if a component in mcs needs another to be used properly it must also be in mcs, e.g., a software component must be hosted on hardware component. To know which components we have to terminate to get to the target configuration, we calculate the component set $toRemove$ by removing mcs from the current configuration $currentConf$, because mcs contains components we can reuse (see line 4 in Algorithm 1). On the other hand, to know which components need to be started we create the set $toStart$, by removing all components in mcs from the set $targetConf$ as we only need to start components which are not in the set of reusable components mcs (see line 5 in Algorithm 1).

Afterwards *terminate* and *start* tasks for each of the sets $toTerminate$ and $toStart$ are created, respectively (see lines 9–16 in Algorithm 1), as well as for their compensation tasks. The ordering of *terminate* activities are to stop first source nodes (see lines 18–20 in Algorithm 1) and the *start* activities start with sink nodes of the graph (see lines 21–23 in Algorithm 1). Note that π_i selects the i-th component of a tuple. In other words, we update components from the 'bottom' of the graph, on the other hand termination tasks are executed in reversed order. We connect the termination and start activities so they are ordered with the goal that everything is terminated first and started after (see lines 24–27 in Algorithm 1) by connecting the sinks of termination tasks with the sources of start tasks. The last step of the algorithm is to add all TASS of the process by finding all paths for which there are compensation activities defined. In addition, all of the compensation activities of such a path must have annotated situations which must hold inside a TASS.

In summary, the main idea of our approach is to model and execute updates tasks based on combining the context of an application with the worst-case execution time of the used management tasks. This combination allows to execute tasks at runtime without the need to reduce the availability, as they can be executed when the overall system and its context are in a suitable state (Fig. 5).

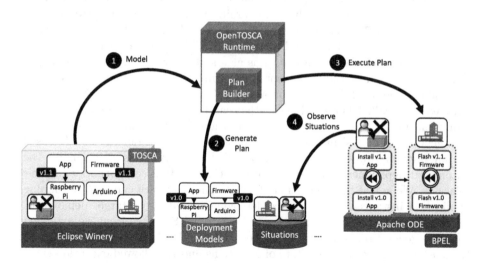

Fig. 5. Prototypical implementation within the OpenTOSCA ecosystem.

4   Prototypical Implementation and Discussion

In this section we describe our prototypical implementation. To validate the practical feasibility of our concepts, we used the deployment modeling language TOSCA [30] for the following reasons: (i) it provides a vendor- and technology-agnostic modeling language and (ii) it is ontologically extensible [4]. Further, for our prototype we extended the OpenTOSCA ecosystem [9][1] providing an open

---

[1] https://github.com/OpenTOSCA/container.

source TOSCA modeling and orchestration implementation. While the declarative modeling within the ecosystem is based on TOSCA, the imperative deployment models are generated and implemented in the workflow language BPEL [29] which use the specified operations of components.

To implement the first two steps of our proposed method we used the TOSCA modeling tool Eclipse Winery [25][2] and modeled a prototypical deployment model based on a Makeblock mBot[3] programmable robot consisting of an embedded device (i.e. an Arduino based mCore Control Board) and different sensors and actuators, such as, ultrasonic sensor or a motor. The robot was also connected to an attached Raspberry Pi 2[4] to enable to control the robot via WiFi by a software adapter that receives control messages via the MQTT protocol. To enable updates while the robot is in use we annotated to each component of the deployment model a situation. The Raspberry Pi represents the commodity hardware hosting software for users, therefore, the *Not in Use* situation is annotated, while the embedded device of the robot was annotated with a *At Station* situation, which where calculated by scripts implemented in Python. We measured the flashing times of the embedded device by the Raspberry Pi and annotated an WCET upper bound of 1 min for the flashing operation. Additionally, we used data by the Deutsche Bahn[5], the german railway, about the local metro, S-Bahn, from the year 2017. A simple analysis of the data delivered that the mean time a train is at a stop is 65.31 and median at 60.0 with a standard deviation of 41.87 s[6]. The minimal time a train was at a station was 60 s, while the longest was to be 101 min, therefore the worst-case time of 1 min of updating the robot is feasible. The WCET, situations and TASS specification annotations where mapped to so-called TOSCA Policies that can be used to specify non-functional requirements, e.g., as in our case, the situation-aware execution of operations. The generation of a situation-aware process in step 3 of our method is based on our previous work on generating so-called TOSCA Plans [7] to enable the automated deployment and configuration of application components and their relations. We added the generation of TOSCA Plans which can update running application instances from a source deployment model to a target deployment model. To implement our Time-Aware Situational Scope concept we extended the code generation according to Subsect. 4.1 to add the subscription to situations, evaluating the current state of situations and the allowed execution time. The generated process, i.e. TOSCA Plans, are implemented in the workflow language BPEL and executed on the compatible workflow engine Apache ODE, while the necessary data, such as TOSCA models, instance data, situations and operations execution time are stored within the OpenTOSCA TOSCA runtime.

---

[2] https://github.com/eclipse/winery.

[3] https://www.makeblock.com/mbot.

[4] https://www.raspberrypi.org/products/raspberry-pi-2-model-b/.

[5] https://data.deutschebahn.com/dataset/data-s-bahn-stuttgart-ris-archiv-daten.

[6] https://github.com/nyuuyn/sbahnstuttgart.

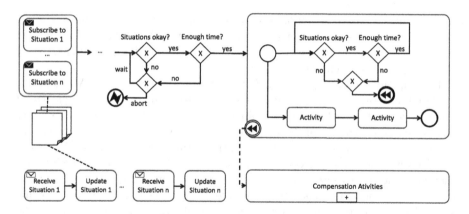

Fig. 6. Mapping TASS to BPMN to illustrate the mapping to BPEL.

4.1 Mapping to Standard-Compliant Process Languages

We implemented our concept of TASS within the OpenTOSCA Plan Builder that can generate imperative processes in the workflow language BPEL [29][7]. The Plan Builder is based on previous work [7] and was extended to enable generation processes able to adapt a running application instance to a new model it belongs to, hence, enable to model and execute updates. However, in the following we will describe a mapping of TASS to BPMN [31][8] which is depicted in Fig. 6, allowing a better understanding of the mapping as BPEL has no standardized graphical notation like BPMN. The mapping assumes that situations are available via a service, such as middlewares sharing context [24]. We used the Situation Recognition Layer from the SitOPT project which we integrated in previous work within OpenTOSCA, it was however extended to enable software components to write the entry- and exit times of situations, i.e., enabling to manipulate the data of how long situations are either active or not.

The general idea of mapping TASS to BPMN (see Fig. 6) is first to subscribe to all situations referenced in the process and, additionally, enable to receive notifications when they change and update internal situation variables. A concrete Time-Aware Situational Scope is added to a BPMN process as follows: At the beginning of the activities to execute, three gateways are used to check whether the situations are active at all and whether the time the situations are active is enough to execute the operations and compensation activities of the scope. If one of the conditions doesn't hold, the control flow either aborts the overall execution of the activities by throwing a fault, or starts a loop for the condition evaluation, depending whether the TASS has the *EntryMode* defined as *abort* or *wait*, respectively. When all of the conditions hold the first time they are evaluated, the activities specified within the TASS are executed according to the control flow. While these are executed, the conditions of the situations and the

---

7 http://docs.oasis-open.org/wsbpel/2.0/OS/wsbpel-v2.0-OS.html.

8 https://www.omg.org/spec/BPMN/2.0/.

available time is continuously monitored in parallel to the actual business logic, and if the conditions aren't met anymore or the business logic takes longer then the available time, the currently running tasks are aborted and compensated by the surrounding compensation handlers.

The implemented mapping to BPEL is almost analogous to BPMN and differs based on wrapping the business functions into their own BPEL *scope* (used as an equivalent to a BPMN in-line subprocess) activity which is added to a *flow* activity (enabling the graph-based ordering of activities) containing two *scope* activities which are used to check the situations state, just as in the BPMN mapping. However, instead of looping via control flow edges we wrap the situation observation activities into a *while* loop activity, as it is not allowed to model cycles in a *flow* activity. When the situations states are checked within the while loop and are found to be not valid anymore a fault will be raised that starts the compensation activities and therefore compensates already completed activities which were added in the generation phase of our approach.

5   Related Work

In the following we describe the related work of our approach, which are from dynamic software updating [26], Context-Aware Systems (CAS) [3,24], real-time systems/transactions [21] and runtime adaptation [38]. While the field of dynamic software updating tries to solve the problem of runtime updates, CAS enable applications to observe their environment to enable reactively or proactively change application behavior and structure, and real-time systems focus on the execution of tasks under timing constraints.

Kramer and Magee [26] present a model to enable Dynamic Software Changes, i.e., the execution of software updates at runtime. One part of the model is to detect a so-called *quiescent* state of software components, i.e., detect software components that are not used or do not affect the running application and its running transactions when updating. In a CPS observing only these types of components is not sufficient as CPS are integrated within physical environments consisting of software, hardware, people and other physical resources, which can create different kinds of errors that can have severe impact on the surrounding. Therefore, runtime update methods must include context information to determine a proper update state, and therefore be Context-Aware.

In the field of Context-Aware Systems the research goal is to enable applications to work contextually, i.e., adapt the behavior or structure according to their context. Context according to Dey [14] is every information that can describe the situation of an entity. To model context different modeling techniques can be used, such as, ontologies, markup or simple key-value models [5,6,36]. On top of these models middlewares can be used to distribute the current state of the context to the applications [3,24]. In research, context-aware systems were applied to multiple different fields, e.g. the Internet of Things [32]. However, most approaches lack the timing aspect in regards to context-aware deployment and management of applications [35]. One application on Context-Awareness to processes is presented by Bucchiarone et al. [10] to enable the runtime adaptation of business processes. The main parts of their method is a main business process containing abstract activities that are implemented at runtime by business process fragments that are added to the main process based on goals. These goals describe what a process or fragments can achieve at runtime and is therefore used to adapt the process to the desired goal of the overall business process. While the presented approach enables context-aware adaptation of processes, it doesn't handle aspects such as timing and therefore robust execution. This is the case in the work of Avenoğlu and Eren [?] as well. They combined a workflow engine with a Complex-Event Processing system to enable observing context. Another Context-Aware Workflow approach is presented by Choi et al. [12] that integrates context data into the workflows on top of the presented middleware, however, it misses the timing as well. Although the presented works integrate context into their approaches they only enable reactive adaptation while to properly manage software updates in CPS the adaptation, i.e., or execution of tasks must be managed proactively. For example, Grabis demonstrates in [15] how the proactive adaptation of workflows can benefit the performance of the adaptation, however, focuses only aspects of the workflow itself not the context as within our approach. Vansyckel et al. [37] present an approach which uses proactive adaptation of application configurations based on context and it's cost to adapt the application in the present and future context. Although they regard timing of the adaptation and context they regard it as a part of a cost function. The proactive context-aware execution of workflows builds on the timing, i.e., how long a particular context is valid in the environment and therefore introduces timing constraints. Specifying time constraints, such as, deadlines on execution of a certain task (e.g. triggering of airbags in the automotive field), are crucial for the development of applications regarding QoS, such as, safety, performance and proper handling of context. In research works integrating time into process models is not new, previous work focused on applying different timing constraints on tasks of a process [11,33], however these do not consider the dynamic change of deadlines, which is natural in context.

In contrast, the field of real-time transactions or scheduling tasks are executed before a certain soft- or hard deadline [13]. A soft deadline is a point in time where a task should be finished, while a hard deadline is a point in time where the task must be finished. The work by Zeller et al. [41] optimized automotive systems in regards to real-time components. In contrast, our approach focuses on the execution of such (re-)configurations at the right time and before a deadline. Most real-time transaction scheduling algorithms work with fixed deadlines, however, in the real world hard deadlines are not always easy to calculate, especially when regarding context and situations. To cope with such problems Litoiu and Tadei [27] presented work which regards deadlines as well as the execution time of tasks as fuzzy. This enables the execution of tasks in uncertain context, whereas our approach assumes hard deadlines for situations. However, it does not regard the compensation of running tasks and assume that behavior of deadlines can be mapped to fixed functions.

In the field of runtime adaptation a related study was done by Grua et al. [16] on self-adaptation in mobile applications, which found that methods for adaptation mostly regarded timeliness in a reactive manner. However, a study by Keller and Mann [22] found contributions that tackle the issue of timing adaptation of an application. Their findings show that there is limited work which handles all parts of an adaptation from the timeliness view, in the study they found only a single paper which handles all phases (time to detect the need for adaptation, executing the adaptation,..) when adapting an application. A detailed view on the issue of timing adaptation is given by Moreno [28]. Moreno tackled the issue of timing adaptation within a MAPE-K loop with different methods such as using a Markov Decision Process or Probabilistic Model Checking.

In general, applying updates in CPS can be viewed as adapting an application under timing constraints to not disrupt its availability. However, which timing constraints are used to manage the adaptation is depending on the use case itself. Some works only regard system properties such as message delays of the approach or the application itself, however, we argue it is equally important to regard the system context to cope with timing issues when adapting.

6   Conclusion and Future Work

The execution of software updates in Cyber-Physical Systems combines challenges from different fields. First they integrate a plethora of heterogeneous software and hardware components that have to be managed differently, but in addition to software and hardware, such systems have to be able to regard the current state in the environment, i.e., Cyber-Physical Systems must be Context-Aware and especially when executing management tasks such as software updates. As updates disrupt the functionality of systems and therefore availability they must regard context at runtime. When the execution is started at the wrong time or is disrupted by the environment itself, they can create serious safety issues and at least reduce the availability of components. In our scenario of trains, components either used by passengers or to control safety-critical functions wouldn't be available if the update would be executed at runtime without regarding context, such as, the current usage of components or the position of a train. Therefore it is beneficial to regard Cyber-Physical Systems as Context-Aware Systems.

In this paper we presented a method to enable the Situation-Aware execution of software updates in Cyber-Physical Systems. The method is based on modeling the update in a declarative model and specifying the situations which have to be active and timing constraints on the operations of the updated components to determine their worst-case execution time. Based on this model our method generates a Situation-Aware process with so-called Time-Aware Situational Scopes which can update the system according to the initial model by calling the component operations, however, these are only executed when the modeled situations are active and their worst case execution time doesn't exceed the available time situations are active. Therefore, operations will only be executed when the context is suitable for updates. We implemented our approach within the OpenTOSCA systems which was already able to start update processes when situations occurred, however, missed the proper timing and therefore could lead to issues as mentioned.

In the future we plan to extend the presented concept to enable Situation-Aware execution of operations with deadlines and execution times that are not crisp, enabling to apply the Situation-Aware execution of operations on cloud resources as well as their execution times are significantly harder to determine, because of multiple virtualization layers on top of the actual hardware. This could be achieved by using measurement-based methods to determine a worst-case execution time of operations, which take the times of previous executions. Another track of future work is the evaluation of the proposed method on available simulation data, such as, a whole countrys' train network.

Acknowledgements. This work was funded by the DFG project DiStOPT (252975529).

References

1. Macana, C.A., Quijano, N., Mojica-nava, E.: A survey on cyber physical energy systems and their applications on smart grids. In: 2011 IEEE PES Conference on Innovative Smart Grid Technologies (ISGT Latin America) (2011). https://doi.org/10.1109/ISGT-LA.2011.6083194

2. Atzori, L., Iera, A., Morabito, G.: The Internet of Things: a survey. Comput. Netw. (2010). https://doi.org/10.1016/j.comnet.2010.05.010

3. Baldauf, M., Dustdar, S., Rosenberg, F.: A survey on context-aware systems. Int. J. Ad Hoc Ubiquitous Comput. (2007). https://doi.org/10.1504/IJAHUC.2007.014070

4. Bergmayr, A., et al.: A systematic review of cloud modeling languages. ACM Comput. Surv. **51**(1), 22:1–22:38 (2018). https://doi.org/10.1145/3150227

5. Bettini, C., et al.: A survey of context modelling and reasoning techniques. Pervasive Mob. Comput. **6**(2), 161–180 (2010). https://doi.org/10.1016/j.pmcj.2009.06.002

6. Bolchini, C., Curino, C.A., Quintarelli, E., Schreiber, F.A., Tanca, L.: A data-oriented survey of context models. SIGMOD Rec. **36**(4), 19–26 (2007). https://doi.org/10.1145/1361348.1361353

7. Breitenbücher, U., Binz, T., Képes, K., Kopp, O., Leymann, F., Wettinger, J.: Combining declarative and imperative cloud application provisioning based on TOSCA. In: International Conference on Cloud Engineering (IC2E 2014), pp. 87–96. IEEE (2014)

8. Breitenbücher, U., Hirmer, P., Képes, K., Kopp, O., Leymann, F., Wieland, M.: A situation-aware workflow modelling extension. In: Proceedings of the 17th International Conference on Information Integration and Web-based Applications & Services, IIWAS '15, pp. 64:1–64:7. ACM, New York, NY, USA (2015). https://doi.org/10.1145/2837185.2837248

9. Breitenbücher, U., et al.: The OpenTOSCA ecosystem - concepts & tools. In: European Space project on Smart Systems, Big Data, Future Internet - Towards Serving the Grand Societal Challenges - Volume 1: EPS Rome 2016, pp. 112–130. INSTICC, SciTePress (2016). https://doi.org/10.5220/0007903201120130

10. Bucchiarone, A., Marconi, A., Pistore, M., Raik, H.: Dynamic adaptation of fragment-based and context-aware business processes. In: Proceedings - 2012 IEEE 19th International Conference on Web Services, ICWS 2012, pp. 33–41 (2012). https://doi.org/10.1109/ICWS.2012.56

11. Chama, I.E., Belala, N., Saidouni, D.E.: Formalization and analysis of timed BPEL. In: Proceedings of the 2014 IEEE 15th International Conference on Information Reuse and Integration (IEEE IRI 2014), pp. 483–491 (2014). https://doi.org/10.1109/IRI.2014.7051928

12. Choi, J., Cho, Y., Choi, J., Choi, J.: A layered middleware architecture for automated robot services. Int. J. Distrib. Sens. Netw. **10**(5), 201063 (2014). https://doi.org/10.1155/2014/201063

13. Davis, R.I., Burns, A.: A survey of hard real-time scheduling for multiprocessor systems. ACM Comput. Surv. **43**(4), 35:1–35:44 (2011). https://doi.org/10.1145/1978802.1978814

14. Dey, A.: Understanding and using context. Pers. Ubiquit. Comput. **5**(1), 4–7 (2001). https://doi.org/10.1007/s007790170019

15. Grabis, J.: Application of predictive simulation in development of adaptive workflows. In: Proceedings of the Winter Simulation Conference 2014, pp. 996–1004 (2014). https://doi.org/10.1109/WSC.2014.7019959

16. Grua, E.M., Malavolta, I., Lago, P.: Self-adaptation in mobile apps: a systematic literature study. In: 2019 IEEE/ACM 14th International Symposium on Software Engineering for Adaptive and Self-Managing Systems (SEAMS), pp. 51–62 (2019). https://doi.org/10.1109/SEAMS.2019.00016

17. Gunes, V., Peter, S., Givargis, T., Vahid, F.: A survey on concepts, applications, and challenges in cyber-physical systems. KSII Trans. Internet Inf. Syst. (2014). https://doi.org/10.3837/tiis.2014.12.001

18. Guo, Y., Hu, X., Hu, B., Cheng, J., Zhou, M., Kwok, R.Y.K.: Mobile cyber physical systems: current challenges and future networking applications. IEEE Access **6**, 12360–12368 (2017). https://doi.org/10.1109/ACCESS.2017.2782881

19. Haque, S.A., Aziz, S.M., Rahman, M.: Review of cyber-physical system in healthcare. Int. J. Distrib. Sens. Netw. **10**(4), 217415 (2014). https://doi.org/10.1155/2014/217415

20. Hassan, R., Markantonakis, K., Akram, R.N.: Can you call the software in your device be firmware? In: Proceedings - 13th IEEE International Conference on E-Business Engineering, ICEBE 2016 - Including 12th Workshop on Service-Oriented Applications, Integration and Collaboration, SOAIC 2016, pp. 188–195 (2017). https://doi.org/10.1109/ICEBE.2016.040

21. Kejariwal, A., Orsini, F.: On the definition of real-time: applications and systems. In: 2016 IEEE Trustcom/BigDataSE/ISPA, pp. 2213–2220 (2016). https://doi.org/10.1109/TrustCom.2016.0341

22. Keller, C., Mann, Z.Á.: Towards understanding adaptation latency in self-adaptive systems. In: Yangui, S., et al. (eds.) ICSOC 2019. LNCS, vol. 12019, pp. 42–53. Springer, Cham (2020). https://doi.org/10.1007/978-3-030-45989-5_4

23. Képes, K., Breitenbücher, U., Leymann, F.: Situation-aware management of cyber-physical systems. In: Proceedings of the 9th International Conference on Cloud Computing and Services Science (CLOSER 2019), pp. 551–560. SciTePress (2019). https://doi.org/10.5220/0007799505510560

24. Knappmeyer, M., Kiani, S.L., Reetz, E.S., Baker, N., Tonjes, R.: Survey of context provisioning middleware. IEEE Commun. Surv. Tutor. **15**(3), 1492–1519 (2013). https://doi.org/10.1109/SURV.2013.010413.00207

25. Kopp, O., Binz, T., Breitenbücher, U., Leymann, F.: Winery – a modeling tool for TOSCA-based cloud applications. In: Basu, S., Pautasso, C., Zhang, L., Fu, X. (eds.) ICSOC 2013. LNCS, vol. 8274, pp. 700–704. Springer, Heidelberg (2013). https://doi.org/10.1007/978-3-642-45005-1_64

26. Kramer, J., Magee, J.: The evolving philosophers problem: dynamic change management. IEEE Trans. Softw. Eng. **16**(11), 1293–1306 (1990). https://doi.org/10.1109/32.60317

27. Litoiu, M., Tadei, R.: Real-time task scheduling with fuzzy deadlines and processing times. Fuzzy Sets Syst. **117**(1), 35–45 (2001). https://doi.org/10.1016/S0165-0114(98)00283-8

28. Moreno, G.A.: Adaptation timing in self-adaptive systems. Ph.D. Thesis. Carnegie Mellon University (2017)

29. OASIS: Web Services Business Process Execution Language (WS-BPEL) Version 2.0. Organization for the Advancement of Structured Information Standards (OASIS) (2007)

30. OASIS: Topology and Orchestration Specification for Cloud Applications (TOSCA) Version 1.0. Organization for the Advancement of Structured Information Standards (OASIS) (2013)

31. OMG: Business Process Model and Notation (BPMN) Version 2.0. Object Management Group (OMG) (2011)

32. Perera, C., Zaslavsky, A., Christen, P., Georgakopoulos, D.: Context aware computing for the Internet of Things: a survey. Commun. Surv. Tutor. **16**(1), 414–454 (2014). https://doi.org/10.1109/SURV.2013.042313.00197

33. Pichler, H., Eder, J., Ciglic, M.: Modelling processes with time-dependent control structures. In: Mayr, H.C., Guizzardi, G., Ma, H., Pastor, O. (eds.) ER 2017. LNCS, vol. 10650, pp. 50–58. Springer, Cham (2017). https://doi.org/10.1007/978-3-319-69904-2_4

34. Shrouf, F., Miragliotta, G.: Energy management based on Internet of Things: practices and framework for adoption in production management. J. Clean. Prod. (2015). https://doi.org/10.1016/j.jclepro.2015.03.055

35. Smanchat, S., Ling, S., Indrawan, M.: A survey on context-aware workflow adaptations. In: Proceedings of the 6th International Conference on Advances in Mobile Computing and Multimedia, MoMM 2008, pp. 414–417. ACM, New York, NY, USA (2008). https://doi.org/10.1145/1497185.1497274

36. Strang, T., Linnhoff-Popien, C.: A context modeling survey. In: First International Workshop on Advanced Context Modelling, Reasoning And Management at UbiComp 2004, Nottingham, England, 7 September 2004 (2004)

37. Vansyckel, S., Schäfer, D., Schiele, G., Becker, C.: Configuration management for proactive adaptation in pervasive environments. In: 2013 IEEE 7th International Conference on Self-Adaptive and Self-Organizing Systems, pp. 131–140 (2013). https://doi.org/10.1109/SASO.2013.28

38. Weyns, D., Iftikhar, M.U., de la Iglesia, D.G., Ahmad, T.: A survey of formal methods in self-adaptive systems. In: Proceedings of the Fifth International C* Conference on Computer Science and Software Engineering, C3S2E 2012, pp. 67–79. Association for Computing Machinery, New York, NY, USA (2012). https://doi.org/10.1145/2347583.2347592

39. Wieland, M., Schwarz, H., Breitenbücher, U., Leymann, F.: Towards situation-aware adaptive workflows: SitOPT - a general purpose situation-aware workflow management system. In: 2015 IEEE International Conference on Pervasive Computing and Communication Workshops, PerCom Workshops 2015 (2015). https://doi.org/10.1109/PERCOMW.2015.7133989
40. Wilhelm, R., et al.: The worst-case execution-time problem—overview of methods and survey of tools. ACM Trans. Embed. Comput. Syst. **7**(3), 36:1–36:53 (2008). https://doi.org/10.1145/1347375.1347389
41. Zeller, M., Prehofer, C., Weiss, G., Eilers, D., Knorr, R.: Towards self-adaptation in real-time, networked systems: efficient solving of system constraints for automotive embedded systems. In: 2011 IEEE Fifth International Conference on Self-Adaptive and Self-Organizing Systems, pp. 79–88 (2011). https://doi.org/10.1109/SASO.2011.19

An IoT Beehive Network for Monitoring Urban Biodiversity: Vision, Method, and Architecture

Mirella Sangiovanni[1]([envelope]), Gerard Schouten[2], and Willem-Jan van den Heuvel[1]

[1] Tilburg University - JADS, 's-Hertogenbosch, The Netherlands
m.sangiovanni@tue.nl
[2] Fontys University of Applied Sciences, Eindhoven, The Netherlands

Abstract. Environmental sustainability issues have received global attention in recent decades, both at scientific and administrative levels. Despite the scrupulous studies and initiatives around such issues, they remain largely unresolved, and sometimes even unknown. A complete understanding of the quality of our living environment that surrounds us, especially urban places, where we spend most of our lives would help improve living conditions for both humans and other species present. The concept of *Intelligent Beehives* for urban biodiversity encapsulates and leverages biotic elements such as bio-indicators (e.g. bees), and pollination, with technologies like AI and IoT instrumentation. Together they comprise a smart service that shapes the backbone of a real-time, AI-enabled environmental dashboard. In this vision paper, we outline and discuss our solution architecture and prototypization for such servified intelligent beehives. We focus our discussion on the hives' predictive modelling abilities that enable Machine-Learning service operations – or MLOps – for increasing the sustainability of urban biodiversity.

Keywords: IoT beehive · Urban biodiversity · MLOps · Data architecture

1 Introduction

Urban areas are expanding rapidly [10]. It is estimated that by 2050 about two-thirds of the global population lives in cities [17]. The consequences of urbanization and large scale loss of natural habitats affect and distort people's health, well-being and quality of life [17]. Moreover, it has pervasive and irremediable effects on biodiversity and the quality of ecosystems [4]. Biodiversity is in accelerated decline [5], both in cities and in rural areas. Supporting and maintaining environmental sustainability[1] is a global challenge and a necessity for the survival of the organisms that are part of it (including humans). It is an indispensable prerogative to guarantee ecosystem services, such as water purification, waste management, pollination, supply of medicines and other natural

---

[1] https://www.un.org/sustainabledevelopment/news/communications-material/.

© Springer Nature Switzerland AG 2020
S. Dustdar (Ed.): SummerSOC 2020, CCIS 1310, pp. 33–42, 2020.
https://doi.org/10.1007/978-3-030-64846-6_3

products. Protection as well as careful design and usage of man-made habitats is of crucial importance [2]. The rapid conversion of natural habitats to urban environments could have severe effects on bees, a key species for pollination [2]. Note that pollinators directly affect 35% of the world's food crop production [7]. Therefore, caring for *bee diversity* and hence *pollination services* becomes an essential responsibility.

In this short paper, we materialize this vision. With a specific simple yet realistic example – a network of IoT beehives – we make it plausible [9,20] how the use and apply software and data engineering, along with state-of-the-art Artificial Intelligence (AI)[2], Internet-of-Things (IoT) instrumentation, and Augmented Reality (AR), can create a breakthrough for biodiversity monitoring and the preservation of ecosystems. AI algorithms are able to spot and expose biological patterns in large and varied multi-sensory datasets. This would allow us to grasp complex natural phenomena [19]. Environmental digital twin platforms based on AR can be build to run simulations, evaluate scenarios, and to do preemptive contingency planning for biodiversity and reach unprecedented levels of sustainability targets. These technologies have the potential to improve the quality of complex decisions beyond state-of-the-art.

The basic concept of the IoT beehive network is to commission bees as biomonitoring agents, and mine their 'data stories'. Bees forage in a substantial area surrounding the hive (radius of 3+ km) and bring back pollen (from flowers) to the hive. More specifically, we envision a network of open transparent beehives with multi-sensory equipment, intermixing such IoT sensing with open environmental data, like satellite surveys and chemical analyzes. We sketch how these unprecedented amounts of (Big) data, collected 24/7 by instrumented hives, can be processed automatically and converted to a biodiversity monitor with a 4-layer architecture.

The IoT beehive network is an ideal vehicle to reach out to citizens, from school children to urban planners. We involve stakeholders in both the development and operational phase of the IoT beehive network and its applications. This increases the awareness about environmental issues [18]. We adopt an iterative and agile way of working, where activities like: (1) experimenting with data, (2) development of the hardware and software, and (3) deployment of the IoT beehives in the field are interwoven, and continuously improved. Continuous integration and delivery, learning and fast feedback loops are thus key elements of this MLOps approach [3]. Systematic exploration, requirements elicitation, design and prototypization of AI-driven solutions are important ingredients of this approach as well.

2   The IoT Beehive Vision

The ambitious, long-term objective is to design cities taking into account biodiversity and maintaining or even improving the quality of urban ecosystems. A network of IoT beehives can significantly contribute to this goal. Honeybees

---

[2] This includes Machine Learning (ML) and Deep Learning (DL).

are excellent bio-indicators [1]. With their intriguing colony behavior, they are extremely sensitive to their natural environment. A few examples how data stories' of bees can be used for assessing biodiversity of the area surrounding the IoT beehive:

- The so-called bee waggle dance communicates the direction and distance to food resources [13] to other unemployed worker bees. This amazing behavior will be detected by camera's in the IoT beehive. Vision AI is used to decode the waggle dance [21]. A convolutional neural network (CNN) and the concept of transfer learning will be considered to implement this function.
- A constant and diverse offering of pollen and nectar is beneficial for the colony health. There are a number of indicators for this, including (1) the number of individual worker bees, (2) the weight of stored honey, and, (3) the number of holes (empty cells) in the honeycomb.
- Bees bring back pollen to the hive. Analyzing and identifying these small particles is a direct indicator of the flower richness in the environment.
- Open environmental data is complementary to this. Important information might be derived from e.g., satellite images, air pollution measurements, water quality samples, etc.

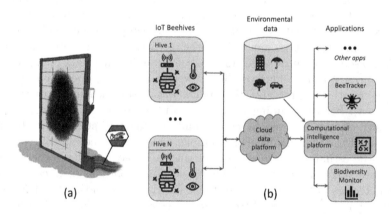

Fig. 1. a) Schematic prototype of the smart beehive. b) Conceptual setup with data collection at IoT nodes, use of other (open) data, data storage and computational services.

We are currently experimenting with large glass-walled beehive housing designs (approximate size: 1m80 × 1m20 × 0m20) that can host two colonies. Two independent colonies provide a better sampling of the biodiversity surrounding the hive. Beekeepers are involved actively in these experiments.

This physical design enables the public to see the actual bee behavior. The first basic IoT design and data processing infrastructure has also already been built and tested.

2.1   Data Collection

In order to monitor and estimate the biodiversity of the surrounding area using data assembled by an IoT beehive enriched with other environmental data from public databases as described above, we need to collect labels as well, i.e., ground-truth measurements of biodiversity collected through traditional methods (e.g., counts of plant and animal species, pollen analysis). In order to minimize inter-person variability and interpretation this should be done with trained observers and strict monitoring protocols. In addition to this, honey from the instrumented IoT beehives could provide a useful indication of soil, plant and air pollution [15].

The lack of models that combines multiple factors to accurately predict urban biodiversity, makes it difficult to set goals for policies and targets for an actionable approach [11]. To simplify the information extraction process, we now experiment with a supervised machine learning model for urban biodiversity that is able to digest a huge amount of data (IoT data, public database records and laboratory data). We foresee a data collection and storage setup as conceptualized in Fig. 1.

2.2   Data Analytics

AI or data analytics is essential for building predictive models for urban biodiversity [8]. Data analytics combines quickly and efficiently huge amounts of data and is able to find patterns in these merged datasets. This approach might provide unexplored solutions that can create breakthrough improvements in biodiversity monitoring. In our case, we aim to infer the biodiversity of an urban area on the basis of two sets of input data: (a) IoT-instrumented beehive data (e.g. processed waggle dances, pollen, colony condition, weight), and, (b) open environmental data (e.g. weather, water and air quality, databases with infrastructure and urban green). For the training part we likewise need labels, i.e., ground-truth biodiversity counts; followed by tuning and optimization steps until obtaining the output of the final model. For example, we expect insect and flower biodiversity to be estimated more accurately with IoT beehives than other species. This is a starting point to evaluate which additional solutions (e.g., camera with motion detectors in the park, drones to survey the open fields, and, eDNA sampling in water [14]) are needed to monitor species that would remain otherwise in the 'shadows'. After the data mining and data cleaning steps we proceed with normalisation, feature engineering, model optimization (hyperparameter tuning) and evaluation steps. Upfront, it is hard to say which type of models perform best. Therefore, we will evaluate and test in a trial-and-error manner the usual state-of-art algorithms like random forest, support vector machines, XGBoost, etc., and will consider meta-heuristics (ensemble learning).

3   MLOps Approach

MLOps has emerged from the DevOps philosophy and associated practices that streamline the software development workflow and delivery processes. In particular, DevOps adopts the continuous integration and continuous testing cycle to produce and deploy production-ready new micro-releases of applications at fast pace [3]. As shown in Fig. 2, MLOps[3] is an extension of this iterative and agile approach, targeted at data-driven (AI-like) applications. In addition to traditional software development, it includes a third experimental 'data' cycle that is composed of the following activities: business understanding, data acquisition, exploratory data analysis, and initial AI modelling. As such MLOps clearly requires sophisticated policies based on metrics and telemetry such as ML performance indicators for accuracy scores (like precision and recall), as well as software quality metrics [12]. It also demands improved dependency management (and thus transparency) between model development, training, validation and deployment.

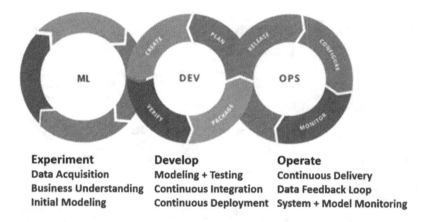

Experiment
Data Acquisition
Business Understanding
Initial Modeling

Develop
Modeling + Testing
Continuous Integration
Continuous Deployment

Operate
Continuous Delivery
Data Feedback Loop
System + Model Monitoring

Fig. 2. MLOps lifecycle steps.

Adopting MLOps implies a culture shift between data analysts, data engineers, deployment, software engineers, and domain experts. In our case domain experts are not only biologists and urban planners (decision makers with respect to city layout and planning) but also school children, the future citizens of our planet. All these stakeholders are involved in the development and operations processes of the IoT beehive network, for requirements elicitation but also to experiment with early designs and prototypization. An MLOps approach is paramount for projects that aim at implementing SDG goals with smart services.

4   Beehive Network Architecture

This project embraces a stratified data architecture, with layers that are separated in terms of the type of data and logic they combine, and, built on top of

---

each other. Each layer is self-contained, and addresses a specific concern, such as data collection and storage, or data analytics, and is inhabited by servified components that can be accessed, queried and managed through a well-defined interface. In this way, a smart service taxonomy for IoT beehives is systematically developed, ranging from coarse-grained servified layers from the IoT beehive architecture, to fine-grained services (hence: micro-services) such as servified (edge) IoT devices.

In the following, we will now further explain our architecture, starting from the physical layers and working up in the stack to the logical (software) layer. We have graphically depicted the IoT beehive stratified data architecture in Fig. 3.

In particular, the IoT beehive architecture encompasses the following two physical layers:

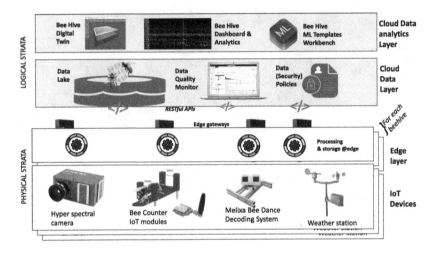

Fig. 3. The IoT beehive stratified data architecture.

4.1   IoT BeeHive Device Layer

Each beehive is to be instrumented with a series of IoT devices to measure several aspects of interest, including, but not restricted to, the number of bees entering and leaving the beehive during day/night, and the type of pollen (if any) collected by bees entering the beehives. For the latter purpose hyperspectral cameras are mounted to the beehive to analyse and better understand the impact of mono- and polyfloral pollen quality and diversity on the physiology of bees. In addition, experimentation with systems such as the Melixa Bee Dance decoding system, will be deployed to better understand how the bee waggle dance encodes polar coordinates to potential supply in the field. Jobless foragers merely check the dancer's movements and based on them start to search for resources. Other IoT devices that are instrumented to each beehive include thermal/optical cameras and a weather station to measure weather conditions 24/7. We also inspect the honeycomb to estimate the heath of the colony.

4.2   IoT BeeHive EdgeLayer

Clearly, the above IoT devices generate huge volumes of (distributed) data, requiring vast amounts of bandwidth for data to be transported from source to target computing environment. The EdgeLayer basically serve as data storage and preprocessing stations close at the source (the edge of the cloud). This can be either achieved through data preprocessing in microprocessors that are embedded in the IoT device (e.g., in the weather station), or by intelligent data gateways (e.g., that fuse images from the hyperspectral camera and the bee waggle decoder and serve as decentral proxies of the central processing unit). Processing at the edge of each device that is attached to each beehive, minimizes communication bandwidth and allows for real-time and local status monitoring at each beehive in the array network.

The following logical layers sit on top of the physical data architecture stratosphere:

4.3   Cloud Data Layer

Data from each geographically distributed beehive is transmitted from the IoT microprocessors or edge-gateways through the RESTful APIs to the central cloud datalake that is the beating heart-and-soul of the cloud data layer. In this way, the datalake collects and stores all data generated by the IoT devices and open sources (e.g., social media, satellite images, lidar). Next to the datalake, this layer also offers dedicated data repositories for test and validation datasets. A data quality monitor continually measures the level of data quality along the axes of consistency, accuracy and timeliness, and employs ML-algorithms to predict and automatically resolve potential data omissions or anomalies. A special facility is in place to guarantee data safety and security, and allow for example citizens (including elementary school kids) and professionals (e.g., policy makers) to access, manipulate and query data according to their own access/control schemes, and organizational/legal rules, norms, and policies.

4.4   Cloud Analytics Layer

This layer provides the central access point for all users of the IoT beehive platform, offering (a) an AI-workbench with preexisting, well-trained and validated AI-models – as well as advanced model development – and testing tools for new models that promote MLOps [6], and, (b) interactive visualization and experimentation that boast user-friendly and easy-to-understand analytics tools, including advanced conversational interface employing natural language processing.

Lastly, this layer will be the habitat of a beehive digital twin that constitutes a digitally designed virtual system that accommodate through the layers below the real-time confluence of data across beehive IoT devices and other information systems (e.g., open source data) for continuous alignment of operational decisions to maintain the beehive, with more policy level decisions with respect to biodiversity. Through mechanisms such as the ability to run "what-if" scenarios the beehive digital twin may be a powerful tool to better predict and appreciate the impact of novel policies on the environment in which we live.

This architecture accommodates several user scenarios. In particular, the interactive visualization tools foster engagement for citizens; the digital twin and AI enables policy makers to come up with urban layouts that are nature friendly. Note that the architecture is generic and open in nature. During the MLOps experimentation we can easily extend it by adding f.e. other IoT devices, or algorithms.

5   Discussion and Conclusions

In this vision paper we have introduced a novel architecture to facilitate cyber-physical IoT instrumented beehives. This stratified architecture forms the foundation for a novel MLOps approach focused on the sustainability of biodiverse urban ecosystems. We will illustrate and explore the proposed architecture elaborating a several urban biodiversity scenarios.

In this way a Big Data approach is facilitated that may assume a high level of automation in mining, processing, analyzing, and visualizing data can be helpful to tackle wicked and complex problems. Environmental issues like for instance climate changes, loss of biodiversity, large-scale urbanization and associated environmental issues are examples of such global challenges. We also emphasize that in order to increase impact this data engineering adopts an MLOps approach.

In the proposed approach we sketch and explain how Big Data can be used to assess the quality of biodiversity in cities with nature-and-tech systems. Because the amount of available biological data increases enormously with this kind of high-tech IoT systems and also because of citizen science we are in need of new and advanced technologies to store and process it [16]. Some specific technical challenges and risks that we foresee are: (1) before decoding the waggle dance we should be able to visually detect real-time the perimetry on the honeycomb ("dance plane"). This requires a high-precision, special-purpose visual detection software module, (2) pollen detection and subsequently physical pollen collection from the back of the bees is still a brittle point in the design because – as of today – it is an off-line process that involves chemical tests for which no IoT devises exist, and, (3) the design should accommodate the fact that the data streaming from the IoT hives to the data lake is noisy and irregular (e.g. not much activity in the night and on rainy days). In addition, we are fully aware that the following bio-socio-technical risks may occur: (1) sections of the bee colony may leave or die, or in the worst case, die at large (e.g., due to extreme weather conditions, or the colony's evolutionary circumstances) (2) our approach assumes active citizen participation which may decrease while time progresses.

This article reports on core research results. We foresee novel research routes in various dimensions. Firstly, we wish to develop reusable models for predicting biodiveristy in rural and urban areas based on observations, and abstractions to built in parameters in the models. Secondly, we wish to further improve the MLOps approach applying it to the beehive project in order to continuously deliver, deploy and operate IoT beehive implementations. Special attention will be placed on approaches that will foster collaboration between the actors involved in the MLOps loops, e.g., school kids and developers. Lastly, research will further flesh out an event and smart service ontology to accommodate semantic reasoning, connecting low-level, discrete and instantaneous events, with society-level, longer-term biodiversity performance indicators.

References

1. Celli, G., Maccagnani, B.: Honey bees as bioindicators of environmental pollution. Bull. Insectology **56**(1), 137–139 (2003)
2. De Palma, A., et al.: Ecological traits affect the sensitivity of bees to land-use pressures in european agricultural landscapes. J. Appl. Ecol. **52**(6), 1567–1577 (2015)
3. Ebert, C., Gallardo, G., Hernantes, J., Serrano, N.: Devops. IEEE Softw. **33**(3), 94–100 (2016)
4. Guetté, A., Gaüzère, P., Devictor, V., Jiguet, F., Godet, L.: Measuring the synanthropy of species and communities to monitor the effects of urbanization on biodiversity. Ecol. Ind. **79**, 139–154 (2017)
5. Hallmann, C.A., et al.: More than 75 percent decline over 27 years in total flying insect biomass in protected areas. PloS One **12**(10), e0185809 (2017)
6. van den Heuvel, W.-J., Tamburri, D.A.: Model-driven ML-Ops for intelligent enterprise applications: vision, approaches and challenges. In: Shishkov, B. (ed.) BMSD 2020. LNBIP, vol. 391, pp. 169–181. Springer, Cham (2020). https://doi.org/10.1007/978-3-030-52306-0_11
7. Klein, A.M., et al.: Importance of pollinators in changing landscapes for world crops. Proc. R. Soc. B: Biol. Sci. **274**(1608), 303–313 (2007)
8. Klein, D.J., McKown, M.W., Tershy, B.R.: Deep learning for large scale biodiversity monitoring. In: Bloomberg Data for Good Exchange Conference (2015)
9. Bublitz, F.M., et al.: Disruptive technologies for environment and health research: an overview of artificial intelligence, blockchain, and internet of things. Int. J. Environ. Res. Public Health **16**(20), 3847 (2019)
10. Maksimović, Č., Kurian, M., Ardakanian, R.: Rethinking infrastructure design for multi-use water services. Springer, Cham (2015)
11. Nilon, C.H., et al.: Planning for the future of urban biodiversity: a global review of city-scale initiatives. BioScience **67**(4), 332–342 (2017)
12. Nogueira, A.F., Ribeiro, J.C., Zenha-Rela, M., Craske, A.: Improving la redoute's CI/CD pipeline and DevOps processes by applying machine learning techniques. In: 2018 11th International Conference on the Quality of Information and Communications Technology (QUATIC), pp. 282–286. IEEE (2018)
13. Nürnberger, F., Keller, A., Härtel, S., Steffan-Dewenter, I.: Honey bee waggle dance communication increases diversity of pollen diets in intensively managed agricultural landscapes. Mol. Ecol. **28**(15), 3602–3611 (2019)
14. Olson, Z.H., Briggler, J.T., Williams, R.N.: An edna approach to detect eastern hellbenders (cryptobranchus a. alleganiensis) using samples of water. Wildl. Res. **39**(7), 629–636 (2012)
15. Porrini, C., et al.: Honey bees and bee products as monitors of the environmental contamination. Apiacta **38**(1), 63–70 (2003)

16. Prajogo, D.I., Sohal, A.S.: The integration of TQM and technology R&D management in determining quality and innovation performance. Omega **34**(3), 296–312 (2006)
17. Reeves, J.P., Knight, A.T., Strong, E.A., Heng, V., Cromie, R.L., Vercammen, A.: The application of wearable technology to quantify health and wellbeing co-benefits from urban wetlands. Front. Psychol. **10**, 1840 (2019)
18. Sebba, R.: The landscapes of childhood: the reflection of childhood's environment in adult memories and in children's attitudes. Environ. Behav. **23**(4), 395–422 (1991)
19. Sedjo, R.A.: Perspectives on biodiversity: valuing its role in an everchanging world. J. For. **98**(2), 45 (2000)
20. Sinha, A., Sengupta, T., Alvarado, R.: Interplay between technological innovation and environmental quality: formulating the SDG policies for next 11 economies. J. Cleaner Prod. **242**, 118549 (2020)
21. Wario, F., Wild, B., Couvillon, M.J., Rojas, R., Landgraf, T.: Automatic methods for long-term tracking and the detection and decoding of communication dances in honeybees. Front. Ecol. Evol. **3**, 103 (2015)

Advanced Application Areas

Data Science Approaches to Quality Control in Manufacturing: A Review of Problems, Challenges and Architecture

Yannick Wilhelm[1(✉)], Ulf Schreier[2], Peter Reimann[1,3], Bernhard Mitschang[1,3], and Holger Ziekow[2]

[1] Graduate School of Excellence Advanced Manufacturing Engineering - University of Stuttgart, Stuttgart, Germany
`{yannick.wilhelm,peter.reimann}@gsame.uni-stuttgart.de`
[2] Business Information Systems - Furtwangen University of Applied Science, Furtwangen, Germany
`{ulf.schreier,holger.ziekow}@hs-furtwangen.de`
[3] Institute for Parallel and Distributed Systems - University of Stuttgart, Stuttgart, Germany
`bernhard.mitschang@ipvs.uni-stuttgart.de`

Abstract. Manufacturing environments are characterized by non-stationary processes, constantly varying conditions, complex process interdependencies, and a high number of product variants. These and other aspects pose several challenges for common machine learning algorithms to achieve reliable and accurate predictions. This overview and vision paper provides a comprehensive list of common problems and challenges for data science approaches to quality control in manufacturing. We have derived these problems and challenges by inspecting three real-world use cases in the field of product quality control and via a literature study. We furthermore associate the identified problems and challenges to individual layers and components of a functional setup, as it can be found in manufacturing environments today. Additionally, we extend and revise this functional setup and this way propose our vision of a future functional software architecture. This functional architecture represents a visionary blueprint for solutions that are able to address all challenges for data science approaches in manufacturing quality control.

Keywords: Data science · Machine learning · Quality control · Challenges · Problems · Functional architecture

1 Introduction

Nowadays, the large amount of available manufacturing data enables opportunities to improve manufacturing systems beyond basic control, administration, and information functions. This is enabled by machine learning (ML) approaches, e.g., for prediction and classification tasks [3,33]. In this overview and vision

S. Dustdar (Ed.): SummerSOC 2020, CCIS 1310, pp. 45–65, 2020.
https://doi.org/10.1007/978-3-030-64846-6_4

paper, we focus on ML or data science approaches to quality control in manufacturing, e.g., to predicting product quality during manufacturing processes. Furthermore, we consider derived analytical tasks, such as error localization and backtracking of root causes for bad quality products that need to be repaired.

According to the standard ISO 9000:2015 [15], quality control focuses on fulfilling quality requirements as operational part of quality management (QM). Quality itself is defined in a wide range as "the degree to which a set of inherent characteristics of an object fulfills requirements" [15]. Thereby, any conceivable object may have quality, including products and manufacturing processes. State of the art methods in QM are *Total Quality Management*, which considers quality as comprehensive target across all areas of a company, *Kaizen* as QM approach for continuous quality and productivity improvement, as well as *Six Sigma* [24].

These state of the art QM methods also incorporate data-driven approaches. Nevertheless, they are restricted to analyzing individual manufacturing process steps with simple statistical methods. Correlations and implications between data characteristics and process steps have to be identified manually by domain experts by interpreting the results of statistical methods. The added value these findings provide for quality control depends on the performance of the QM methods and on the skills of domain experts. Especially in case of high-dimensional correlations and patterns along several process steps, domain experts often reach their limits. This is exactly where data science and ML approaches come into play [3,33]. These approaches may be used to discover patterns and relationships even in high-dimensional data spaces along multiple process steps as well as across multiple interdependencies between processes and products. Data science approaches can be applied profitably where the limits of classical QM methods and classical manufacturing information systems are reached.

However, the step from theory to really applying data science approaches in practice is not as trivial as it sometimes seems to be. Manufacturing environments are characterized to be non-stationary, to have rapidly varying conditions, to have complex process interdependencies and to deal with a high number of process and product variants [3,27,33]. This is exactly the opposite of what standard data science approaches expect in order to achieve reliable and accurate predictions. Through our work and experiences with three real-world use cases in the field of quality control and via a literature study, we systematically identified a comprehensive list of common problems and challenges for data science approaches to quality control in manufacturing. In this overview and vision paper, we discuss the main problems and challenges. In addition, we extend the classical functional setup of QM in manufacturing environments to a more complete functional software architecture. This functional architecture represents our visionary proposal of a blueprint solution that is able to address all challenges for data science approaches in manufacturing quality control.

The rest of the paper is structured as follows: Sect. 2 presents related work and our own preliminary work on three use cases in the field of quality control in manufacturing. In Sect. 3, we discuss the most important problems and challenges for data science approaches to quality control. The proposed functional software architecture to address the problems and challenges is introduced in Sect. 4. Section 5 summarizes the paper and lists future research directions.

2   Related Work

We have carried out an literature study to identify challenges that data science approaches for manufacturing data have to address. We summarize the major results of this literature study in Sect. 2.1. Nevertheless, we have found that most related work look at only a few challenges and do not provide a complete list of all the challenges that are relevant in the use cases of our industry partners. Because of this, we took a deeper look into these real-world use cases to derive a first comprehensive list of analytical challenges. We introduce three of these use cases in Sects. 2.2, 2.3 and 2.4. The resulting challenges are discussed in Sect. 3.

2.1   Literature

We have analyzed several review articles that summarize literature describing applications of machine learning to manufacturing use cases [3, 4, 9, 18, 33]. However, most of these reviews only highlight the potentials of machine learning. Wüst et al. and Cheng et al. are the only ones that provide first overviews on real problems or challenges that limit the scope and performance of machine learning techniques in real-world manufacturing environments [3, 33]. For instance, Wüst et al. discuss that manufacturing data often involves lots of redundant or even irrelevant information, which may lead to a decreased prediction performance of learning algorithms [33]. Cheng et al. highlight that manufacturing environments are non-stationary [3]. This leads to uncertainty and dynamic changes in data, which for instance causes many concept drifts, i.e., continuous changes in the patterns learned by algorithms [6, 21].

We have also examined several real-world use cases that are not covered by the reviews of Wüst et al. and Cheng et al. For instance, Kassner et al. use machine learning, especially text analytics, to identify the root causes of quality problems related to customer warranty claims [16]. The authors discuss a few challenges for this kind of data analytics, e.g., many real-world data contain a multiplicity of class labels that occur in an imbalanced way. This class imbalance leads to the problem that learning algorithms often ignore the patterns of many classes, finally leading to a decreased prediction performance [2]. Leitner et al. apply binary classification techniques to support fault detection of products after an assembly line [20]. They go in line with the argumentation of Kassner et al. in that the class imbalance is an inherent problem in manufacturing data. Thalmann et al. discuss analytical challenges for three use cases for fault detection, fault diagnosis, and predictive maintenance [27]. They especially mention that underlying data often represent diverse product variants with different physical properties. This adds another kind of imbalance to the data, i.e., not only the classes, but also the product variants are represented in an imbalanced way.

2.2 Proactive Error Prevention in Manufacturing Based on an Adaptable Machine Learning Environment (PREFERML)

PREFERML is a project working on the development of machine-learning-based methods to predict and proactively avoid production errors in current and future production processes [8,34]. These methods promise to reduce production costs and wasted workpieces. Production companies carry out many production processes which are changing over time. This requires to generate and use numerous machine learning models for different processes and process versions. As a big consequence and challenge, it is necessary to increase the degree of automation in creating and maintaining models. To come up with a corresponding solution, we test prediction methods at specific production lines of an industry partner that produces a diverse range of intelligent sensors and solutions for factories, logistics, and process automation.

The proposed solution is a combination of machine learning technology and knowledge modeling. The underlying idea is to leverage domain knowledge about the production processes and about collected data to improve the degree of automation in model generation and model maintenance. A domain expert with concrete process knowledge can often name relevant relationships, e.g., between processes, process steps, and data sources. For example, when selecting data for a prediction model at a particular process, it is critical to select only relevant and non-redundant sources related to the process-specific predicted value [33]. This selection can be done to some extend by heuristics, but more effectively by domain experts. Our approach is to create a domain-oriented model that can be used to capture the required knowledge and to make it available for automated data processing, model generation, and model maintenance.

2.3 End-of-Line Testing of Complex Products

End-of-Line (EoL) testing constitutes the final quality check of products after all process steps of the production or assembly line. Here, we consider a use case for quality control of truck engines from an industry partner from the automotive area [10,12]. These truck engines are composed of more than 100 parts within a multi-step assembly line. Example engine parts are cylinders or a turbo charger. After the whole assembly line, the engines are transferred to a sophisticated test bench to carry out fault detection [14]. The test bench delivers a multitude of sensor signals to test certain characteristics of the engine, e.g., its oil consumption. Based on these sensor signals, a binary classification model decides whether a particular engine is either classified as functioning or as defective.

For each defective engine, a quality engineer carries out a fault diagnosis by manually inspecting all sensor signals from the test bench [14]. The goal of this fault diagnosis is to identify one of the more than 100 engine parts that caused the quality issue. Thereupon, operators replace the identified engine part. The engine is then tested again on the test bench to clarify if the replaced part was the real cause of the quality issue. In a previous study, we discuss how to support quality engineers in their decision-making by transforming the fault diagnosis into a data-driven classification problem [10]. Thereby, we consider the sensor signals as features and the several engine parts as classes. So, we have a multi-class problem, i.e., the final classifier has to decide on exactly one of multiple possible classes. We tested several techniques for data pre-processing and classification and finally came up with an approach using Random Forest [1].

2.4 Prediction of Product and Process Quality at Highly Automated Multi-step Assembly Lines

The next use case considers a highly automated and multi-step assembly line for flow production of pneumatic solenoid valves. The assembly line consists of 20 assembly steps. Additionally, seven fully automated test steps at the end of the assembly line are used as an EoL test, i.e., to check whether each assembled valve fulfills the quality requirements. Similar to the use case introduced in Sect. 2.3, this decision is based on evaluating sensor signals and on checking whether the signals comply with specific tolerance bands. Bad quality valves are either repaired manually by a worker or they are directly repassed to a previous process step of the highly automated assembly line.

Data science approaches may be used to predict product and process quality directly within previous steps of the assembly line to mitigate bottlenecks at the EoL test. For instance, we may use data analytics to detect process anomalies before the error rate increases at the EoL test. Furthermore, a goal is to backtrack root causes of quality problems, e.g., to identify the assembly step that caused a problem [12]. Each of these approaches is characterized by high-dimensional data dependencies and data patterns along many process and test steps. The underlying data hence cannot be analyzed by simple monitoring methods, but requires more sophisticated data sciences approaches and statistical analyses.

3 Problems and Challenges for Data Analytics in Manufacturing Environments

Driven by our own use cases and based on our literature survey, we have identified common problems and challenges for data-driven approaches to quality control in manufacturing environments. This section describes these typical problems and challenges. The starting point for the following considerations is Fig. 1 that gives an overview of the functional setup of data-driven approaches within manufacturing environments, as they can typically be found today. The emphasis is on domain-oriented functional requirements, not on non-functional requirements like performance, security, etc. This way, the functional setup helps to describe the identified challenges and to locate their origin in typical QM setups. A typical functional setup for current implementations consists of three basic layers:

- All physical manufacturing equipment, the products, and manufacturing processes are contained in the *manufacturing layer*. This layer represents all parts of the manufacturing system, i.e., production planning, part manufacturing,

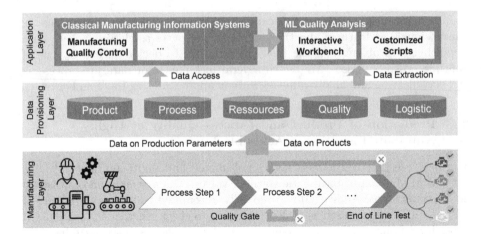

Fig. 1. Overview of the functional setup for quality control and data science approaches as it can be found in today's manufacturing environments. The figure depicts the typical manufacturing environment and components to digitize this environment.

assembly, and quality control. The manufacturing of products is typically organized in multiple successive process steps with several inline quality gates for quality checking and a final *End-of-Line* (EoL) test.

- Above the manufacturing layer, the *data provisioning layer* combines all data on production parameters and products from all parts of the manufacturing system. Furthermore, this layer provides all necessary data to the systems in the application layer above.
- The top layer, the *application layer*, contains systems implementing the domain functions. The figure distinguishes *Classical Manufacturing Information Systems* and *Quality Analysis based on ML*. Classical Manufacturing Information Systems include traditional systems for *Manufacturing Quality Control* that provide information and functions for many tasks without explicitly making use of machine learning. Examples of these systems are computer-integrated manufacturing (CIM) systems, Enterprise Resource Planning (ERP) systems, and manufacturing execution systems (MES) with all their components, e.g., production and machine data acquisition (PDA, MDA), and computer-aided quality (CAQ) [29]. Operational staff carrying out corresponding tasks in the context of quality control are workers, quality engineers and data scientists. A first and simple approach towards *Quality Analysis based on ML* is using scripting solutions (e.g., based on Python or R) or interactive ML workbenchs (e.g., WEKA). Either way, ML-based solutions use information from classical manufacturing information systems or directly from data sources provided by the data provisioning layer.

As indicated in Fig. 2, 3 and 4, each of the three layers may bring in certain problems and challenges for data science approaches to quality control. As already mentioned, we found many representative challenges during our own work on the ML use cases introduced in Sect. 2. In addition, our literature study has shown that several of our challenges are known and confirmed in literature. The problems and challenges for data analytics in manufacturing environments can be related (M) to the manufacturing domain, (D) to the characteristics of underlying data and data sources, (A) to the properties of analytics themselves, and (S) to software and their interfaces. Therefore, we categorize the problems and challenges into these four groups and discuss them in the next subsections.

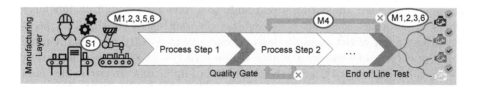

Fig. 2. The manufacturing layer and its related challenges and problems.

3.1 Challenges Related to the Manufacturing Domain

This group includes problems and challenges for data analytics that arise due to the nature of manufacturing environments and due to the typical domain-specific characteristics. Problems and challenges of this group mainly concern the manufacturing layer in manufacturing environments as shown in Fig. 2.

M1 - Heterogeneous Product Families and Operating Equipment. Typically, manufacturing environments are characterized by several product variants and different versions of operating equipment, e. g, machinery, tools, or shop floor equipment. These product variants and versions of operating equipment differ in their composition and in their physical properties [13]. This variety of products and equipment likewise increases the variety of underlying data [27,33]. It leads to complex data relations, to high data dimensionalities, and to a complicated interpretability of data. For instance, the value ranges representing one particular class pattern often differ among individual product variants or in different versions of operating equipment [10]. This finally makes it hard for ML algorithms to detect clearly distinguishable patterns.

M2 - Diverse Error Types. As discussed in Sect. 2.3, fault detection may be implemented using a binary classification. Here, the two classes are usually represented as labels "OK" (functioning product) or "Not OK" (defective product). The subsequent fault diagnosis is however a multi-class classification, i.e., where ML algorithms have to distinguish patterns for multiple class labels. In manufacturing scenarios, these class labels usually represent diverse error types. Examples of such error types are the approximately 100 different product parts in the EoL testing scenario introduced in Sect. 2.3. This multiplicity and diversity of class labels usually leads to a high complexity of the whole classification problem [16,20]. It oftentimes reduces the prediction performance, e.g., in terms of accuracy, that is in general achievable with common ML algorithms [10].

M3 - Imbalanced Data Distributions. Manufacturing data is typically highly imbalanced [10,16,33]. In general, we may distinguish between three different kinds of imbalance. The first kind is related to the binary classification of fault detection. Here, the majority of the samples in the training data have the label "OK". In fact, only a few percent of the samples have the more interesting label "Not OK" indicating a real fault [20]. The second kind of imbalance occurs in use cases for fault diagnosis, i.e., in multi-class classification problems. Here, a few of the multiple classes occur very frequently, while many other classes only have a less amount of data samples [10,16]. The high product variety discussed for challenge M1 adds the third kind of imbalance. In particular, individual classes or error types are unevenly distributed among individual product variants [10,27]. These three kinds of imbalance lead to many underrepresented classes and product variants. ML algorithms often tend to ignore such underrepresented classes or product variants, which may significantly degrade prediction performance [2,10].

M4 - Non-linear Production Processes and Self-loops. Manufacturing processes are characterized by several process and test steps. In successful cases, each product or workpiece passes each process and test step exactly once and in the right linear processing order. The data collection of such a manufacturing line then represents exactly this linear processing order, i.e., the process data and test data of each product or workpiece occur only once in the data set. However, in case a product or workpiece does not pass a test, the processing order of this product or workpiece does not follow the predefined order. Manufacturing processes then become non-linear [3]. Here, the processing order typically includes loops from one step back to another preceding step, or even self-loops within a single manufacturing step. This means that data samples of a specific product or workpiece occur multiple times in the related data set, but with different timestamps for one and the same process or test step, respectively.

M5 - Concept Drifts. The standard way to create a ML model is to train it on a data set with a fixed, although mostly unknown probability distribution of labeled training samples. The objective is to learn a description of a concept representing all relevant patterns identified in the training samples. This concept is then encoded in the ML model, e.g., as a decision tree. However, if the concept depends on some varying or time-dependent hidden context, the meaning of a concept can change over time. Such changes in the meaning of a concept are called concept drifts. They are usually caused by changes or drifts in the data distribution [6,21]. Concept drifts are very common in manufacturing environments as these environments and also underlying data are inherently nonstationary and show varying and uncertain conditions [3]. For instance, machines or tools at individual process steps may continuously change their mechanical properties. This may also alter the threshold values of sensor signals that indicate whether a product should pass a quality control gate or not. To ensure consistent ML-based decision outcomes and predictions in such varying and uncertain conditions, concept drifts have to be handled accurately [6,21]. Requirements for an ideal system for handling concept drifts are: (1) Capability to rapidly detect changing environments and to adapt ML models to occurring concept drifts, (2) robust differentiation between concept drifts and noise, and (3) ability to detect and cope with recurring contexts [6,21].

M6 - Cost-Sensitive Modeling. A promising approach to maximize classification accuracy is cost-sensitive boosting, e. g, AdaBoost.NC [30]. Such cost-sensitive techniques consider costs as penalty of a misclassification. The idea is to iteratively train and test a ML model until the overall misclassification costs are minimal or below a certain threshold. One difficulty in applying such techniques is that the real costs are often unknown or hard to calculate for a given problem domain [25]. This also holds for the manufacturing domain [10]. In this domain, it is additionally of utmost importance to distinguish the costs of different types of misclassifications. For instance, consider a real-world fault detection use case, where a product is either classified as "OK" (negative) or "NOT OK" (positive). Here, we require different misclassification costs of false positives and false negatives [26]. A false positive means that we classify a product as "NOT OK" that actually did not have any quality issue. This leads to an unnecessary subsequent fault diagnosis and repair tasks. This however causes much less costs than a false negative. In this case, the product is classified as "OK" and is hence delivered to the customer. Due to the false negative, the customer however gets a faulty product, which then has to be returned to the supplier.

3.2   Challenges Related to Characteristics of Data and Data Sources

As shwon in Fig. 3, these problems and challenges mainly refer to the data provisioning layer and to its dependencies to the manufacturing layer.

D1 - Complex Data Fusion from Multimodal Data Sources. Manufacturing environments comprise several machines and assembly units. Each machine or assembly unit may offer different data acquisition techniques, e.g., different measurement instruments or sensors, to obtain data or information about one particular product or process step. According to Lahat et al. [19], each combination of one data source and an associated data acquisition technique is called a *modality*. Furthermore, each modality has to provide some new and unique additional information that is not available from other modalities. So, the *overall set of modalities* in a manufacturing environment comprises several data sources and data acquisition techniques, all of which are inevitably required to retrieve the full set of generally available information [19].

In theory, a manufacturing company needs to select and integrate all data sources and data acquisition techniques that together cover such a set of modalities. This way, they obtain the greatest possible amount of information with a minimum number of data sources and data acquisition techniques. In practice, this is however a challenging task. The individual modalities, i.e., both the data sources and the data acquisition techniques show a high degree of heterogeneity. Some data sources contain time-series data, while others store relational data or even textual data [3,16]. This makes it necessary to apply data fusion techniques on all relevant modalities to get a unified view on heterogeneous data [17,19]. However, several articles report on various problems and challenges that arise from a multimodal data fusion [17,19]. For instance, many sensors deliver their data in different time resolutions. So, it is very complicated to compare and combine these data. The following challenges D2 to D4 discuss additional detailed challenges that arise from this setup with multimodal data sources.

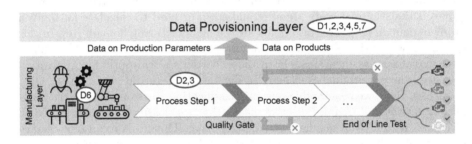

Fig. 3. The challenges and problems related to the characteristics of data and data sources are associated with the manufacturing layer and the data provisioning layer.

D2 - Missing Primary and Foreign Key Relations. During data acquisitions along multiple process steps in manufacturing environments, we have to ensure that the acquired data is uniquely and correctly mapped to the related products. This requires a consistent and unique primary and foreign key relation between a product and all the different information along multiple process steps. However, many data structures and data formats used in real-world manufacturing use cases do not contain such unique primary and foreign key relations [10,33].

D3 - Unsynchronized Timestamps Along Manufacturing Process Steps. Many manufacturing lines follow a defined processing order of successive process and test steps. Many data analyses have to explicitly take into account the chronological sequence of these process and test steps. This is especially important for time-critical and real-time analyses. Consider an example, where we want to analyse all data obtained from several quality control units in a manufacturing line. Each control unit thereby uses its own clock as time signal. If we acquire data directly from the control units, we have to ensure that these time signals are synchronized. One solution for synchronizing time signals is to use the Network Time Protocol (NTP). If this is not implemented by the underlying devices, one has to come up with appropriate time alignment capabilities.

D4 - Duplicate and Invalid Data Samples. Manufacturing data often contain duplicate and invalid data samples [10, 33]. This is due to undesired effects at data acquisition processes, e.g., disturbed sensor measurements. Another reason is that some products pass the same process or test step over and over again, thus generating the same or similar data samples several times (cf. challenge M4). Both, duplicate and invalid data samples have to be identified and filtered out to create a valid dataset for machine learning algorithms.

D5 - Missing Specifications and Explanations of Data. Before applying a ML algorithm to train a model, data scientists have to decide which variables or features in a dataset are relevant to learning the target concept. For parts of this feature selection, data scientists require a priori knowledge about the meaning of variables and their causal relationships. This a priori knowledge about data and variables may be encoded in specifications such as data schemas or in further explanations of data. However, such data specifications and explanations are rarely or only partially available in many real-world manufacturing use cases [10].

D6 - Insufficient Data Acquisition. Most manufacturing processes underlie time-continuous physical processes. Measurement devices, e, g., sensors, hence also record time-continuous signals describing properties of these physical processes. These time-continuous signals provide the maximum possible information content. However, data acquisition techniques reduce this information content, because they need to discretize time-continuous signals using a specific sample rate. Usually, a lower sample rate leads to a less information content. In the worst case, we even get a strongly condensed representation of the underlying physical process by acquiring only a single nominal value for each sensor, e.g., a mean value [10]. In such a case, data scientists are not capable to derive information-rich features due to this condensed representation of the manufacturing process.

D7 - Non-traceable Data Schema Changes. In a manufacturing process, data is usually acquired over a long time period and stored in a database. The data schema of this database may be subject to several changes. For example, consider that the firmware of a sensor device is updated to a new version and that this update lets the sensor device deliver values for additional attributes. A new test software version at the quality gate with new measurements and new test output parameters is another example. Then, the data schema of the underlying database has to be changed by adding new columns. This may be handled by schemaless NoSQL databases, but then data-accessing applications have to interpret the meaning of data on their own.

3.3 Challenges Related to Analytics

The analytics-related problems and challenges are mainly related to the application layer (see Fig. 4). Nevertheless, they also concern the backtracking of learned concepts and analysis results to the manufacturing layer.

Fig. 4. The challenges related to analytics and to software that are mapped to the components of the application layer.

A1 - Missing Trust in ML Models and Analysis Results. ML models are an abstract representation of the underlying learned concepts, e.g., a decision tree. This abstraction may make it hard to comprehend how a ML model has been created via the used algorithm and how this model is projected to the underlying use case. This is especially true for non-data-scientists such as quality engineers and workers on the shop floor. Hence, these non-data-scientists often do not trust the analysis results, e.g., the decisions made by ML models. While decision trees may be easily interpretable, other ML models such as artificial neural networks are hard to interpret. It is however essential to be able to understand and interpret the results, how they have been constructed, and what they mean for the underlying use case. For instance, false positives in quality control have an financial impact, while false negatives could have security implications (see challenge M6 in Sect. 3.1). This missing trust and its domain-specific implications often significantly reduces user acceptance of ML-based solutions.

A2 - Backtracking of Analysis Results to Root Causes. As ML models are abstract representations of the underlying concepts, it may be difficult to project the meanings of analysis results back to the corresponding process step or root cause in a production line. A typical use case in manufacturing environments is to predict the quality of a product, i.e., whether it is "OK" or "NOT OK". In case of a "NOT OK" prediction, one normally wants to know two further points about the fault. One point is the root cause within the production line, e.g., a particular process step, which is responsible for the bad quality [12]. Here, standard feature importance measures may help, but they give only rough guidance for the user. Recently, new methods have been proposed to interpret or to explain models at a more detailed level. One example are SHAP values [22]. An application to manufacturing quality control is discussed by Ziekow et al. [35]. The other point is to identify the root cause within an assembled product, e.g., which product part caused a quality issue [10]. This information gives hints for fixing the fault in a rework step after the assembly line (see Sect. 2.3).

The possibility of backtracking analysis results to a root causes mainly depends on how the learning problem is modeled. As an example, a binary classifier can just predict two states, e.g., the labels "OK" and "NOT OK". On basis of this binary output, it is not possible to make any assumptions about what and where the root cause is. The information content of the input data set for machine learning has a big influence. The more fine-grained a manufacturing process is mapped into this data set the more accurate a root cause can be backtracked.

A3 - Management of Manifold Machine Learning Models. All products of a company require quality management and at least the important production errors should be controlled by machine learning. As a consequence, a company has to manage many machine learning models for various products and production errors. These ML models are of different technical types, e.g., a decision tree or forest, matrices, neural networks or something else. Furthermore, each model is associated with characteristics about used features, class labels, model evaluations such as a confusion matrix or a ROC curve, as well as attributes of training data or data sources. Meanwhile, first systems are available which manage models and their characteristics, e.g., ModelDB [28]. These systems are however too generic to be directly suitable for manufacturing use cases. A new challenge is the linking between technical meta data of ML model management to domain-specific information about products, production and investigation goals [31].

A4 - Feature Engineering, Selection of Models and Parameters. A basic challenge in machine learning is to find the best input in the form of selected and prepared features. Feature engineering refers to derived combinations of other features, e.g., as result of mathematical functions. Other challenges are to select a suitable model type (e.g., decision tree or neural network), an appropriate ML algorithm, and the best hyper-parameters for the algorithm. A manual search for the best option among all diverse solution alternatives is a very cumbersome task. AutoML is an approach to automate this task by constructing machine learning programs without human assistance [5]. Based on the input data, an AutoML system tries to optimize some classification or regression objective.

3.4   Challenges Related to Software

S1 - Missing Modern Data Access Interfaces. The individual machines or assembly units of a manufacturing environment offer their data via specific software interfaces and heterogeneous communication solutions. Modern industrial communication approaches such as the Open Platform Communication Unified Architecture (OPC UA) promise to offer unified data access mechanisms across different machine and equipment vendors [32]. However, the experiences with the real-world use cases of our industry partners revealed that many vendors still offer their own proprietary interfaces for data storage and data access. These vendor-specific interfaces are often characterized by proprietary data export formats. So, a manufacturing company has to spend lots of effort to implement specialized wrapper functions that extract, transform and load the data into a format that is suitable for the given use case. Often, this even requires to change the source code of the control units that are mounted on the machines. This challenge arises along several layers of the functional setup shown in Figs. 2, 3 and 4, as it concerns the interfaces between the layers. Nevertheless, it is less related to the data analytics process itself, rather it is caused by the given technical circumstances and the nature of manufacturing environments.

S2 - Scripting Individual Solutions. A usual approach to data science is exploring a specific problem, analyzing possible solution approaches and writing a specific solution for the given problem. Some scripting languages like R or Python with their libraries are specialized for this task. The most complicated part has to be done before actually applying machine learning algorithms. Data scientists usually spend a vast amount of time to implement scripts that access the right data and prepare data for machine learning, taking into account the various problems and challenges discussed in Sects. 3.1 and 3.2. The problems for machine learning itself are selecting appropriate algorithms and tuning of algorithm hyper-parameters. After applying these algorithms, the results need to be evaluated, where visualizations with many kinds of plots are useful.

With various products and diverse production steps, many individual script solutions are coming up written by several groups of data scientists. This may lead to source codes which are hard to maintain. Furthermore, it hinders reusability of existing script solutions, which in turn leads to likewise high efforts for the next data science task. Hence, software engineering and software design are important issues as well. A domain-oriented analytics application for production quality control using meta data is one part of an answer to this problem. Section 4 sketches a functional architecture for this purpose. Another part of an answer is using automated machine learning (AutoML) [5] (see challenge A3).

4   Future Functional Architecture

Figure 5 sketches a blueprint architecture which should be used by data science applications for manufacturing quality control. The individual systems instantiating the blueprint and its components may come in different flavors: as a generic application suitable for many companies, as an extension of existing quality control systems, or as a specific implementation for a special work plant or for a particular production line. All variations should satisfy the constraints described below. The blueprint comprises a comprehensive mapping of all problems and challenges to the components of the functional architecture. Note that it is beyond the scope of the paper to describe solutions of individual components.

The next subsections describe the five main functions of the functional architecture. The *Application Layer* addresses most of the challenges, since a change in the manufacturing layer and its information system architectures may result in significant technical interventions in existing production systems. This might

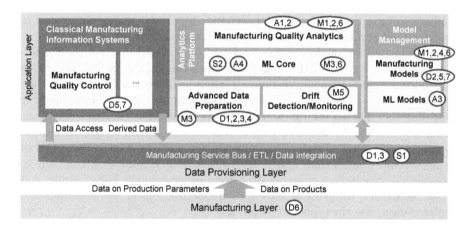

Fig. 5. Overview of the proposed functional architecture. Furthermore, the figure maps challenges to components that contribute to solutions addressing the challenges.

have a negative impact on these production systems, which might even worsen the problems and challenges from Sect. 3 (an exception is D6). In addition to the two essential functions of ML-based prediction (Sect. 4.3) and analysis of quality-related ML results (Sect. 4.4), the Application Layer comprises three preparing functions: manufacturing modeling (Sect. 4.1), data preparation and model training (Sect. 4.2), and concept drift detection and re-training (Sect. 4.5). The function of data provisioning (Sect. 4.6) addresses three challenges related to the *Data Provisioning Layer*.

4.1   Manufacturing Modeling

One basic idea of the blueprint architecture is to define and use domain knowledge about products, production processes, and procedures for quality tests. This idea is based on our experiences with all real-world use cases introduced in Sect. 2. The *Management of Manufacturing Models* provides required domain knowledge, and the components *Advanced Data Preparation, ML Core, Manufacturing Quality Analytics* and *ML Models* may benefit profoundly from this meta data. Usually, quality engineers and workers are able to enter domain knowledge. Alternatively, it is possible to extract it from other systems. For instance, product information is one basic ingredient and may be retrieved from an ERP system. In particular, knowledge about product families and product hierarchies is important. It may be used to address challenge M1, i.e., to conquer the complexity of ML-based approaches dealing with diverse product variants [11]. Additional information that may be used here are costs for wrong predictions, which are needed for cost-sensitive modeling (challenge M6). Another basic ingredient is the testing model, which may be derived from a manufacturing quality control system. It comprises knowledge about test results used as features, diverse error types and their grouping to error families (M2). Furthermore, a manufacturing model has to include relationships between individual tests and quality gates, in particular their chronological order in a non-linear production line (M4).

If machine, operational resources and environment features are used, additional knowledge is helpful. Here, data schemata can change, hence the system has to manage different schema versions (D7). For instance, a test software update with new test parameters or a new production step implies a new data schema. One way to address a missing information problem is to postulate the definition of the missing information. As discussed in Sect. 3.2, there is usually no documentation for dependencies between data, i.e., unknown primary and foreign keys (D2) or missing specifications of data (D5). Nevertheless, it is helpful for a company to define this documentation or to obtain it from other systems. For example, it is anyway useful for a company to have formal specifications of test programs and associated data, e. g, the types of test parameters.

4.2   Advanced Data Preparation and Training of ML Models

A quality engineer should be able to start model training for selected products and process steps based on error statistics coming from the classical quality control system. To cope with many product variants (M1) and error types (M2), a *ML Core* component may use AutoML [5] to find learning algorithms, hyperparameters and features for model training per product group and error type (A4). This relieves data scientists from the cumbersome task of scripting and testing different solution alternatives in a trial-and-error manner (S2, A4). Here, the *ML Core* may use domain knowledge from model management, e.g., for enhanced feature engineering or for a thorough selection of algorithms which can deal with small numbers (M3) of diverse errors (M2). Furthermore, an important optimization criteria for AutoML approaches may be business costs to support cost-sensitive modeling (M6).

The *Advanced Data Preparation* component incorporates existing technologies to support the task of data preparation before model training. This includes means for data profiling, cleaning, normalization, sampling, or encoding [7]. As a first step, the component has to get the right data from the *Data Provisioning Layer*. Instead of hard coding of queries and access procedures, *Advanced Data Preparation* should use meta data from *Manufacturing Model Management* in order to specify domain-specific queries to data. Biased and imbalanced data (M3) is a known problem in many domains. Hence, many solutions such as sampling techniques exist that may cope with this problem [7]. The challenge of duplicate and invalid data samples (D4) is also part of data preparation. Complex setups with multimodal data sources (D1) may be solved by an interplay of domain knowledge from *Manufacturing Model Management* and *Advanced Data Preparation* as well. In addition, information about the production line permits the system to join test and production data from each step. Here, the *Advanced Data Preparation* component has to cope with missing primary and foreign key relations in these data sources (D2). Since a work piece can repeatedly pass a production step (M4), joining has to keep the chronological ordering, thereby coping with unsynchronized timestamps along manufacturing steps (D3).

4.3   ML-Based Predictions and ML Model Management

The *Model Management* component addresses challenge A3, i.e. it copes with the manifold ML models that are available in a company. For instance, data scientists or the *ML Core* may use this component to store their ML models along with specific technical characteristics. Other users may then query the component to find the right model for their classification or regression task [31]. At any quality gate of the *Manufacturing Layer*, we may use ML models for error prediction. Therefore, new data samples trigger the *ML Core* to retrieve the right model from the *Model Management* component. As mentioned in Sect. 3.3, this requires to link technical meta data of ML models with domain-specific information, e.g., about production steps. This is the reason why the *Model Management* component not only covers information about ML models, but also about manufacturing models (see Fig. 5).

4.4   Manufacturing Quality Analytics

The *Manufacturing Quality Analytics* provides quality engineers and workers with a domain-oriented view on machine learning results. This component uses meta data on product families (M1) and error types (M2) to provide aggregated information to this domain-oriented view. Furthermore, it implements solutions to enhance the interpretation and explanation of complex analysis results, e.g., of ML models. This way, it addresses the challenge of missing trust in complex ML algorithms and models (A1). This may include presentations of correlations between features derived by feature engineering of AutoML. In addition, this component may calculate and visualize dependencies between errors and features, which are the basis to backtrack analysis results to their root causes (A2). Furthermore, it supports cost-sensitive modeling (M6) by incorporating costs of false predictions together with typical evaluation metrics for ML models.

4.5   Concept Drift Detection and Re-training of ML Models

Since concept drifts may happen (M5), the quality of error predictions in a production line has to be monitored constantly. The *Drift Detection/Monitoring* component is responsible for the tasks of monitoring ML models that are currently in use and for detecting concept drifts. When it detects a concept drift for an error type of a product, re-training of affected ML models becomes indispensable. For this purpose, the *Drift Detection/Monitoring* component inquires other system components and coordinates their work. The *ML Core* has to define which training and test data are needed. It then commissions the *Advanced Data Preparation* component to obtain the data. Afterwards, the *ML Core* re-learns the new ML model and stores it within the ML Model Management.

4.6   Data Provisioning Layer

Challenges D1, D3, and S1 cover typical problems of information integration for manufacturing data. These problems may be solved by generic ETL tools or via service bus technologies. For instance, we may use the manufacturing services bus (MSB) proposed by Minguez et al. [23]. The MSB offers a proven solution to integrate various applications and information systems from a whole manufacturing environment. As shown in Fig. 5, we use it to provide data from the manufacturing layer to all systems in the application layer. Furthermore, we may use it to deliver derived data, i.e., the results from *Classical Manufacturing Information Systems* to our new components shown in blue in the figure. Hence, a direct connection at the application layer between new and old applications as in the functional setup of Fig. 1 is no longer required.

5   Conclusion

This paper summarizes our experiences from three industrial use cases and from a literature survey regarding data science approaches to manufacturing quality control. Bringing together this knowledge from several research groups evidences many commonalities and a long list of requirements and difficulties for data science. It turns out that four categories of problems and challenges are important. The first category is clustered around the manufacturing domain itself, i.e., data science approaches have to be specialized to satisfy domain constraints. A second list of issues is related to the characteristics of data and data sources. In particular, data from operating equipment, products or test stations are not well structured or come with diverse and continuously changing formats. The third category reflects challenges related to the properties of analytical applications. For instance, domain experts need more detailed explanations of the outcomes of classification or regression models, because they otherwise doubt the results. The fourth category of software-related problems reveals the immature state of software interfaces, as they are used in today's manufacturing environments.

In addition, we propose a functional software architecture that extends the current functional setup of QM in manufacturing environments by novel components. This architecture represents a visionary blueprint for solutions addressing all identified problems and challenges for data science approaches to manufacturing quality control. We thereby sketch how individual components of this architecture may solve particular problems and challenges.

Due to its visionary nature, this functional architecture constitutes a good basis for future research opportunities. Individual software components need to be further researched and devised. This also requires to supplement existing ML approaches so that they reflect the inherent characteristics of quality control applications in manufacturing environments. Another interesting idea for research is to develop and evaluate software design patterns for problems and solutions.

Acknowledgement. We would like to thank the German Research Foundation (DFG) for financial support of parts of this work in the Graduate School of advanced Manaufacturing Engineering (GSC 262). Parts of this work is based on earlier publications of the PREFERML project. PREFERML is funded by the German Federal Ministry of Education and Research, funding line "Forschung an Fachhochschulen mit

Unternehmen (FHProfUnt)", contract number 13FH249PX6. The responsibility for the content of this publication lies with the authors.

References

1. Breiman, L.: Random Forests. Mach. Learn. **45**(1), 5–32 (2001). https://doi.org/10.1023/A:1010933404324
2. Chawla, N., Japkowicz, N., Kołcz, A.: Editorial: Special issue on learning from imbalanced data sets. SIGKDD Explor. **6**, 1–6 (2004). https://doi.org/10.1145/1007730.1007733
3. Cheng, Y., et al.: Data and knowledge mining with big data towards smart production. J. Ind. Inf. Integr. **9**, 1–13 (2018). https://doi.org/10.1016/j.jii.2017.08.001
4. Choudhary, A., Harding, J., Tiwari, M.: Data mining in manufacturing: A review based on the kind of knowledge. J. Intell. Manuf. **20**, 501–521 (2009). https://doi.org/10.1007/s10845-008-0145-x
5. Feurer, M., et al.: Efficient and robust automated machine learning. In: Proceedings of the 28th International Conference on Neural Information Processing Systems (NIPS 2015), pp. 2755–2763. MIT Press, Cambridge, MA, USA (2015)
6. Gama, J., et al.: A survey on concept drift adaptation. ACM Comput. Surv. **46**(4), 44:1–44:37 (2014)
7. García, S., Luengo, J., Herrera, F.: Data Preprocessing in Data Mining. Intelligent Systems Reference Library, vol. 72. Springer International Publishing, Cham (2015). https://doi.org/10.1007/978-3-319-10247-4
8. Gerling, A., et al.: A reference process model for machine learning aided production quality management. In: Proceedings of the 22nd International Conference on Enterprise Information Systems, pp. 515–523. SCITEPRESS - Science and Technology Publications, Prague, Czech Republic (2020). https://doi.org/10.5220/0009379705150523
9. Harding, J., Shahbaz, M.: Data mining in manufacturing: A review. J. Manuf. Sci. Eng. Trans. ASME **128**(4), 969–976 (2006). https://doi.org/10.1115/1.2194554
10. Hirsch, V., Reimann, P., Mitschang, B.: Data-driven fault diagnosis in end-of-line testing of complex products. In: Proceedings of the 6th IEEE International Conference on Data Science and Advanced Analytics (DSAA), pp. 492–503. IEEE, Washington, D.C., USA (2019). https://doi.org/10.1109/DSAA.2019.00064
11. Hirsch, V., Reimann, P., Mitschang, B.: Exploiting domain knowledge to address multi-class imbalance and a heterogeneous feature space in classification tasks for manufacturing data. Proc. VLDB Endowment **13**(12), 3258–3271 (2020). https://doi.org/10.14778/3415478.3415549
12. Hirsch, V., et al.: Analytical approach to support fault diagnosis and quality control in End-Of-Line testing. Procedia CIRP, 51st CIRP Conf. Manuf. Syst. **72**, 1333–1338 (2018)
13. Hu, S., et al.: Product variety and manufacturing complexity in assembly systems and supply chains. CIRP Ann. **57**(1), 45–48 (2008). https://doi.org/10.1016/j.cirp.2008.03.138
14. Isermann, R.: Fault-Diagnosis Systems: An Introduction from Fault Detection to Fault Tolerance. Springer-Verlag, Berlin Heidelberg (2006)
15. ISO 9000:2015: Quality management systems - Fundamental and vocabulary. Standard, International Organization for Standardization, ISO/TC 176/SC 1 Concepts and terminology, Geneva, CH (2015)

16. Kassner, L., Mitschang, B.: Exploring text classification for messy data: An industry use case for domain-specific analytics technology. In: Proceedings of the 19th International Conference on Extending Database Technology (EDBT 2016), pp. 491–502. ACM, Bordeaux, France (2016). https://doi.org/10.5441/002/edbt.2016.47

17. Khaleghi, B., et al.: Multisensor data fusion: A review of the state-of-the-art. Inf. Fusion **14**(1), 28–44 (2013). https://doi.org/10.1016/j.inffus.2011.08.001

18. Köksal, G., Batmaz, İ., Testik, M.C.: A review of data mining applications for quality improvement in manufacturing industry. Expert Syst. Appl. **38**(10), 13448–13467 (2011). https://doi.org/10.1016/j.eswa.2011.04.063

19. Lahat, D., Adali, T., Jutten, C.: Multimodal data fusion: An overview of methods, challenges, and prospects. Proc. IEEE Multimodal Data Fusion **103**(9), 1449–1477 (2015). https://doi.org/10.1109/JPROC.2015.2460697

20. Leitner, L., Lagrange, A., Endisch, C.: End-of-line fault detection for combustion engines using one-class classification. In: Proceedings of the IEEE International Conference on Advanced Intelligent Mechatronics (AIM), pp. 207–213. Banff, AB, Canada (2016). https://doi.org/10.1109/AIM.2016.7576768

21. Lu, J., et al.: Learning under concept drift: A review. Trans. Knowl. Data Eng. **31**, 2346–2363 (2019). https://doi.org/10.1109/TKDE.2018.2876857

22. Lundberg, S.M., Lee, S.I.: A unified approach to interpreting model predictions. In: Guyon, I., et al. (eds.) Advances in Neural Information Processing Systems 30, pp. 4765–4774. Curran Associates, Inc., New York (2017)

23. Minguez, J., et al.: A service bus architecture for application integration in the planning and production phases of a product lifecycle. Int. J. Syst. Service-Oriented Eng. **2**(2), 21–36 (2011). https://doi.org/10.4018/978-1-4666-2470-2.ch010

24. Schmitt, R.: Quality assurance. In: Chatti, S., Laperrière, L., Reinhart, G., Tolio, T. (eds.) CIRP Encyclopedia of Production Engineering, pp. 1402–1406. Springer, Berlin Heidelberg, Berlin, Heidelberg (2019)

25. Sun, Y., Wong, A.K.C., Kamel, M.S.: Classification of imbalanced data: A review. Int. J. Pattern Recognit. Artif. Intell. **23**(04), 687–719 (2009). https://doi.org/10.1142/S0218001409007326

26. Thai-Nghe, N., Gantner, Z., Schmidt-Thieme, L.: Cost-sensitive learning methods for imbalanced data. In: Proceedings of the 2010 International Joint Conference on Neural Networks (IJCNN) (2010). https://doi.org/10.1109/IJCNN.2010.5596486

27. Thalmann, S., et al.: Cognitive decision support for industrial product life cycles: A position paper. In: Proceedings of the 11th International Conference on Advanced Cognitive Technologies and Applications, pp. 3–9. IARIA, Venice, Italy (2019)

28. Vartak, M., et al.: ModelDB: A system for machine learning model management. In: Proceedings of the Workshop on Human-In-the-Loop Data Analytics (HILDA), San Francisco, CA, USA (2016). https://doi.org/10.1145/2939502.2939516

29. VDI 5600 Part 1 - Manufacturing Execution Systems (MES). Standard, Verein Deutscher Ingenieure e.V. (VDI), Düsseldorf, DE (2016)

30. Wang, S., Yao, X.: Multiclass imbalance problems: Analysis and potential solutions. IEEE Trans. Syst. Man Cybern. B Cybern. **42**(4), 1119–1130 (2012). https://doi.org/10.1109/TSMCB.2012.2187280

31. Weber, C., Hirmer, P., Reimann, P.: A model management platform for industry 4.0 - Enabling management of machine learning models in manufacturing environments. In: Abramowicz, W., Klein, G. (eds.) Business Information Systems, vol. 389, pp. 403–417. Springer International Publishing, Cham (2020)

32. Wollschlaeger, M., Sauter, T., Jasperneite, J.: The future of industrial communication: Automation networks in the era of the internet of things and industry 4.0. IEEE Ind. Electron. Mag. **11**(1), 17–27 (2017)
33. Wüst, T., et al.: Machine learning in manufacturing: Advantages, challenges, and applications. Prod. Manuf. Res. **4**, 23–45 (2016)
34. Ziekow, H., et al.: Proactive error prevention in manufacturing based on an adaptable machine learning environment. In: Artificial Intelligence: From Research to Application: Proc. of the Upper-Rhine Artificial Intelligence Symposium UR-AI, pp. 113–117. Offenburg, Germany (2019)
35. Ziekow, H., et al.: Technical Report: Interpretable machine learning for quality engineering in manufacturing - Importance measures that reveal insights on errors. Tech. rep., Furtwangen University of Applied Science (2019). https://nbn-resolving.de/urn:nbn:de:bsz:fn1-opus4-55331

The NISQ Analyzer: Automating the Selection of Quantum Computers for Quantum Algorithms

Marie Salm$^{(\boxtimes)}$, Johanna Barzen , Uwe Breitenbücher , Frank Leymann ,
Benjamin Weder , and Karoline Wild

Institute of Architecture of Application Systems, University of Stuttgart,
Universitätsstraße 38, Stuttgart, Germany
{salm,barzen,breitenbuecher,leymann,weder,wild}@iaas.uni-stuttgart.de

Abstract. Quantum computing can enable a variety of breakthroughs in research and industry in the future. Although some quantum algorithms already exist that show a theoretical speedup compared to the best known classical algorithms, the implementation and execution of these algorithms come with several challenges. The input data determines, for example, the required number of qubits and gates of a quantum algorithm. A quantum algorithm implementation also depends on the used Software Development Kit which restricts the set of usable quantum computers. Because of the limited capabilities of current quantum computers, choosing an appropriate one to execute a certain implementation for a given input is a difficult challenge that requires immense mathematical knowledge about the implemented quantum algorithm as well as technical knowledge about the used Software Development Kits. In this paper, we present a concept for the automated analysis and selection of implementations of quantum algorithms and appropriate quantum computers that can execute a selected implementation with a certain input data. The practical feasibility of the concept is demonstrated by the prototypical implementation of a tool that we call NISQ Analyzer.

Keywords: Quantum computing · Quantum algorithms · Hardware selection · Implementation selection · Decision support · NISQ analyzer

1 Introduction

Quantum computing is a promising field that may enable breakthroughs in various areas such as computer science, physics, and chemistry [25]. The unique characteristics of quantum mechanics, such as *superposition* and *entanglement*, are the reasons quantum computing is more powerful than classical computing for specific problems [2,29,32]. In fact, some quantum algorithms already exist that show a theoretical speedup over their best known classical counterparts. For example, the *Shor* algorithm provides an exponential speedup in factorizing numbers [34]. With a large enough quantum computer, this algorithm could break cryptosystems such as the commonly used RSA [29].

© Springer Nature Switzerland AG 2020
S. Dustdar (Ed.): SummerSOC 2020, CCIS 1310, pp. 66–85, 2020.
https://doi.org/10.1007/978-3-030-64846-6_5

However, there are several challenges regarding the execution of quantum algorithms. There is a multitude of different implementations for quantum algorithms that are only applicable to certain input data, e.g., in terms of the number of qubits required for its encoding. These implementations differ from each other in various aspects, e.g., the required number of qubits and operations [11]. Both numbers often depend on the input data. Thus, the input data influences whether a particular quantum algorithm implementation is executable on a certain quantum computer: If the number of required qubits or operations is higher than the number of qubits or the decoherence time, i.e. the time the states of qubits are stable, of the quantum computer, the implementation with the given input cannot be executed successfully. Error rates, fidelity, and qubit connectivity of current so-called *Noisy Intermediate-Scale Quantum (NISQ)* computers also play an important role in the decision [17,29].

Moreover, there is no accepted common quantum programming language [19]. As a result, most quantum computer vendors have their proprietary Software Development Kit (SDK) for developing and executing implementations on their quantum computers [16]. However, this tightly couples the implementation of a quantum algorithm to a certain quantum computer. As a result, choosing an implementation for a quantum algorithm to be executed for given input data and selecting an appropriate quantum computer is a multi-dimensional challenge. It requires immense mathematical knowledge about the implemented algorithm as well as technical knowledge about the used SDKs. Hence, *(i) the selection of a suitable implementation of a quantum algorithm for a specific input* and *(ii) the selection of a quantum computer with, e.g., sufficient qubits and decoherence time* is currently one of the main problems of quantum computing in practice.

In this paper, we present the concept of the *NISQ Analyzer* for analyzing and selecting *(i) an appropriate implementation* and *(ii) suitable quantum computers based on the input data for a chosen quantum algorithm.* The approach is based on defined selection criteria for each implementation described as first-order logic rules. Rule-based selection mechanisms have been established as proven principles and concepts [21]. We consider the number of required qubits of the implementation and the number of qubits of eligible quantum computers, while vendor-specific SDKs are also heeded. In addition, the number of operations of an implementation is determined and the corresponding decoherence times of the different quantum computers are considered. To determine the number of qubits and operations of an implementation, hardware-specific transpilers, e.g., provided by the vendors, are used. For demonstrating the practical feasibility of the proposed NISQ Analyzer, a prototypical implementation is presented. It is designed as a plug-in based system, such that additional criteria, e.g., error rates, fidelity, or qubit connectivity, can be added.

The paper is structured as follows: Sect. 2 introduces the fundamentals, current challenges, and the problem statement. Section 3 shows an overview of our approach. Section 4 presents the overall system architecture. Section 5 presents the prototypical implementation and our validation. Section 6 discusses related work. Section 7 concludes the paper and presents future work.

2   Background, Challenges and Problem Statement

In this section, we introduce the fundamentals and current challenges when using quantum computers during the Noisy Intermediate-Scale Quantum (NISQ) era [29]. Afterward, quantum algorithms and the current state of their implementations are presented. Finally, we formulate the problem statement and the resulting research question of this paper.

2.1   Quantum Computers and NISQ Era

Instead of working with classical bits, quantum computers, or more precisely *Quantum Processing Units (QPUs)*, use so-called *qubits* [26]. As classical bits can only be in one of the two states 0 or 1, qubits can be in both states at the same time [26,32]: A unit vector in a two-dimensional complex vector space represents the state of a qubit [26]. Operators applied to these vectors are *unitary* matrices. Qubits interact with their environment, and thus, their states are only stable for a certain time, called *decoherence time* [7,26,32]. The required operations have to be applied in this time frame to get proper results from computations. Furthermore, different quantum computing models exist, e.g., *one-way* [30], *adiabatic* [1], and *gate-based* [26]. In this paper, we only consider the gate-base quantum computing model, as many of the existing quantum computers, e.g., from IBM[1] and Rigetti[2], base on this model [16]. Thereby, *gates* represent the unitary operations. Combined with qubits and measurements they form a *quantum circuit* [26]. Such quantum circuits are gate-based representations of *quantum algorithms*. The number of gate collections to be sequentially executed defines the *depth* of a quantum circuit. Within such a collection, called *layer*, gates are performed in parallel. The number of qubits defines the *width* of the circuit. Both properties determine the required number of qubits and the minimum decoherence time a suitable quantum computer has to provide.

Each quantum computer has a set of physically implemented gates [32]. However, the sets of implemented gates differ from quantum computer to quantum computer. Thus, to create quantum circuits for specific problems, non-implemented gates must be realized by a subroutine of available gates of the specific quantum computer [19]. The substitution of non-implemented gates by subroutines is done by the hardware-specific transpiler of the vendor. Therefore, the transpiler maps the gates and qubits of the circuit to the gate sets and qubits of the regarded quantum computers. The resulting transpiled circuit may have a different depth and width from the circuit. Especially the resulting depth of the transpilied circuit can differ greatly between different quantum computers [17]. The mapping process is known to be NP-hard [8,36]. Thus, transpiling the same circuit several times can lead to slightly different values of width and depth and depends on the mapping algorithm of the transpiler.

Today's quantum computers only have a few qubits and short decoherence times [41]. Further, high error rates limit the number of operations that can

---

[1] https://www.ibm.com.
[2] https://www.rigetti.com.

be executed before the propagated error makes the computation too erroneous on these quantum computers. However, it is assumed that quantum computers will have up to a few hundred qubits and can perform thousands of operations reliably soon[3,4] [29]. But these qubits will be error-prone as the correction of such errors requires many more qubits [25,29].

> **Challenge I**: *There are a variety of quantum computers that are different regarding their number of qubits, their decoherence time, and their set of physically implemented gates. Therefore, there is serious heterogeneity of available quantum computers, and not every quantum algorithm implementation can be executed on every quantum computer.*

2.2 Quantum Algorithms and Implementations

Many quantum algorithms show a theoretical speedup over their best known classical counterparts. The number of required qubits and operations for the execution of quantum algorithms often depends on the input data. For example, the Shor algorithm requires $2n$ qubits for factorizing the integer N with a binary size of n [11]. Some implementations require additional qubits for executing the algorithm. For example, *Quantum Phase Estimation (QPE)* [27] for computing the eigenvalues of a unitary matrix, needs in many of the existing implementations additional qubits to define the precision of the result. There are also implementations that can only process limited input data. Thus, selecting an appropriate quantum computer to execute a certain quantum algorithm not only depends on the mathematics of the algorithm itself, but also on the physical requirements of its implementations.

In addition, current implementations of quantum algorithms are tightly coupled to their used SDKs. Vendors like IBM and Rigetti offer their proprietary SDKs for their quantum computers, called *Qiskit*[5] and *Forest*[6], respectively. There are also SDKs that support quantum computers of multiple vendors, e.g., *ProjectQ* [38] or *XACC* [22]. Nonetheless, most of the SDKs only support quantum computers of a single vendor for executing quantum circuits [16]. Furthermore, implementations are not interchangeable between different SDKs because of their different programming languages and syntax. As a result, most of the developed implementations are only executable on a certain set of quantum computers provided by a specific vendor.

> **Challenge II**: *An implementation of a quantum algorithm implies physical requirements on a quantum computer. In addition, an implementation usually depends on the used SDK.*

---

[3] https://www.ibm.com/blogs/research/2020/09/ibm-quantum-roadmap/.

[4] https://ionq.com/news/october-01-2020-most-powerful-quantum-computer.

[5] https://qiskit.org.

[6] http://docs.rigetti.com/en/stable/.

2.3   Problem Statement

In this section, we summarize the challenges presented before and formulate the research question regarding the selection of quantum computers capable of executing a quantum algorithm for certain input data. For executing a certain quantum algorithm for given input data, the user has to consider different aspects regarding available quantum algorithm implementations and quantum computers. First, the user has to find manually a suitable implementation of the quantum algorithm that can process the desired input. With the chosen quantum algorithm implementation, the user has to select a suitable quantum computer that can execute the implementation. Thereby, the heterogeneity of quantum computers, with their different qubit counts, decoherence times, and available gate sets, has to be taken into account (*Challenge I*). Additionally, the mathematical, physical, and technical requirements on the quantum computer and the used SDK of the implementation have to be considered for the quantum computer selection (*Challenge II*). Thus, the selection of quantum algorithm implementations and suitable quantum computers requires an immense manual effort and sufficient knowledge on the user side. Hence, the resulting research question can be formulated as follows:

> *Problem Statement*: *How can the selection of the quantum algorithm implementation and the suitable quantum computer be automated based on a certain input data of the chosen quantum algorithm?*

3   Analysis and Selection Approach

In this section, we introduce our concept of a *NISQ Analyzer*, which enables an automated analysis and selection of quantum algorithm implementations and quantum computers depending on the chosen quantum algorithm and input data. Figure 1 depicts an overview of the approach. First, a quantum algorithm is selected. Second, implementations of the algorithm are analyzed and selected. Third, quantum computers are analyzed and selected. Finally, the selected implementation is executed on the suitable quantum computer. In the following, the individual phases are described in detail.

3.1   Algorithm Selection

In the *(1) Algorithm Selection* phase, the user selects one of the provided quantum algorithms for solving a particular problem, e.g., the Shor algorithm for factorization as shown in Fig. 1. Thus, a repository with a set of descriptors of different quantum algorithms is provided, as proposed by [18]. The selected quantum algorithm and the input data serves as input for the analysis and selection phase. In the example, the user wants to factorize 9, thus, $N = 9$.

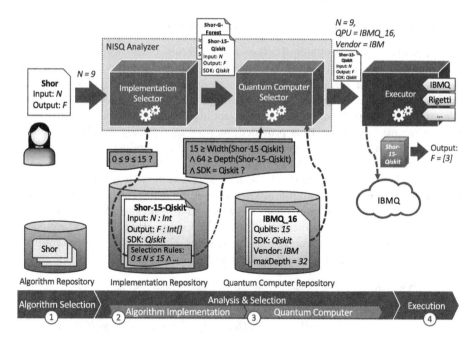

Fig. 1. Approach for automated selection of implementations and quantum computers.

3.2 Algorithm Implementation Analysis and Selection

In the *(2) Algorithm Implementation Analysis and Selection* phase, available implementations of the selected quantum algorithm are browsed to identify applicable implementations that can process the input. Therefore, a repository containing descriptors of different implementations is provided. The descriptors include metadata, such as input and output parameters, and the required SDK. For the identification, selection rules described by first-order logic are attached to the implementations. A rule describes the restrictions for the input data of the respective implementation. The selection rules of the considered implementations are evaluated based on the input data. As exemplary shown in Fig. 1, the selection rule for the implementation *Shor-15-Qiskit* is defined as follows:

$$
y \in \mathcal{I} \forall n \in \mathbb{N} \exists l_0, l_1 \in \mathbb{N} : (InputRange(l_0, l_1, y) \land GreaterEquals(n, l_0) \\
\land SmallerEquals(n, l_1)) \Leftrightarrow Processable(n, y)
\tag{1}
$$

Thereby, $y = Shor\text{-}15\text{-}Qiskit$ is in the set of implementations $\mathcal{I}$ and n is the input data, e.g. $n = N = 9$. $InputRange(l_0, l_1, y)$ describes the range of processable input data of y, e.g., $l_0 = 0$ and $l_1 = 15$ for lower and upper bound. $GreaterEquals(n, l_0)$ defines "$n \geq l_0$" and $SmallerEquals(n, l_1)$ defines "$n \leq l_1$", such that n has to be between 0 and 15. This is all true if and only if $Processable(n, y)$ is true and, thus, $Shor\text{-}15\text{-}Qiskit$ can process $n = N = 9$. The selection rule is implementation-specific and has to be defined by the developer. All implementations that can process n are considered in the next phase.

3.3   Quantum Computer Analysis and Selection

In the *(3) Quantum Computer Analysis and Selection* phase, appropriate quantum computers are identified for the considered implementations. Therefore, the width and depth of the implementations are analyzed and compared with the number of qubits and the estimated maximum depths provided by the available quantum computers. Thus, a corresponding repository with the properties of given quantum computers is provided, as presented in Fig. 1. The estimated maximum depth of a specific quantum computer is determined by dividing the average decoherence time of the supported qubits through the maximum gate time [33]. The width and depth of the implementation with the input data on the considered quantum computer are determined by using the hardware-specific transpiler. The supported transpilers are wrapped as a service. Additionally, the SDKs used by the implementations and the SDKs supporting the quantum computers are considered. The general rule for selecting a suitable quantum computer for a particular implementation is defined as follows:

$$
\begin{aligned}
\forall x \in \mathcal{Q} \forall y \in \mathcal{R} \subseteq \mathcal{I} \exists s \in \mathcal{S} \exists q_0, q_1, d_0, d_1 \in \mathbb{N} : \\
(\mathit{Qubits}(q_0, x) \wedge \mathit{Qubits}(q_1, y) \wedge \mathit{GreaterEquals}(q_0, q_1) \\
\wedge \mathit{Depth}(d_0, x) \wedge \mathit{Depth}(d_1, y) \wedge \mathit{GreaterEquals}(d_0, d_1) \\
\wedge \mathit{Sdk}(s, x) \wedge \mathit{Sdk}(s, y)) \Leftrightarrow \mathit{Executable}(y, x)
\end{aligned}
\tag{2}
$$

Thereby, x is a quantum computer of the set of available quantum computers $\mathcal{Q}$, e.g., *IBMQ_16*. y is an implementation of the set of remaining implementations $\mathcal{R} \subseteq \mathcal{I}$. $\mathit{Qubits}(q_0, x)$ defines the provided number of qubits q_0 of x. $\mathit{Qubits}(q_1, y)$ defines the required number of qubits, or the width, q_1 of y. $\mathit{GreaterEquals}(q_0, q_1)$ defines that "$q_0 \geq q_1$" to ensure that the quantum computer x does not have less qubits than required by y. $\mathit{Depth}(d_0, x)$ defines the maximum depth d_0 executable by x. $\mathit{Depth}(d_1, y)$ defines the depth d_1 of the transpiled circuit of y. $\mathit{GreaterEquals}(d_0, d_1)$ defines that "$d_0 \geq d_1$", such that the maximum executable depth of the quantum computer x is not smaller than required by the implementation y. Furthermore, the SDK $s \in \mathcal{S}$, e.g. *Qiskit*, used by the implementation, defined by $\mathit{Sdk}(y, s)$, must also support the selected quantum computer, defined by $\mathit{Sdk}(x, s)$, to ensure their compatibility. This all is true, if and only if *Executable(y, x)* is true. In the example in Fig. 1, *IBMQ_16* can execute *Shor-15-Qiskit*. If more than one executable implementation remains, the user decides which one to execute. Furthermore, the user also decides, in case, more than one quantum computer can execute the chosen implementation.

3.4   Execution

In the *(4) Execution* phase, the selected implementation is executed by the selected quantum computer, as seen in Fig. 1. The *Executor* supports the different SDKs and can be extended by further plug-ins. Thereby, the required SDK, e.g. *Qiskit*, is used to deliver the quantum circuit to the specific vendor via the cloud. Eventually, the result is returned and displayed to the user.

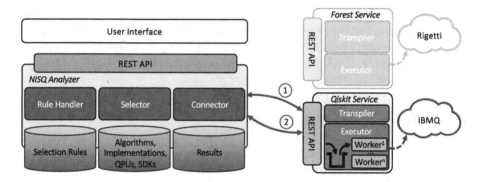

Fig. 2. System architecture for automated analysis and selection.

4   System Architecture

In this section, we introduce the overall system architecture, as shown in Fig. 2. It comprises a *User Interface (UI)*, the *NISQ Analyzer*, and *Services* wrapping the transpilation and execution logic of, e.g., vendor-specific SDKs. The NISQ Analyzer provides a HTTP REST API used by the UI. The *Rule Handler* component, which is part of the NISQ Analyzer, generates, adds, updates, and accesses the selection rules defined in Sect. 3. The *Selector* component identifies suitable implementations and quantum computers dependent on the selected quantum algorithm and input data by invoking the Rule Handler and the Services. The descriptors containing the metadata about algorithms, implementations, quantum computers, and SDKs are stored in a respective repository. A Service invokes the hardware-specific *Transpiler* and *Executor* of a specific SDK. For example, the *Qiskit Service* transpiles and executes Qiskit implementations on quantum computers provided via the cloud on IBMQ[7]. Each Service provides its own HTTP REST API. A *Results* repository stores analysis and execution results.

To start the analysis and selection, the user selects the desired quantum algorithm and provides the input data using the UI. The Selector invokes the Rule Handler to evaluate which implementations of the quantum algorithm can process the input. Therefore, the selection rules defined by the developers are stored in a repository. For determining the width and depth of an implementation on a certain quantum computer, the Selector calls the Transpiler of the required Service using the *Connector* (see (1) in Fig. 2). The resulting values are returned to the Selector and passed to the Rule Handler for evaluating the quantum computer selection rule defined in Sect. 3. The invocation of the transpiler and the evaluation of the general selection rule is performed for each supported quantum computer. With the analysis results presented by the UI, the user selects an implementation and a recommended quantum computer for execution. Next, the NISQ Analyzer invokes the Executor of the specific Service to deliver the implementation to the specific vendor, e.g. IBMQ (see (2) in Fig. 2). Finally, the

---

[7] https://quantum-computing.ibm.com.

Service returns the result to the user. Since multiple transpiler and execution frameworks exist, further Services providing a HTTP REST API and the defined interface can be implemented and invoked by the NISQ Analyzer. On the side of the NISQ Analyzer, the Uniform Resource Locators (URLs) of further Services have to be passed as configuration parameters.

5   Prototype and Validation

In this section, we present our prototypical implementation of the NISQ Analyzer, the UI, and, as a proof of concept, the Qiskit Service. For the validation of our approach, three use cases are presented. Afterward, we discuss the limitations of our prototype.

5.1   Prototype

The prototypical UI of the NISQ Analyzer, as shown in Fig. 2, is implemented in TypeScript. The NISQ Analyzer[8] is implemented in Java using the Spring Boot framework. The descriptors of available quantum computers, SDKs, quantum algorithms, and implementations, as well as the analysis and execution results, are stored in a relational database.

Rule Handling and Selection with Prolog. For the implementation of the first-order logic rules presented in Sect. 3, we use the logic programming language Prolog. For handling Prolog programs, the NISQ Analyzer uses the library and interpreter of SWI-Prolog[9]. The program logic in Prolog is expressed by facts and rules. For computations, facts and rules are queried and evaluate to true or false. A fact is, e.g., "providesQubits(ibmq_16, 15).". It defines that the number of qubits provided by *ibmq_16* is 15. Querying facts always evaluates to true. For the implementation selection, the required rules are defined by the developers and queried with the input data of the user. For the selection of suitable quantum computers, the general rule is defined as follows:

```
executable(CircuitWidth, CircuitDepth, Implementation, Qpu) :-
    providesQubits(Qpu, ProvidedQubits),
    ProvidedQubits >= CircuitWidth,
    t1Time(Qpu, T1Time),
    maxGateTime(Qpu, GateTime),
    CircuitDepth =< T1Time/GateTime,
    requiredSdk(Implementation, Sdk),
    usedSdk(Qpu, Sdk).
```

---

[8] https://github.com/UST-QuAntiL/nisq-analyzer.
[9] https://www.swi-prolog.org.

The general rule is applied on the facts that are automatically generated based on the metadata of implementations and quantum computers. The fact `providesQubits` defines the number of qubits supported by the considered quantum computer. The number of qubits is compared to the width of the considered implementation by `ProvidedQubits >= CircuitWidth`. The facts `t1Time` and `maxGateTime` define the decoherence time and the maximum gate time of the quantum computer to compare the estimated maximum depth with the depth of the implementation: `CircuitDepth =< T1Time/GateTime`. `requiredSdk` defines the SDK of the implementation. This has to match with `usedSdk` which specifies the SDK supporting the specific quantum computer. The general rule evaluates to true, if the properties of the implementation match the properties of the considered quantum computer.

Transpilation and Execution Service. The Qiskit Service[10] is implemented in the programming language Python. For transpiling and executing an implementation on a specific quantum computer, the Python module of the Qiskit SDK[11] is used. Qiskit supports the quantum computers of IBMQ. For transpilation, the NISQ Analyzer examines if the implementation and the quantum computer is supported by Qiskit. This reduces the number of invocations of the Qiskit Service and improves the performance of the overall system. Then, the NISQ Analyzer sends a HTTP request to the Qiskit Service. The request contains the source code location of the implementation, the name of the quantum computer, and the input data of the user. The Qiskit Service retrieves the source code, passes the input data, and transpiles the resulting quantum circuit of the implementation. Thereby, the transpilation process is done locally. The corresponding HTTP response of the Qiskit Service contains the width and depth of the transpiled quantum circuit. The transpiler supports several optimization levels[12]. For our prototype, the light optimization level is used. Higher optimization levels require more classical compute resources and, therefore, more computing time. However, they may further reduce the depth and width of a quantum circuit.

For executing an implementation on a quantum computer, e.g. at IBMQ, jobs are put in queues. Thus, the response of IBMQ containing the execution result is delivered asynchronously. Therefore, execution requests of the NISQ Analyzer are received by the Qiskit Service via HTTP and then placed in a queue using Redis Queue[13]. With several *Workers* listening on the queue, multiple implementations can be executed in parallel, see Fig. 2. The corresponding HTTP response contains the content location of the long-running task, where the execution result is later provided by a relational database of the Qiskit Service.

---

[10] https://github.com/UST-QuAntiL/qiskit-service.
[11] https://github.com/Qiskit.
[12] https://qiskit.org/documentation/stubs/qiskit.compiler.transpile.html.
[13] https://python-rq.org.

Table 1. Analysis results of the Qiskit transpiler for *simon-general-qiskit*.

Input	Width	Depth	Backend
	2	4	ibmq_qasm_simulator
01	2	4	ibmq_5_yorktown
	2	4	ibmq_16_melbourne
	3	8	ibmq_qasm_simulator
0110	3	26	ibmq_5_yorktown
	3	39	*ibmq_16_melbourne**
	3	6	ibmq_qasm_simulator
1000	3	15	ibmq_5_yorktown
	3	23	ibmq_16_melbourne
	3	12	ibmq_qasm_simulator
1111	3	48	ibmq_5_yorktown
	3	74	*ibmq_16_melbourne**
	5	52	ibmq_qasm_simulator
10110010	5	81	ibmq_5_yorktown
	5	132	*ibmq_16_melbourne**
11111111	7	196	ibmq_qasm_simulator
00000000	–	–	*ibmq_5_yorktown**
	7	471	*ibmq_16_melbourne**

Table 2. Analysis results of the Qiskit transpiler for *grover-general-sat-qiskit*.

Input	Width	Depth	Backend
$(A \vee B) \wedge (A \vee \neg B)$	7	29	ibmq_qasm_simulator
$\wedge(\neg A \vee B)$	7	150	*ibmq_16_melbourne**
$(A \vee B \vee \neg C) \wedge (\neg A \vee B \vee C)$	8	103	ibmq_qasm_simulator
$\wedge(\neg A \vee \neg B \vee \neg C)$	15	296	*ibmq_16_melbourne**
$(\neg A \vee \neg B \vee \neg C)$	12	173	ibmq_qasm_simulator
$\wedge(\neg A \vee B \vee C) \wedge (A \vee \neg B \vee C)$			
$\wedge(A \vee B \vee \neg C) \wedge (A \vee \neg B \vee \neg C)$	15	526	*ibmq_16_melbourne**

5.2   Case Studies for Validation

For validating our approach, three quantum algorithms and exemplary implementations are considered as use cases. The implementation selection rules evaluated by the NISQ Analyzer, the results of the transpiler, and the resulting
recommendations of the NISQ Analyzer are presented in the following. The first
considered quantum algorithm is *Simon's* algorithm for the distinction of two
function classes [35]. The second algorithm is the *Grover* algorithm for searching
an item in an unsorted list [9,31]. The third is the *Shor* algorithm for factorizing
an integer with exponential speedup [34]. For each algorithm, implementations
using the Qiskit SDK are provided in our GitHub repository[14]. Thereby, the considered general implementations use functions provided by Qiskit[15] for automatically generating quantum circuits dependent on the input data. For validation,
the quantum computers *ibmq_16_melbourne* [12], supporting 15 qubits and a calculated maximum depth of 32 levels, and the *ibmq_5_yorktown* [13], supporting
5 qubits and a calculated maximum depth of 96 levels, of IBMQ are considered.
In addition, the IBMQ quantum computer simulator *ibmq_qasm_simulator*, sim-
ulating 32 qubits, is considered. The simulator is not restricted in its maximum
depth. The properties of the quantum computers are accessible by the Qiskit
SDK[16]. We group the simulator and the quantum computers as backends.

Simon's Algorithm. A function $f : \{0,1\}^n \rightarrow \{0,1\}^n$ exists with $f(x_1) =$
$f(x_2)$ if $x_1 = x_2 \oplus s$, whereby $s \in \{0,1\}^n$ [24,35]. If $s = 0^n$, the function f
is a one-to-one mapping from source to target set, otherwise it is a one-to-two
mapping [24]. The secret string s has to be found with a minimum number of
function calls by a quantum computer. Such black box functions are often called
oracles [32]. A sample general implementation for Simon's Algorithm is *simon-
general-qiskit*. The input data is s which defines the oracle for the resulting
quantum circuit. As required by the specific oracle-generating function[17] used,
the length of s has to be a power of two. Thus, the implementation selection rule
is defined as follows:

```
processable(S, simon-general-qiskit) :-
    S =~ '^[01]+$',
    atom_length(S, X), X is X /\ (-X).
```

`simon-general-qiskit` is the name of the respective implementation. First,
the rule body specifies a regular expression for the non-empty secret string S such
that it only contains the characters 0 or 1. The second line counts the length of
S and evaluates if it is a power of two. Therefore, the bit-wise AND operation
with the two's complement of the length of S is used. Valid input data for S are

---

[14] https://github.com/UST-QuAntiL/nisq-analyzer-content.
[15] https://qiskit.org/documentation/apidoc/qiskit.aqua.algorithms.html.
[16] https://quantum-computing.ibm.com/docs/manage/account/ibmq.
[17] https://qiskit.org/documentation/stubs/qiskit.aqua.components.oracles.
TruthTableOracle.html.

shown in Table 1. To determine if `processable` evaluates to true for a certain input, e.g. '0110', the NISQ Analyzer evaluates such Prolog rules as follows:

```
?- processable('0110', simon-general-qiskit).
```

Depending on the backend, Table 1 shows the width and depth of the transpiled `simon-general-qiskit` implementation. The resulting values show a correlation to the length of s. Quantum computers marked with * in Table 1 do not support the required number of qubits or maximum depth for execution. Thus, they are excluded by the general selection rule defined in 5.1 and are not recommended by the NISQ Analyzer. For the input '1111111100000000', the required number of qubits is higher than the provided number of *ibmq_5_yorktown*. The transpiler denies the transpilation and provides no result.

Grover Algorithm. The Grover algorithm searches an item in an unsorted list of M items with a quadratic speedup compared to classical search algorithms [9,14]. The input for the algorithm is a Boolean function that defines the searched item [32]. For the computation, briefly, superposition of all M items and *amplitude amplification* is used to measure the searched item on a quantum computer. The Grover algorithm can also be used to solve the *Boolean satisfiability problem (SAT)*. The input for the sample implementation *grover-general-sat-qiskit* are Boolean formulas, as shown in Table 2. Therefore the selection rule used by the NISQ Analyzer can be defined as follows:

```
processable(Formula, grover-general-sat-qiskit) :-
    Formula =~ '^[0-9A-Za-z|&()~^ ]+$'.
```

The regular expression matches all alphanumerical characters, round brackets, and logical operators in the required format. "|" defines a logical OR. "&" specifies a logical AND. "~" is a NOT and "^" a XOR. Additionally, `Formula` has to be non-empty. Width and depth of the transpiled *grover-general-sat-qiskit* implementation for valid formulas are presented in Table 2. It shows that more complex Boolean formulas require more resources. For each input, *ibmq_16_melbourne* is excluded (marked with *). It has enough qubits, but the required depth is already too high and, therefore, the NISQ Analyzer does not recommend the quantum computer.

Shor Algorithm. The input for the Shor algorithm is an odd integer $N = pq$, where p and q are the searched prime factors [14]. Part of the algorithm is the computation of the period of a function by a quantum computer [31]. Therefore, superposition and the *Quantum Fourier Transform (QFT)*, a quantum variation of the classical Discrete Fourier Transform (DFT), is used to measure the period. By further post-processing with the Euclidean algorithm on classical computers, the searched prime factors can be obtained [32]. The first considered implementation of the Shor algorithm is *shor-general-qiskit* [3]. It can process all odd integers greater than 2. Therefore, the rule for the implementation selection of the NISQ Analyzer is defined as follows:

```
processable(N, shor-general-qiskit) :- N > 2, 1 is mod(N, 2).
```

Transpiling the *shor-general-qiskit* implementation with several demonstrative valid input data results in extremely high depths, as presented in Table 3. As none of the considered quantum computers can compute such quantum circuits, only the *ibmq_qasm_simulator* is recommended by the NISQ Analyzer.

Table 3. Analysis results of the Qiskit transpiler for *shor-general-qiskit*.

Input	Width	Depth	Backend
3	10	2401	ibmq_qasm_simulator
9	18	15829	ibmq_qasm_simulator
15	18	14314	ibmq_qasm_simulator
21	22	27515	ibmq_qasm_simulator
33	26	48503	ibmq_qasm_simulator
35	26	49139	ibmq_qasm_simulator
39	26	48379	ibmq_qasm_simulator

In comparison, an exemplary fix implementation of the Shor algorithm is *shor-fix-15-qiskit*[18]. It only factorizes $N = 15$, as it implements a concrete quantum circuit. Thus, the implementation itself does not assume any input data. The attached rule for the implementation selection is defined as follows:

```
processable(N, shor-fix-15-qiskit) :- N is 15.
```

Transpiling *shor-fix-15-qiskit* for all considered backends results in small values of width and depth, as shown in Table 4. In contrast to the general implementation, each of the backends can execute *shor-fix-15-qiskit* according to the NISQ Analyzer with the limitation that only the input $N = 15$ can be processed.

Table 4. Analysis results of the Qiskit transpiler for *shor-fix-15-qiskit*.

Input	Width	Depth	Backend
15	3	5	ibmq_5_yorktown
15	4	11	ibmq_16_melbourne
15	5	5	ibmq_qasm_simulator

---

[18] https://quantum-circuit.com/app_details/HYLMtcuK6b7uaphC7.

5.3 Discussion and Limitations

Currently, the prototype of our approach only supports implementations for Qiskit and quantum computers of IBMQ. Thus, only implementations using Qiskit can be transpiled and considered for the quantum computer selection. However, our plug-in based system supports extensibility for further SDKs. For transpiling and executing given implementations by the Qiskit Service, the resulting quantum circuits are returned from the source code. Furthermore, the response time of the NISQ Analyzer depends on the response time of the transpilation process. Especially general implementations, such as *shor-general-qiskit*, are computationally intensive as the circuit is constructed after passing the required input data. As each implementation that can process a given input is transpiled for each backend, this could result in performance issues - especially with an increasing set of different quantum computers. Therefore, one approach is to define lower bounds for width and depth. For example, the lower bounds for the *shor-fix-15-qiskit* implementation could be determined by counting the number of qubits, which is 5, and the number of gate layers, which is 7, of the original circuit. But, as shown in Table 4, both values can be smaller depending on the target backend. This results from the hardware-specific optimization functionalities of the transpiler. Thus, pre-filtering the set of quantum computers by defined lower bounds of width and depth could result in excluding suitable quantum computers. Dividing the average decoherence time of all qubits by the maximum gate time to determine the maximum depth of a quantum computer can only be considered as a rough estimate [33]. Currently, no further functional or non-functional requirements, such as costs, execution time, and quality of qubits, are considered. Thus, the user has to select the desired solution if more than one suitable implementation or backend is recommended. If no implementation or backend suits the input data, no recommendation is given.

As the definition of Prolog rules for the implementation selection have to be provided by the developer, knowledge in logic programming and the implementation itself is required. Nevertheless, the defined rules enable the automated selection of suitable implementations for other users. Furthermore, Prolog does only support Horn clauses, which are formulas in conjunctive normal form (CNF). Horn clauses contain at most one positive literal. For example, a formula of type $(A \land B \Leftrightarrow C)$, as concretely defined in Sect. 3, is equivalent to the Horn clause $(\neg A \lor \neg B \lor C) \land (A \lor \neg C) \land (B \lor \neg C)$. Negating A or B leads to a formula with more than one positive literal which is not a Horn clause. To prevent this limitation, the closed-world assumption and the negation as failure inference rule are assumed. Since the system generates or provides all required data, we can expect that the closed-world assumption holds true.

6 Related Work

For the comparison of different quantum computers, several metrics were developed, such as *quantum volume* [5] or *total quantum factor (TQF)* [33]. Additionally, several benchmarks for the quantification of the capabilities of quantum computers were proposed [2,4]. However, these metrics only give a rough comparison of the capabilities of the regarded quantum computers. They do not consider the aspects of specific quantum algorithms. Hence, selecting the quantum computer with the highest score independent of the quantum algorithm and the input data does not always lead to a suitable decision.

Suchara et al. [40] introduce the *QuRE Toolbox*, a framework to estimate required resources, such as qubits or gates, to execute a quantum algorithm on quantum computers of different physical technologies. Thereby, the quantum algorithm description is used as input for resource estimation. Additionally, they consider error-correction. Thus, they approximate the number of additional gates and qubits required to compare the efficiency of different error-correction codes in diverse setups. However, their focus is on building a suitable quantum computer, not on selecting an existing one. Therefore, they do not consider the current set of different quantum computers, their supporting SDKs, and their limitations.

Sivarajah et al. [37] present the quantum software development platform $t|ket\rangle$. It supports implementations of several quantum programming languages and their execution on quantum computers of different vendors. For cross-compilation an intermediate representation is used. Their internal compiler optimizes given implementations in several phases and maps them to the architecture of the desired quantum computer. Before execution, it is validated if an implementation is executable on the selected quantum computer. Thereby, the used gate set, the required number of qubits and the required connection between the qubits is compared with the properties of the quantum computer. However, they do not estimate the maximum depth of the supported quantum computers and, therefore, do not compare it to the depth of an implementation. Additionally, they do not support the recommendation of suitable quantum computers as their scope is the cross-compilation and optimization of implementations.

Furthermore, JavadiAbhari et al. [15] estimate and analyze required resources of implementations in their compilation framework *ScaffCC*. Thereby, they track width and depth, the number of gates, and the interaction between qubits. However, their work focuses on hardware agnostic compilation and optimization and, therefore, does not recommend suitable quantum computers.

Also in other domains approaches for decision support exist. In cloud computing, different approaches for automating the service and provider selection are presented. Zhang et al. [43] propose an approach to map user requirements automatically to different cloud services and their suited configuration using a declarative language. Han et al. [10] introduce a cloud service recommender system based on quality of service requirements. Strauch et al. [39] provide a decision support system for the migration of applications to the cloud. For *Service Oriented Architecture (SOA)*, decision models are introduced to support the design of application architectures [44,45]. Manikrao et al. [20] propose a service selection framework for web services. It semantically matches functional and non-functional requirements of the service providers and the user and recommends based on previous user feedback. Brahimi et al. [6] present a proposal for recommending *Database Management Systems (DBMSs)* based on the requirements of the user. However, none of these systems include quantum technologies and their special characteristics, such as the limited resources of quantum computers or the varying requirements of quantum algorithms dependent on the input data.

7 Conclusion and Future Work

In this paper, we presented the concept of a NISQ Analyzer. It analyzes and selects (i) an appropriate algorithm implementation and (ii) a suitable quantum computer for executing a given quantum algorithm and input data by means of defined selection rules. Thereby, the width and depth of the implementations are dynamically determined using hardware-specific transpilers and are compared with the properties of available quantum computers. Implementations of quantum algorithms are tightly coupled to the used SDKs. Thus, the compatibility between the SDK used by the implementation and the SDK supporting the quantum computer has to be considered. The selected implementation is then sent to the corresponding quantum computer for execution.

The implemented NISQ Analyzer will be part of a platform for sharing and executing quantum software as proposed in [18,19]. It is currently realized by the project PlanQK[19]. As part of PlanQK, we plan to use established deployment automation technologies to automate the deployment of quantum algorithms [42]. In the future, we want to analyze the source code of implementations to consider further properties, such as error rates, fidelity, and qubit connectivity. We also plan to implement further services to support additional vendors of quantum computers and hardware-specific transpilers. In addition, we plan to determine and develop further metrics for a more precise analysis and selection of implementations and quantum computers. Thereby, we plan to integrate further functional and non-functional requirements. We also want to support variational quantum algorithms [23,28]. This approach uses quantum computers and classical computers alternately for optimization problems in a hybrid manner: This allows to limit the time spend on a quantum computer, i.e. it avoids problems resulting from decoherence and the lack of gate fidelity. Thus, it overcomes the current limitations of NISQ computers to a certain extent.

Acknowledgements. This work was partially funded by the BMWi project *PlanQK* (01MK20005N) and the DFG's Excellence Initiative project *SimTech* (EXC 2075 - 390740016).

References

1. Aharonov, D., Van Dam, W., Kempe, J., Landau, Z., Lloyd, S., Regev, O.: Adiabatic quantum computation is equivalent to standard quantum computation. SIAM Rev. **50**(4), 755–787 (2008)

---

[19] https://planqk.de/en/.

2. Arute, F., Arya, K., Babbush, R., Bacon, D., Bardin, J.C., Barends, R., et al.: Quantum supremacy using a programmable superconducting processor. Nature **574**(7779), 505–510 (2019)

3. Beauregard, S.: Circuit for Shor's algorithm using 2n+3 qubits. Quant. Inf. Comput. **3**(2), 175–185 (2003)

4. Benedetti, M., Garcia-Pintos, D., Perdomo, O., Leyton-Ortega, V., Nam, Y., Perdomo-Ortiz, A.: A generative modeling approach for benchmarking and training shallow quantum circuits. NPJ Quant. Inf. **5**(1), 45 (2019)

5. Bishop, L.S., Bravyi, S., Cross, A., Gambetta, J.M., Smolin, J.: Quantum volume. Technical report (2017)

6. Brahimi, L., Bellatreche, L., Ouhammou, Y.: A recommender system for DBMS selection based on a test data repository. In: Pokorný, J., Ivanović, M., Thalheim, B., Šaloun, P. (eds.) ADBIS 2016. LNCS, vol. 9809, pp. 166–180. Springer, Cham (2016). https://doi.org/10.1007/978-3-319-44039-2_12

7. Chuang, I.L., Yamamoto, Y.: Creation of a persistent quantum bit using error correction. Phys. Rev. A **55**, 114–127 (1997)

8. Cowtan, A., Dilkes, S., Duncan, R., Krajenbrink, A., Simmons, W., Sivarajah, S.: On the qubit routing problem (2019)

9. Grover, L.K.: A fast quantum mechanical algorithm for database search. In: Proceedings of the Twenty-Eighth Annual ACM Symposium on Theory of Computing, pp. 212–219 (1996)

10. Han, S.M., Hassan, M.M., Yoon, C.W., Huh, E.N.: Efficient service recommendation system for cloud computing market. In: Proceedings of the 2nd International Conference on Interaction Sciences: Information Technology, Culture and Human, pp. 839–845 (2009)

11. Häner, T., Roetteler, M., Svore, K.M.: Factoring using 2n+2 qubits with toffoli based modular multiplication. Quant. Inf. Comput. **18**(7–8), 673–684 (2017)

12. IBMQ team: 15-qubit backend: IBM Q 16 Melbourne backend specification V2.3.1 (2020). https://quantum-computing.ibm.com

13. IBMQ team: 5-qubit backend: IBM Q 5 Yorktown backend specification V2.1.0 (2020). https://quantum-computing.ibm.com

14. Abhijith, J., et al.: Quantum algorithm implementations for beginners (2018)

15. JavadiAbhari, A., et al.: Scaffcc: a framework for compilation and analysis of quantum computing programs. In: Proceedings of the 11th ACM Conference on Computing Frontiers. CF 2014. Association for Computing Machinery, New York (2014)

16. LaRose, R.: Overview and comparison of gate level quantum software platforms. Quantum **3**, 130 (2019)

17. Leymann, F., Barzen, J.: The bitter truth about gate-based quantum algorithms in the NISQ era. Quant. Sci. Technol. **5**, 1–28 (2020)

18. Leymann, F., Barzen, J., Falkenthal, M.: Towards a platform for sharing quantum software. In: Proceedings of the 13th Advanced Summer School on Service Oriented Computing, pp. 70–74. IBM Technical report, IBM Research Division (2019)

19. Leymann, F., Barzen, J., Falkenthal, M., Vietz, D., Weder, B., Wild, K.: Quantum in the cloud: application potentials and research opportunities. In: Proceedings of the 10th International Conference on Cloud Computing and Services Science. SciTePress (2020)

20. Manikrao, U.S., Prabhakar, T.V.: Dynamic selection of web services with recommendation system. In: International Conference on Next Generation Web Services Practices (NWeSP 2005), p. 5 pp. (2005)

21. Masood, S., Soo, A.: A rule based expert system for rapid prototyping system selection. Robot. Comput. Integr. Manuf. **18**(3–4), 267–274 (2002)

22. McCaskey, A.J., Lyakh, D., Dumitrescu, E., Powers, S., Humble, T.S.: XACC: a system-level software infrastructure for heterogeneous quantum-classical computing. Quant. Sci. Technol. **5**, 1–17 (2020)
23. Moll, N., et al.: Quantum optimization using variational algorithms on near-term quantum devices. Quant. Sci. Technol. **3**(3), 030503 (2018)
24. Nannicini, G.: An introduction to quantum computing, without the physics (2017)
25. National Academies of Sciences: Engineering, and Medicine: Quantum Computing: Progress and Prospects. The National Academies Press, Washington, DC (2019)
26. Nielsen, M.A., Chuang, I.L.: Quantum Computation and Quantum Information, 10th edn. Cambridge University Press, Cambridge (2011)
27. O'Brien, T.E., Tarasinski, B., Terhal, B.M.: Quantum phase estimation of multiple eigenvalues for small-scale (noisy) experiments. New J. Phys. **21**(2), 1–43 (2019)
28. Peruzzo, A., et al.: A variational eigenvalue solver on a photonic quantum processor. Nat. Commun. **5**(1) (2014)
29. Preskill, J.: Quantum computing in the NISQ era and beyond. Quantum **2**, 79 (2018)
30. Raussendorf, R., Briegel, H.J.: A one-way quantum computer. Phys. Rev. Lett. **86**, 5188–5191 (2001)
31. Rieffel, E., Polak, W.: An introduction to quantum computing for non-physicists. ACM Comput. Surv. **32**(3), 300–335 (2000)
32. Rieffel, E., Polak, W.: Quantum Computing: A Gentle Introduction. 1st edn. The MIT Press, Cambridge (2011)
33. Sete, E.A., Zeng, W.J., Rigetti, C.T.: A functional architecture for scalable quantum computing. In: IEEE International Conference on Rebooting Computing, pp. 1–6 (2016)
34. Shor, P.W.: Polynomial-time algorithms for prime factorization and discrete logarithms on a quantum computer. SIAM J. Comput. **26**(5), 1484–1509 (1997)
35. Simon, D.R.: On the power of quantum computation. In: Proceedings of the 35th Annual Symposium on Foundations of Computer Science, SFCS 1994, pp. 116–123. IEEE Computer Society, USA (1994)
36. Siraichi, M.Y., Santos, V.F., Collange, S., Quintão Pereira, F.M.: Qubit allocation. In: CGO 2018 - International Symposium on Code Generation and Optimization, pp. 1–12 (2018)
37. Sivarajah, S., Dilkes, S., Cowtan, A., Simmons, W., Edgington, A., Duncan, R.: t|ket⟩: a retargetable compiler for NISQ devices. Quant. Sci. Technol. (2020)
38. Steiger, D.S., Häner, T., Troyer, M.: ProjectQ: an open source software framework for quantum computing. Quantum **2**, 49 (2018)
39. Strauch, S., Andrikopoulos, V., Bachmann, T., Karastoyanova, D., Passow, S., Vukojevic-Haupt, K.: Decision support for the migration of the application database layer to the cloud. In: 2013 IEEE 5th International Conference on Cloud Computing Technology and Science, vol. 1, pp. 639–646. IEEE (2013)
40. Suchara, M., Kubiatowicz, J., Faruque, A., Chong, F.T., Lai, C.Y., Paz, G.: QuRE: the quantum resource estimator toolbox. In: IEEE 31st International Conference on Computer Design (ICCD), pp. 419–426. IEEE (2013)
41. Tannu, S.S., Qureshi, M.K.: Not all qubits are created equal: a case for variability-aware policies for nisq-era quantum computers. In: Proceedings of the Twenty-Fourth International Conference on Architectural Support for Programming Languages and Operating Systems, ASPLOS 2019, pp. 987–999. Association for Computing Machinery, New York (2019)

42. Wild, K., Breitenbücher, U., Harzenetter, L., Leymann, F., Vietz, D., Zimmermann, M.: TOSCA4QC: two modeling styles for TOSCA to automate the deployment and orchestration of quantum applications. In: 2020 IEEE 24th International Enterprise Distributed Object Computing Conference (EDOC). IEEE Computer Society (2020)

43. Zhang, M., Ranjan, R., Nepal, S., Menzel, M., Haller, A.: A declarative recommender system for cloud infrastructure services selection. In: Vanmechelen, K., Altmann, J., Rana, O.F. (eds.) GECON 2012. LNCS, vol. 7714, pp. 102–113. Springer, Heidelberg (2012). https://doi.org/10.1007/978-3-642-35194-5_8

44. Zimmermann, O., Grundler, J., Tai, S., Leymann, F.: Architectural decisions and patterns for transactional workflows in SOA. In: Krämer, B.J., Lin, K.-J., Narasimhan, P. (eds.) ICSOC 2007. LNCS, vol. 4749, pp. 81–93. Springer, Heidelberg (2007). https://doi.org/10.1007/978-3-540-74974-5_7

45. Zimmermann, O., Koehler, J., Leymann, F., Polley, R., Schuster, N.: Managing architectural decision models with dependency relations, integrity constraints, and production rules. J. Syst. Softw. **82**(8), 1249–1267 (2009)

Pattern Views: Concept and Tooling for Interconnected Pattern Languages

Manuela Weigold$^{(\boxtimes)}$, Johanna Barzen , Uwe Breitenbücher ,
Michael Falkenthal , Frank Leymann , and Karoline Wild

Institute of Architecture of Application Systems, University of Stuttgart,
Universitätsstrasse 38, Stuttgart, Germany
{manuela.weigold,johanna.barzen,uwe.breitenbuecher,michael.falkenthal,
frank.leymann,karoline.wild}@iaas.uni-stuttgart.de

Abstract. Patterns describe proven solutions for recurring problems.
Typically, patterns in a particular domain are interrelated and can be
organized in pattern languages. As real-world problems often require
to combine patterns of multiple domains, different pattern languages
have to be considered to address these problems. However, cross-domain
knowledge about how patterns of different pattern languages relate to
each other is mostly hidden in individual pattern descriptions or not
documented at all. This makes it difficult to identify relevant patterns
across pattern languages. To address this challenge, we introduce pattern
views (i) to document the set of related patterns for a certain problem
across pattern languages and (ii) to make this knowledge about combin-
able patterns available to others. To demonstrate the practical feasibility
of pattern views, we integrated support for the concept into our pattern
toolchain, the Pattern Atlas.

Keywords: Patterns · Pattern languages · Cross-language relations ·
Pattern language composition · Pattern graph

1 Introduction

Patterns describe proven solutions for recurring problems. After the first patterns were published in the domain of city and building architecture by Alexander et al. [1], the concept of patterns has been adopted in various other fields.
Especially in software and information technology, publishing patterns has
become a popular way to convey expert knowledge in different domains, e.g.,
object-oriented programming [2], enterprise application architecture [3], messaging [4], or security [5]. Since patterns can often be used in combination or offer
alternative solutions, the relations between patterns are essential for identifying
all relevant patterns and are therefore often documented. For example, the pattern *Public Cloud* of the cloud computing pattern language by Fehling et al. [6]
describes how cloud providers can offer IT resources to a large customer group.
It further refers to patterns that describe the different service models for offering

© Springer Nature Switzerland AG 2020
S. Dustdar (Ed.): SummerSOC 2020, CCIS 1310, pp. 86–103, 2020.
https://doi.org/10.1007/978-3-030-64846-6_6

resources, e.g., as *Infrastructure as a Service* (IaaS) [6]. When using the *Public Cloud* pattern, those related patterns should also be considered, because they solve related problems. In conjunction with the relations between them, patterns can be organized in pattern languages [1]. As a result, a pattern language describes how patterns work together to solve broader problems in a particular domain [7].

However, real-world problems often require the use of patterns of different domains. However, in many cases not all relevant patterns belong to the same pattern language. Therefore, some authors include relations to other languages. For example, in the cloud computing pattern language [6], the authors state that the message queues of the *Message-oriented Middleware* pattern are introduced by Hophe & Woolf's [4] *Message Channel* pattern. Unfortunately, not all relevant pattern languages are referred to. Many pattern languages refer only to a few related patterns of other languages or none at all. For example, distributed cloud applications typically have to meet security requirements regarding the communication of the distributed components. To ensure secure communication, Schumacher et al.'s [5] *Secure Channel* pattern could be applied. However, this pattern language is not mentioned in the cloud computing patterns at all [6]. As relations to other pattern languages are often missing, it is difficult to identify related patterns of other languages.

One reason for missing relations is the way pattern languages are documented. Most pattern languages are published in books or scientific publications. Once they are published, they can hardly be changed and, therefore, the pattern languages remain static. This was not intended by Alexander et al. [1], who described them as *"living networks"*. Some authors created dedicated websites for their pattern languages (e.g., [8–10]), which eases their adaptation. Nevertheless, most websites represent only one particular language. For this reason, pattern repositories have been developed that aim to collaboratively collect patterns of various domains and provide tooling support to edit or extend patterns and relations. Although several pattern repositories support the collection of patterns, patterns of different domains are not organized in pattern languages (e.g., [11,12]) and are thus treated as a single set of patterns and their relations. In contrast to that, a pattern language is more than a collection of patterns and reflects the higher-level *domain* for which the patterns are relevant [13], e.g., for realizing cloud applications. A few repositories organize patterns in pattern languages (e.g., [14,15]), but do not reflect explicit cross-domain relations between patterns in different languages. This knowledge is hidden in individual pattern descriptions. However, without explicit cross-domain relations, and without the context in which these relations are relevant, it is difficult to identify relevant patterns for a given problem. This leads to the overall research question: *"How can relevant patterns and their relations be identified for a problem across different domains?"*

In this paper, we address this problem by introducing a concept to explicitly document cross-domain knowledge relevant for a particular problem. For this, patterns and their relations from different pattern languages can be selected and further relations can be defined as relevant in a specific context. The relations between patterns of different languages are *cross-language relations* that express cross-domain knowledge, i.e. relations between patterns of different pattern languages. Thus, it is possible to combine and extend pattern languages – a truly *living network of patterns*. Based on our previous experience with pattern repositories, we show how support for the concept can be integrated into a pattern repository by adapting our previous toolchain [16–18] which we refer to as the *Pattern Atlas* [19]. The remainder of the paper is structured as follows: Sect. 2 describes fundamentals and a motivating scenario. In Sect. 3, we introduce our concept and show how tooling support for it can be integrated into a pattern repository. In Sect. 4, we present a concrete use case and describe the realization of our prototype. Section 5 describes related work and is followed by a discussion in Sect. 6. Finally, Sect. 7 concludes the paper.

2   Background and Motivation

In this section, we first introduce patterns and pattern languages and then motivate that for real-world problems often patterns from multiple domains have to be considered. Based on the motivating scenario, we further refine the research question.

2.1   Patterns and Pattern Languages

As already mentioned, patterns are used to gather knowledge about proven solutions for recurring problems in many different fields, especially in the domain of software and information technology [7] but also in humanities it is a common concept [20]. They describe the core idea of the solution in a general manner, which means in case of software engineering patterns that they are independent of a specific technology or programming language. The general solution concept of a pattern can therefore be applied to a variety of use cases in different ways. Each pattern is identified by its name which we write in italics throughout this paper. Since humans are the targets, patterns are documented as textual descriptions according to a defined pattern format. Even if the pattern formats differ slightly from pattern language to pattern language [21], typical formats for patterns in software and information technology domains contain several common sections [22]: A section about the addressed *problem*, the *context* in which the problem might arise, *forces* which direct the problem, the proposed *solution*, the *resulting context* describing which forces have been resolved, and a section showing a *sketch* of the solution. Often other patterns are only referenced in the textual description of one of these sections. Some authors have introduced explicit sections to describe the relations of the pattern and give them defined semantics [23], such as *"Variations"* [6,9], *"See also"* [5], or *"Next"* [4]. Further examples of semantics for relations between patterns can be found in [24–26].

Patterns and relations are the basic building blocks of pattern languages. In this work, we build on the premise that a pattern language is more than a collection of patterns, but a designed system [27]. This means that (i) relations of a pattern language are designed to guide the reader towards suitable patterns and (ii) each pattern solves a specific problem that is related to the overall context of the pattern language [13,28], e.g., in the domain of cloud computing, enterprise integration, or security.

2.2 Motivating Scenario and Problem Statement

Often patterns of several domains have to be considered for a real-world problem. For example, suppose a software developer wants to build a secure elastic cloud application. An elastic application responds to changing workload by adjusting the amount of resources allocated to the application [6]. This ensures that neither too many resources (which is costly) nor too few resources are allocated over a long period.

The cloud computing patterns in Fig. 1 on the left provide several patterns relevant for an elastic cloud application: For example, an *Elastic Infrastructure* provides a dynamically adjustable infrastructure to a customer to deploy an application and an *Elastic Queue* can be used to monitor the number of messages in a queue and to adjust the number of *Processing Components* handling the requests. In the context of an elastic cloud application, the *Processing Components* are often implemented as *Competing Consumers* as any of the instances can receive and process an incoming request. Therefore, this enterprise integration pattern is explicitly referred to in the *Processing Component* pattern. Since messaging is often used for integrating cloud application components, several cloud computing patterns also refer to other enterprise integration patterns. For example, the authors state that the *Message-oriented Middleware* pattern summarizes selected enterprise integration patterns that are not explicitly listed. However, often explicit references to related pattern languages would be helpful.

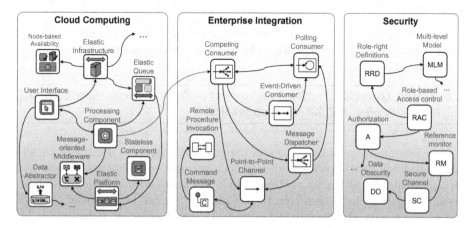

Fig. 1. Patterns and their documented relations of multiple pattern languages: Cloud computing patterns [6], enterprise integration patterns [4], and security patterns [5].

An example of missing cross-language relations can also be found in our motivating scenario: The enterprise integration patterns were published before the cloud computing patterns and thus never reference them. And although most elastic cloud applications must meet certain security requirements, such as secure communication between application components, as provided by the *Secure Channel* pattern of the security patterns, no security patterns are mentioned and, thus, no cross-language relations exist. It can easily be seen that cross-language relations are also important for pattern languages of other areas than software, e.g., for realizing a film scene, patterns from different domains (costumes, music, and film settings) are needed [26].

But even if cross-language relations exist, they are often not properly documented. The pattern languages depicted in Fig. 1 are published in books [4–6] or on dedicated websites [8,10]. Besides scientific publications and dedicated websites, patterns are published in repositories that aim to collect patterns in collaboration [16]. However, even with the tooling support of current repositories, it is challenging to find related patterns for a given problem: Several repositories do not organize patterns in pattern languages [11,12] and treat patterns only as a simple interconnected set. Thus, the domain of the pattern language is not visible and cannot serve as an entry-point for the reader. The few repositories organizing patterns in pattern languages [14,16] list cross-language relations in individual pattern descriptions which are therefore not obvious. None of the repositories known to us enables to document patterns and relations for a specific context (e.g., secure elastic cloud applications). Consequently, finding suitable patterns across pattern languages for a certain problem is a cumbersome, manual process. And especially if a large number of patterns must be considered, this process can be time-consuming. For example, the cloud computing pattern language comprises 74 patterns while the enterprise integration pattern language consists of 65 patterns. Among these patterns, often only a subset is relevant for a certain problem. In Sect. 1, we questioned how this subset and their relations can be identified across different domains. The domain of the problem may be addressed by either one or multiple pattern languages. In this work, we focus on pattern languages as they also define sophisticated relations and we do not consider simple pattern collections. As a result, the research question can be reformulated as follows:

> **Research Question I**: *"How can relevant patterns in one or more pattern languages be identified for a certain problem?"*

The main purpose of patterns and pattern languages is to document knowledge. The additional knowledge about which patterns and relations are relevant for a particular cross-domain problem area is also worth documenting. Especially if multiple pattern languages have to be considered, it can be beneficial to share and extend this knowledge in collaboration. Therefore, a second question can be derived from the original question:

> ***Research Question II***: *"How can this knowledge about relevant patterns be documented in a reusable manner?"*

To address these questions, sufficient tooling support is needed to document this knowledge that may span different pattern languages. As mentioned earlier, documenting patterns and relations for a specific problem is currently not supported by any existing pattern repository known to us.

3   Pattern Views

In this section, we introduce our concept and tooling support to tackle the research questions introduced in Sect. 2. First, we introduce *pattern views* as a concept to document cross-domain knowledge for a particular context that requires patterns and relations across pattern languages. A pattern view can then be used to identify relevant patterns for the problem that is defined by the context of the pattern view (***Research Question I***). Then, a formal definition of pattern views is given. Finally, the integration of pattern views in a pattern repository is shown (***Research Question II***).

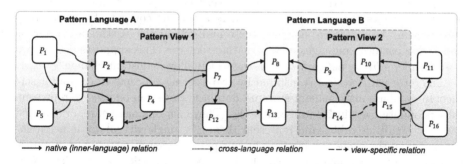

Fig. 2. The concept of pattern views: Pattern views can contain patterns of either multiple pattern languages (pattern view 1) or one single pattern language (pattern view 2).

3.1   The Concept of Pattern Views

Alexander et al. [1] already mentioned in the publication of the first pattern language that if a certain problem requires patterns of different pattern languages, patterns of different domains can be combined as needed. Based on this idea we introduce *pattern views* as a concept (i) to explicitly define the context in which a set of patterns and relations is relevant, (ii) to specify new relations between patterns that are relevant in this specific context, and (iii) to preserve knowledge about the pattern languages from which the patterns originate.

Figure 2 illustrates our concept: A pattern view comprises patterns of either different pattern languages (pattern view 1) or a single pattern language (pattern view 2). For example, patterns from different languages are relevant for a secure elastic cloud application, while only a subset of the cloud computing patterns are relevant for the deployment of a cloud application. The relations between the contained patterns in a pattern view are either those already defined in the original language or newly defined relations that are relevant in the defined context of the pattern view. We distinguish between (i) *native relations*, which are inner-language relations defined by a pattern language, (ii) *cross-language relations*, which are either described in a pattern language or newly introduced by a pattern view, and (iii) *view-specific relations*, which are newly introduced inner-language relations. Especially cross-language relations are often poorly documented in pattern languages. The relevance of a pattern view for a certain use case is determined by its context: The context guides the pattern users, e.g., software architects, to identify a pattern view for his or her particular problem. Thus, pattern views enable to document knowledge about the joint use of patterns and pattern languages for a particular problem explicitly and reusable for other users. In Sect. 4.1, a pattern view containing patterns relevant in the context of *secure elastic cloud applications* is described in detail as a sample. As a result, an individual pattern can be considered from different perspectives: It is primarily anchored in its original pattern language, but can also be part of different views that place the pattern in a specific context of an overarching problem. As a pattern view can reuse and extend the existing structure of underlying pattern languages, new structures emerge. This supports one aspect of Alexander's *living network of patterns* which allows constant change.

The term *pattern view* is inspired by two existing concepts in computer science: In database management systems, database views can be used to represent subsets of data contained in regular tables. They can join, aggregate, or simplify data from multiple tables and represent them as a single virtual database table. For patterns, the same can be done by our pattern views: Patterns from multiple sources (pattern languages) can be included in a single pattern view. New relations for the pattern view can be defined, just like a database view can refer to other tables. Another analogy to pattern views is the notion of architecture views in architecture descriptions [29]. An architecture view represents the architecture of a system from a specific viewpoint that is in accordance with a certain set of stakeholders' concerns [29]. Depending on the concerns of the different stakeholders, a suitable architecture description can be created, e.g. a process view for process architects or a software distribution view for software developers. Avgeriou & Zdun [30] use this definition to assign architectural patterns to their primary architectural view, e.g., the *Client-Server* pattern to the component-interaction view. We go beyond this and define pattern views as a representation of pattern languages based on problem scopes. Such a scope of a pattern view represents the context in which the patterns and pattern languages may be used to address the concerns of the pattern user.

In Sect. 4.1, we present a pattern view for *secure elastic cloud applications* that is aimed towards cloud software architects and contains several patterns for the integration of the application components. Although our work is based on information technology pattern languages, our concept does not rely on specific properties of patterns of this domain. Therefore, our concept may be applied, e.g., to patterns for costumes [31] or building architecture [1] in the future.

3.2 Formalization of Pattern Views

Being composed of patterns and relations, pattern languages are commonly formalized as graphs [7,23,32,33]. This notation is also used in Fig. 2 for the pattern languages A and B: Patterns are represented by nodes, and edges define the relations between them. Some authors assume a hierarchical ordering of the patterns and restrict the graph to be acyclic [1,7,13]. Because in practice arbitrary relations are used in pattern languages [23], we do not enforce hierarchical ordering. Therefore, we allow cyclic edges in our definition of a pattern language graph that is based on our previous work [23]:

Definition 1 (Pattern Language). *A pattern language is a directed, weighted graph $G = (N, E, W) \in \mathfrak{G}$, where $\mathfrak{G}$ is the set of all pattern languages, N is a set of patterns, $E \subseteq N \times N \times W$ is a set of relations, and W is a set of weights used to reflect the semantics of the relations between patterns. Thereby applies that $W \subseteq \mathfrak{W}$ where $\mathfrak{W}$ is the set of all"meaningful"weights.*

In our concept introduced in Sect. 3.1, we distinguish three kinds of relations between patterns for which we formally define three categories of relations:

Definition 2 (Pattern Relation Categories). *Let $G = (N, E, W) \in \mathfrak{G}$. Then $e \in E$ is called **native relation** (more precisely **G-native** relation). With $\hat{G} = (\hat{G}, \hat{E}, \hat{W}) \in \mathfrak{G}$ $(\hat{G} \neq G)$, $(n, \hat{n}, w) \in N \times \hat{N} \times \mathfrak{W}$ is called **cross-language relation** (more precisely **cross-$(\mathbf{G}, \hat{\mathbf{G}})$** relation). Finally, $(n, n', w) \in (N \times N \times \mathfrak{W}) \setminus E$ $(n \neq n')$ is called **view-specific relation** (more precisely **view-G-specific** relation).*

Note that these categories are mutually exclusive. Relations of all three categories can be part of a pattern view which is defined as follows:

Definition 3 (Pattern View). *A graph (P, R, S) is called **pattern view:** $\Leftrightarrow$ $\exists \mathfrak{H} \subseteq \mathfrak{G}$:*

(i) $P \subseteq \bigcup_{(N,E,W) \in \mathfrak{H}} N$

(ii) $R = R_n \cup R_c \cup R_s$ with
  (a) $\forall e \in R_n \; \exists G \in \mathfrak{H} : e$ is G-native
  (b) $\forall e \in R_c \; \exists G, \hat{G} \in \mathfrak{H} : e$ is cross-$(G, \hat{G})$
  (c) $\forall e \in R_s \; \exists G \in \mathfrak{H} : e$ is view-G-specific
(iii) $S \subseteq \mathfrak{W}$

While both pattern languages and pattern views are directed graphs and thus structurally similar, pattern views reuse selected structures of pattern languages (patterns and native relations) and extend by view-specific relations and cross-language relations.

3.3   Tooling for Pattern Views

In previous works, our toolchain has been introduced as a collaborative tool for documenting and managing patterns and pattern languages [16], as well as concrete solutions [18,34] that are implementations of the patterns with a particular technology or in a particular programming language in case of software engineering patterns. Pattern research is actively supported as experts can analyze concrete solutions in collaboration and as a result identify best practices and document patterns [16]. Based on an analogy to cartography we refer to our toolchain as the *Pattern Atlas* [19].

Figure 3 illustrates the abstract architecture of the Pattern Atlas with the newly developed components in black. In the pattern repository, patterns and relations between them are managed. The patterns as well as their relations are organized in pattern languages. The metadata defines the pattern formats for the different pattern languages as well as the semantics of the relations. Analogously, the solution repository stores concrete solutions and their relations, which are organized in solution languages. Concrete solutions are related to patterns: While a pattern captures the essence of multiple concrete solutions, the documentation of a concrete solution eases the application of its pattern to a specific problem [17]. In addition, aggregation descriptors are stored that specify how different concrete solution artifacts can be combined [17]. These combined solutions are especially relevant if multiple patterns (and thus their concrete solutions) need to be applied to a broader problem. The solution repository for managing solution languages highly depends on the domain of the solution, e.g., for concrete solutions of costumes detailed descriptions of clothing pieces are relevant [35] whereas solutions of software patterns can be code snippets [16]. The repositories facilitate to add patterns and solutions as textual descriptions and browse the pattern languages as well as solution languages. For this work, we enriched our previous realization of the toolchain [16,18,34] by the concept of pattern views and added a graphical editor. Further details of the implementation are described in Sect. 4.

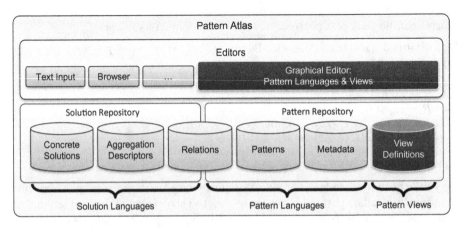

Fig. 3. Abstract system architecture of the Pattern Atlas.

4   Case Study and Prototypical Implementation

In our motivating scenario described in Sect. 2.2, we stated that patterns from multiple domains are needed for realizing a secure elastic cloud application. In this section, we first present a case study with the pattern view for the context of *secure elastic cloud applications*. We then describe our prototypical implementation which can be used to facilitate the documentation of a pattern view.

4.1   Case Study

Users expect a high availability of certain applications. To fulfill this expectation, cloud providers offer infrastructure and services that can be used to guarantee the availability of an application even for a sudden increase in demand, i.e. scalability of the services. Elastic cloud applications deal with changing demand by adjusting the amount of resources that are used for the application [6]. In addition, data security plays a major role, especially when data is exchanged between communication partners.

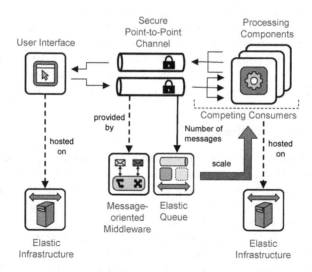

Fig. 4. Architecture of a secure elastic cloud application.

Figure 4 depicts the architecture of a secure elastic cloud application. The application consists of a *User Interface* component that communicates with *Processing Components* via messaging. Both components are hosted on an *Elastic Infrastructure*. The number of messages in the channel is monitored to determine the workload of the *Processing Component* instances. Depending on the number of messages, the *Elastic Queue* adjusts the number of instances. As any *Processing Component* instance can answer a request, the component is implemented as *Stateless Component* and its instances act as *Competing Consumers* listening on a *Point-to-Point* channel provided by a *Message-Oriented Middleware*. After consuming and processing a message the *Processing Component* instance can send a response via another *Point-to-Point Channel*. To ensure data security, the communication between the component must be encrypted.

For such an application, there is a number of patterns that should be taken into account during implementation. In Fig. 5, the pattern view for secure elastic cloud applications is shown. It includes patterns from the cloud computing, enterprise integration, and security pattern languages that are relevant in this specific context. Besides native relations and one cross-language relation from the original pattern languages, three new cross-language relations and two view-specific relations are contained in the pattern view. In addition to the already named patterns also a *Message Dispatcher* can be used to delegate the message to one specific consumer, i.e. one *Processing Component* instance. Each *Competing Consumer* can be implemented as *Polling Consumer*, *Event-Driven Consumer*, or a combination of both [4]. A *Message-oriented Middleware* provides the functionality for communication via messaging and therefore also the secure message channels for the *Competing Consumer* instances. To ensure that a message is consumed only once, the consumers must all listen to the same *Point-to-Point Channel*. As all transferred data of the application must be encrypted, the *Point-to-Point Channel* must also implement the *Secure Channel* pattern. Once defined, this pattern view can be used by other cloud application architects to realize their secure elastic cloud applications. Since the existing knowledge is only enriched by the pattern views, further relevant patterns outside the view can be identified by the native relations in the pattern languages.

4.2 Prototypical Implementation

In the course of this work, we not only extended the pattern repository conceptually but also refactored the implementation of our previous toolchain. The user interface of the pattern repository was implemented as an Angular frontend[1] and we used Spring Boot for implementing a RESTful backend[2].

In the pattern repository, patterns are created in the scope of a pattern language that specifies a certain pattern format. After the creation of a pattern, it can be added to a pattern view. For both, pattern languages and pattern views, we implemented a graphical editor that visualizes their graph structure. In Fig. 6, this is shown for the pattern view presented in Sect. 4.1. Patterns from all pattern languages of the repository can be added via drag and drop. The layout of the graph can be adapted by re-positioning nodes, zooming in and out, and triggering an automatic reformatting of the graph based on the edges. After the selection of a pattern, related patterns are highlighted. New relations can be added by drawing arrows between two pattern nodes and are further defined by a description and specification of the relation type. These new relations are either cross-language relations or view-specific relations. Users can therefore directly

---

[1] https://github.com/PatternAtlas/pattern-atlas-ui.
[2] https://github.com/PatternAtlas/pattern-atlas-api.

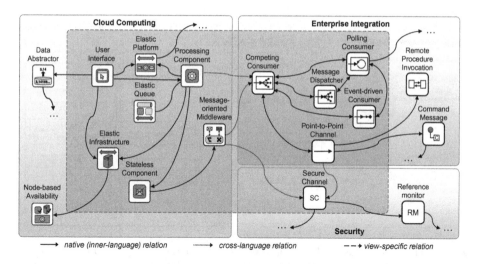

Fig. 5. Pattern view for secure elastic cloud applications.

edit or interact with the visualized pattern graph and observe how new relations or patterns lead to structural changes as the overall structure of the network of patterns can be grasped immediately. For pattern views, native relations of a pattern can be displayed and selectively imported into the pattern view. This enables the user to reuse the structure that is defined by relations in a pattern language.

5   Related Work

Several authors have examined relations and patterns across multiple pattern languages. Avgeriou and Zdun [30] reviewed architectural views and patterns from different languages. They assigned each architectural pattern to its primary architectural view and defined relations between the patterns. As each of their collection of patterns and relations for an architectural view is worth documenting, we adopted the idea of views as a concept that is not limited to the domain of IT architecture. Caiza et al. [36] standardize the relations of various privacy pattern languages to combine them into a new pattern language. Porter et al. [32] derived a method to combine pattern languages based on pattern sequences. In contrast, pattern views contain only those patterns of different languages and their relations that are relevant in a certain context. Thus, pattern views are more specific and less complex than potentially large combined pattern languages.

Buschmann et al. [37] introduce pattern stories as textual descriptions that walk a reader through the application of multiple patterns. In an exemplary pattern story, they demonstrate how patterns of multiple languages are used together. The information that is contained in a story - the patterns and the relations described in it - can also be captured in pattern views. However, pattern

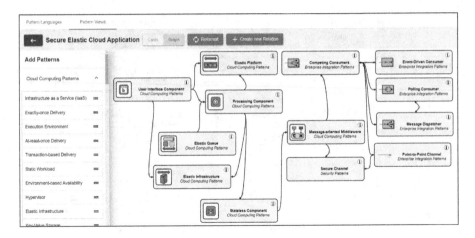

Fig. 6. The secure elastic cloud applications view in the graphical editor. Via drag & drop (left side of the figure), patterns from pattern languages can be added to the pattern view.

stories are targeted at illustrating common pattern sequences. Pattern views are not limited to express sequential steps but can express arbitrary relationships.

Reinfurt et al. [38] present an algorithm for finding entry points in pattern languages. Their algorithm can be used to support several manual steps that are needed to document pattern views: For a formalized set of problems related to the context of the pattern view, their algorithm suggests suitable languages and a pattern that serves as a starting point.

Köppe et al. [39] elaborated on requirements for online pattern repositories. They used the term pattern views in the sense that there should be different options (pattern views) for displaying a pattern, e.g., for smaller screens or optimized for printing. Their notion of a pattern view, therefore, defines the visual representation of a pattern whereas we use the term pattern view for a concept to encompass patterns and relations that are relevant for a particular context. Apparently similar terms from other domains are *process views* and *process viewing patterns* [40]. Process views are used to represent a complex business process regarding certain aspects, e.g. by reducing the process to its essentials parts [40]. They are obtained by applying transformations on the process graph of the business process [41]. These transformations have been described by process viewing patterns [40]. In contrast to pattern views that are created by selecting suitable nodes (patterns) and redefine the relations (edges) between them, the former transformations can be far more sophisticated, e.g., nodes of a process graph can be aggregated.

Pavlič et al. [42] introduced the concept of pattern-containers to represent pattern collections. They formalized how patterns represent knowledge in an ontology. Relations are modeled by specifying that a pattern is related to another pattern. But in their ontology, the relation cannot be described further, and thus, the type of the relation cannot be defined. They define pattern-containers as a way to create pattern collections: Pattern-containers can include patterns and other pattern-containers. A pattern can be included in multiple pattern-containers. But given their ontology, pattern-containers cannot be used to represent pattern views: As it cannot be defined which relations are relevant for a pattern-container, they represent a simple subset of patterns.

Graph-based representations for pattern languages are commonly used to reflect Alexander's description of a network of patterns [23,33,37]. Another pattern repository, *The Public Sphere Project*, mentions that a graph representation of all their patterns and relations was once created [14], but only a sub-graph of it (8 patterns and their relations) can still be found on their website. Nevertheless, even the complete graph is still a static representation of their underlying living pattern network. Schauer & Keller [43] developed a tool for documenting software systems. Although they use patterns to enhance multiple graph-based views for a software system (e.g. as annotations in UML diagrams), they do not offer a general view on patterns. Welicki et al. [44] developed a visualization tool that can be used to search and create relations (including cross-language relations) between patterns in their software pattern catalog. They also implemented different views on a pattern that display e.g. a summary or software-specific views (e.g. source-code of a concrete implementation). The MUSE repository of Barzen [45] offers a graph-based representation of concrete costumes that occur in films and are understood as concrete solutions for costume patterns. However, these tools and repositories do not offer different perspectives on the relations of the patterns or pattern languages. Therefore, no other pattern repository or tool known to us offers graph-based representations of pattern languages and the ability to dynamically combine patterns from different languages to pattern views for a particular problem context.

6   Discussion

Once a pattern view has been documented for a particular problem, the (cross-domain) knowledge about the patterns is made explicit. When initially documenting a pattern view, expert knowledge or experience in the domain of the corresponding pattern languages is required. While this is an additional manual step, it enables other users of the pattern repository to reuse and extend the knowledge captured in the pattern view. In future work, the documentation of pattern views could be further simplified by further tooling support that, e.g., suggests related patterns.

In contrast to pattern languages, patterns of a pattern view can belong to different pattern languages. Thus, independent of the underlying pattern format, each pattern can be integrated into a pattern view. However, since the patterns are unchanged, their pattern descriptions may use different terminologies. For example, the patterns of the pattern view in Sect. 4.1 use either *"message channel"* [4] or *"message queue"* [6] to describe the same concept. This is due to the fact that the overall context of the pattern language is not the same:

Hohpe & Woolf [4] describe solutions in the context of integrating enterprise applications via a shared message-based communication channel, called message channel. Fehling et al. [6] use the term message queue in the context of cloud computing to emphasize that multiple messages are stored in a queue and can be retrieved by one of the multiple receivers. This behavior of the message queue can be used for scaling as discussed in Sect. 4.1. Besides the differences in the overall context (or domain) of a pattern language, *pattern primitives* may be used inconsistently by different pattern authors [46]. Pattern primitives are fundamental elements of patterns and can be used as common elements in patterns [47]. However, in the future, the approach may be extended to adapt or standardize pattern descriptions in the context of a pattern view.

Finally, we want to point out that our approach is not based on specific properties of software patterns and, thus, seems to be applicable to pattern languages of other areas.

7   Conclusion and Future Work

In this paper, we introduced the concept of pattern views to explicitly document cross-domain knowledge relevant for a particular problem context. Patterns from either different pattern languages or a single pattern language relevant for a specific problem can be combined into a so-called pattern view. In addition to the patterns and native relations of the underlying pattern languages, view-specific relations can be defined if necessary and cross-language relations can be documented as relevant for the given context. Therefore, cross-domain knowledge expressed by these relations is documented explicitly and within a meaningful context.

We extended the implementation of our pattern repository that was presented in previous works [16,17,19] by the concept of pattern views. Therefore, our repository allows to collect multiple pattern languages and to define pattern views that can combine, reuse, and extend the structure of pattern languages that are given by their patterns and relations. Our repository also offers a graph-based representation for pattern views and pattern languages that visualizes the network of patterns. We plan to collect further pattern languages in the repository, such as Internet of Things patterns [48] or green IT patterns [49] and to extend our collection of pattern views. We will further evaluate if some patterns need to be adapted to be used in the context of a pattern view. For future research, we will especially consider patterns from new research areas such as music [50] or Quantum Computing [51]. Patterns for quantum computing are especially interesting as new technologies need to be integrated into our current software systems (for which we already have patterns at hand). Also, an open access hosting of the pattern repository would offer multiple advantages in the future.

Acknowledgment. This work was partially funded by the BMWi projects *PlanQK (01MK20005N)* and *IC4F (01MA17008G)*. The authors would like to thank Lisa Podszun for her help with the documentation of existing patterns.

References

1. Alexander, C., Ishikawa, S., Silverstein, M.: A Pattern Language: Towns, Buildings. Oxford University Press, Construction, Oxford (1977)
2. Gamma, E., Helm, R., Johnson, R., Vlissides, J.: Design Patterns: Elements of Reusable Object-Oriented Software. Addison-Wesley, Boston (1994)
3. Fowler, M.: Patterns of Enterprise Application Architecture. Addison-Wesley, Boston (2002)
4. Hohpe, G., Woolf, B.: Enterprise Integration Patterns: Designing, Building, and Deploying Messaging Solutions. Addison-Wesley, Boston (2004)
5. Schumacher, M., Fernandez-Buglioni, E., Hybertson, D., Buschmann, F., Sommerlad, P.: Security Patterns: Integrating Security and Systems Engineering. Wiley, Hoboken (2013)
6. Fehling, C., Leymann, F., Retter, R., Schupeck, W., Arbitter, P.: Cloud Computing Patterns: Fundamentals to Design, Build, and Manage Cloud Applications. Springer, Heidelberg (2014). https://doi.org/10.1007/978-3-7091-1568-8
7. Coplien, J.O.: Software Patterns. SIGS Books & Multimedia (1996)
8. Cloud computing patterns. https://cloudcomputingpatterns.org/
9. Internet of things patterns. http://internetofthingspatterns.com/
10. Hohpe, G.: Enterprise integration patterns. https://www.enterpriseintegration patterns.com/
11. Ui patterns. https://ui-patterns.com/
12. Pattern catalog. http://designpatterns.wikidot.com/pattern-catalog
13. Borchers, J.O.: A pattern approach to interaction design. In: Gill, S. (ed.) Cognition, Communication and Interaction: Transdisciplinary Perspectives on Interactive Technology. HCIS, pp. 114–131. Springer, Heidelberg (2008). https://doi.org/10.1007/978-1-84628-927-9_7
14. The public sphere project https://www.publicsphereproject.org/
15. Open pattern repository for online learning systems. https://www.learningen vironmentslab.org/openpatternrepository/
16. Fehling, C., Barzen, J., Falkenthal, M., Leymann, F.: PatternPedia – collaborative pattern identification and authoring. In: Proceedings of PURPLSOC (Pursuit of Pattern Languages for Societal Change). The Workshop 2014, August 2015, pp. 252–284 (2015)
17. Falkenthal, M., Barzen, J., Breitenbücher, U., Leymann, F.: Solution languages: easing pattern composition in different domains. Int. J. Adv. Softw. 263–274, (2017)
18. Falkenthal, M., Barzen, J., Breitenbücher, U., Fehling, C., Leymann, F.: Efficient pattern application: validating the concept of solution implementations in different domains. Int. J. Adv. Softw. **7**(3&4), 710–726 (2014)
19. Leymann, F., Barzen, J.: Pattern Atlas. arXiv:2006.05120 [cs], [Online], June 2020. http://arxiv.org/abs/2006.05120
20. Barzen, J., Leymann, F.: Patterns as formulas: patterns in the digital humanities. In: Proceedings of the Ninth International Conferences on Pervasive Patterns and Applications (PATTERNS), pp. 17–21. Xpert Publishing Services, Athen
21. Henninger, S., Corrêa, V.: Software pattern communities: current practices and challenges. In: Proceedings of the 14th Conference on Pattern Languages of Programs - PLOP 2007, p. 1. ACM Press (2007)
22. Coplien, J.O.: Software patterns. SIGS, New York; London (1996)
23. Falkenthal, M., Breitenbücher, U., Leymann, F.: The nature of pattern languages. In: Proceedings of the International Conference on Pursuit of Pattern Languages for Societal Change (PURPLSOC), pp. 130–150, October 2018

24. Noble, J.: Classifying relationships between object-oriented design patterns. In: Proceedings 1998 Australian Software Engineering Conference (cat. no. 98ex233), pp. 98–107. IEEE (1998)
25. Zimmer, W.: Relationships between design patterns. Pattern Lang. Progr. Des. **57**, 345–364 (1995)
26. Falkenthal, M., et al.: Leveraging pattern application via pattern refinement. In: Proceedings of the International Conference on Pursuit of Pattern Languages for Societal Change (PURPLSOC 2015). epubli, June 2015
27. Winn, T., Calder, P.: A pattern language for pattern language structure. In: Proceedings of the 2002 Conference on Pattern Languages of Programs, vol. 13, pp. 45–58 (2003)
28. Meszaros, D.J., Doble, J.: A pattern language for pattern writing. In: Proceedings of International Conference on Pattern Languages of Program Design (1997), vol. 131, p. 164 (1997)
29. IEEE Standards Association: IEEE Std 1471 (2000): IEEE Recommended Practice for Architectural Description of Software-Intensive Systems, Std. (2000)
30. Avgeriou, P., Zdun, U.: Architectural patterns revisited – a pattern language. In: 10th European Conference on Pattern Languages of Programs (EuroPlop 2005). UVK - Universitaetsverlag Konstanz, July 2005
31. Barzen, J., Leymann, F.: Costume languages as pattern languages. In: Baumgartner, P., Sickinger, R. (eds.) Proceedings of PURPLSOC (Pursuit of Pattern Languages for Societal Change). The Workshop 2014, Krems: PURPLSOC 2015, June 2015, Workshop-Beitrag, pp. 88–117 (2015)
32. Porter, R., Coplien, J.O., Winn, T.: Sequences as a basis for pattern language composition. Sci. Comput. Program. **56**(1–2), 231–249 (2005)
33. Zdun, U.: Systematic pattern selection using pattern language grammars and design space analysis. Softw. Pract. Exp. (9), 983–1016 (2007)
34. Falkenthal, M., Barzen, J., Breitenbücher, U., Fehling, C., Leymann, F.: From pattern languages to solution implementations. In: Proceedings of the Sixth International Conferences on Pervasive Patterns and Applications (PATTERNS 2014), pp. 12–21. Xpert Publishing Services, May 2014
35. Barzen, J., Falkenthal, M., Leymann, F.: Wenn Kostüme sprechen könnten: MUSE - Ein musterbasierter Ansatz an die vestimentäre Kommunikation im Film, Digital Humanities. Perspektiven der Praxis, pp. 223–241. Frank und Timme, Berlin, May 2018
36. Caiza, J.C., Martín, Y.-S., Del Alamo, J.M., Guamán, D.S.: Organizing design patterns for privacy: a taxonomy of types of relationships. In: Proceedings of the 22nd European Conference on Pattern Languages of Programs, EuroPLoP 2017, pp. 32:1–32:11. ACM (2017)
37. Buschmann, F., Meunier, R., Rohnert, H., Sommerlad, P., Stal, M.: Pattern-Oriented Software Architecture: A System of Patterns, vol. 1. Wiley, Hoboken (1996)
38. Reinfurt, L., Falkenthal, M., Leymann, F.: Where to begin: on pattern language entry points. SICS Softw. Intens. Cyber-Phys. Syst. (2019)
39. Köppe, C., Inventado, P.S., Scupelli, P., Van Heesch, U.: Towards extending online pattern repositories: supporting the design pattern lifecycle. In: Proceedings of the 23rd Conference on Pattern Languages of Programs, PLoP 2016. The Hillside Group, USA (2016)
40. Schumm, D., Leymann, F., Streule, A.: Process viewing patterns. In: Proceedings of the 14th International Conference on Enterprise Distributed Object Computing (EDOC 2010), pp. 89–98. IEEE, October 2010

41. Schumm, D., Leymann, F., Streule, A.: Process views to support compliance management in business processes. In: Buccafurri, F., Semeraro, G. (eds.) EC-Web 2010. LNBIP, vol. 61, pp. 131–142. Springer, Heidelberg (2010). https://doi.org/10.1007/978-3-642-15208-5_12

42. Pavlič, L., Hericko, M., Podgorelec, V.: Improving design pattern adoption with ontology-based design pattern repository, pp. 649–654, July 2008

43. Schauer, R., Keller, R.K.: Pattern visualization for software comprehension. In: Proceedings of the 6th International Workshop on Program Comprehension, IWPC 1998 (Cat. No.98TB100242), pp. 4–12, June 1998

44. Welicki, L., Sanjuán, O., Manuel, J., Cueva Lovelle, J.: A model for meta-specification and cataloging of software patterns. In: Proceedings of the 12th Conference on Pattern Languages of Programs (PLoP 2012), January 2005

45. Barzen, J.: Wenn Kostüme sprechen - Musterforschung in den Digital Humanities am Beispiel vestimentärer Kommunikation im Film. Ph.D. dissertation, Universität zu Köln (2018)

46. Fehling, C., Barzen, J., Breitenbücher, U., Leymann, F.: A process for pattern identification, authoring, and application. In: Proceedings of the 19th European Conference on Pattern Languages of Programs (EuroPLoP 2014). ACM, January 2014

47. Zdun, U., Avgeriou, P., Hentrich, C., Dustdar, S.: Architecting as decision making with patterns and primitives. In: Proceedings of the 3rd International Workshop on Sharing and Reusing Architectural Knowledge (SHARK 2008), pp. 11–18. ACM, May 2008

48. Reinfurt, L., Breitenbücher, U., Falkenthal, M., Leymann, F., Riegg, A.: Internet of things patterns for devices. In: Ninth International Conferences on Pervasive Patterns and Applications (PATTERNS). Xpert Publishing Services (XPS), pp. 117–126 (2017)

49. Nowak, A., Leymann, F., Schleicher, D., Schumm, D., Wagner, S.: Green business process patterns. In: Proceedings of the 18th Conference on Pattern Languages of Programs (PLoP 2011). ACM, October 2011

50. Barzen, J., Breitenbücher, U., Eusterbrock, L., Falkenthal, M., Hentschel, F., Leymann, F.: The vision for MUSE4Music. Applying the MUSE method in musicology. Comput. Sci. Res. Dev. **32**, 323–328 (2017)

51. Leymann, F.: Towards a pattern language for quantum algorithms. In: Feld, S., Linnhoff-Popien, C. (eds.) QTOP 2019. LNCS, vol. 11413, pp. 218–230. Springer, Cham (2019). https://doi.org/10.1007/978-3-030-14082-3_19

Cloud and Edge

Investigating Possibilites for Protecting and Hardening Installable FaaS Platforms

Mike Prechtl, Robin Lichtenthäler$^{(\boxtimes)}$, and Guido Wirtz

Distributed Systems Group, University of Bamberg, Bamberg, Germany
mike-uwe.prechtl@stud.uni-bamberg.de,
{robin.lichtenthaeler,guido.wirtz}@uni-bamberg.de

Abstract. Function as a Service is a popular trend in the area of cloud computing and also for IoT use cases. Thus, in addition to cloud services, installable open source platforms for FaaS have recently emerged. To deploy such an installable FaaS platform in production, the security aspect needs to be considered which has not been investigated in detail yet. Therefore, this work presents possible security threats and recommended security measures for protecting and hardening installable FaaS platforms. Currently available FaaS platforms are analyzed according to the possibilities they offer to implement such security measures. Although most platforms provide necessary security measures, there is still potential to improve the platforms by offering advanced measures and facilitate a secure deployment.

Keywords: Function as a Service · FaaS platform · Comparison · Security

1 Introduction

The popularity of cloud-based computing offerings is continuously increasing [11] and the offerings itself are evolving. In addition to the established delivery models Infrastructure as a Service (IaaS), Platform as a Service (PaaS), and Software as a Service (SaaS) recently serverless computing has evolved. The term serverless actually is a misnomer. Of course, servers are still required, however, developers can focus on application development without worrying about the underlying infrastructure [12,27]. To be more precise, serverless computing is therefore differentiated into two essential delivery models: Backend as a Service (BaaS) and Function as a Service (FaaS) [12,27]. While BaaS offerings replace server-side components with off-the-shelf services, FaaS provides a platform where *serverless functions* can be deployed. That means, applications are built by deploying several functions that can be triggered by events or Hypertext Transfer Protocol (HTTP) requests. The actual provisioning of computing resources and execution of the function is then managed transparently by the FaaS platform. Cloud providers, like Amazon, Google, Microsoft, and IBM provide FaaS platforms

© Springer Nature Switzerland AG 2020
S. Dustdar (Ed.): SummerSOC 2020, CCIS 1310, pp. 107–126, 2020.
https://doi.org/10.1007/978-3-030-64846-6_7

with a set of complementary BaaS services that offer added-value but also lock-in their consumers. In contrast to such hosted platforms, over the last years also installable platforms were developed which can be installed on an own infrastructure. An installable FaaS platform can be of importance in the Internet of Things (IoT) area [7] where it is more efficient to process data closer to where it is created rather than transferring it to the cloud. Popular installable FaaS platforms are OpenFaaS, OpenWhisk, Fission, Knative, and Kubeless (see Table 1).

FaaS has also been discovered as an important topic in scientific literature [6,12,18–20,33]. One aspect, however, which has not gained much attention yet, is the security of hosted and installable FaaS platforms. Kritikos and Skrzypek have analyzed installable FaaS platforms in a recent review [16] and state that *"security and access control in particular over functions seem not to be well supported by the frameworks"*. To integrate the recent trend of serverless computing in the industry sector, however, users need to be confident about how to deploy and operate FaaS platforms in a secure way. Security manifests itself in many ways and can be expressed through security objectives which are deduced from the specific situation and application requirements. Important security objectives are availability, confidentiality, integrity and authenticity. Usually, these security objectives are achieved by relying on security mechanisms such as encryption, digital certificates, and signatures. Such security mechanism are applied and combined in protocols and standards such as OAuth, OpenID Connect (OIDC), and Transport Layer Security (TLS) which can be used in applications to ensure specific security objectives like user authenticity or data transfer confidentiality.

The aim of this work therefore is an investigation of security measures for protecting and hardening installable FaaS platforms to fulfill security objectives as well as an evaluation of the most popular platforms according to the possibilities they offer to implement these measures. This evaluation should help to assess how such platforms can be used securely in practice and highlight possibilities for further improving such platforms. This is summarized in our research questions:

RQ1: Which security measures are supported by installable FaaS platforms for securing the platform and the deployed functions?

RQ2: In which way can the security of FaaS platforms be improved?

To answer these questions, Sect. 2 explains the technical foundations to infer security requirements for FaaS platforms. In Sect. 3 our approach for examining the different FaaS platforms is presented while Sect. 4 shows the results of the security evaluation as the main contribution of this work. We reflect on these results in Sect. 5 and discuss the implications for deploying FaaS platforms in practice. Section 6 sets our work in relation to others before we conclude our investigation in Sect. 7.

2   Fundamentals

2.1   Containerization

The basis for enabling FaaS is *containerization*, a recent trend in virtualization techniques. In contrast to the virtual machine approach, where the hardware is virtualized, in containerization the operating system (OS) is virtualized. Several containers share the kernel of the host OS, but run as isolated processes offering similar isolation and allocation benefits as virtual machines. However, containers are more lightweight, leading to lower computing resource requirements and especially faster start up times [22]. To run containers, a *container runtime* is required. The most popular container runtime is Docker[1]. The container runtime can start and run containers based on a container image. A container image has a certain format, like the Docker image format or the Open Container Initiative (OCI) image format. Docker provides tooling to build a container image from a so-called *Dockerfile* and, once built, container images can be shared and provided through container registries, such as the Docker Hub[2]. A Docker image is layered with the *bootfs* and *rootfs* as the bottom layers [32]. For the rootfs, an OS can be chosen and for building an application, additional layers with respective software can be added, representing again a new image. When a container is created from an image, the image layers are made read-only and a new writable layer is put on top of them. Docker calls this layer container layer. All changes that are made, such as modifying files, are written to the container layer. When files are changed, they are copied from the read-only layer below into the read-write layer. The read-only version still exists, but is now hidden underneath the copy [32].

Docker itself can only be used to run containers on a single node. To enable the usage of containers in a cluster of nodes, *container orchestration systems* can be used [9,14]. This is especially relevant for systems which consist of numerous interconnected containers, such as in a microservices architecture [5]. The container orchestration system automates several tasks such as scaling the number of running containers to adjust to the current load, enforcing resource limits on containers, or restarting containers which have become unhealthy. Therefore, it becomes feasible to run systems consisting of numerous interconnected containers in a scalable and fault tolerant way without an excessive increase of the operational effort to do so. The most prominent container orchestration system is Kubernetes[3]. In Kubernetes, the unit of deployment is a *pod*. Each pod can contain one or several containers which are included in the pod in the form of their container images. Through the pod abstraction, Kubernetes is less dependent on Docker, although Docker is the most popular approach to run containers in Kubernetes. A pod is a so-called kubernetes *resource*. For resources, Kubernetes offers mechanisms to monitor them and react on specified events at runtime. This concept is used by the *replica set* resource which represents a replicated set of pods. If one pod of this set crashes, an event is emitted based on which

---

[1] https://www.docker.com/.

[2] https://hub.docker.com/.

[3] https://kubernetes.io.

Kubernetes can automatically start a new pod to reconcile the actual state with the expected state for the replica set resource [8]. This concept of resources can also be used to extend Kubernetes by creating *custom resource definitions* for which again custom events and actions can be defined.

Internally, Kubernetes differentiates between the control plane on which the *kube-api-server* is running and worker nodes which run a so-called *kubelet* agent. The kube-api-server manages the global state of the cluster and offers a single point of access on which it accepts requests to create, modify or remove resources. These requests are fulfilled by orchestrating the pods via the kubelet agents over the available nodes. Because this is in complete control of the container orchestration system, it happens transparently to the Kubernetes user. In addition, Kubernetes also offers specific resources for handling security, such as the ability to store *secrets* or define access *roles* and *groups*.

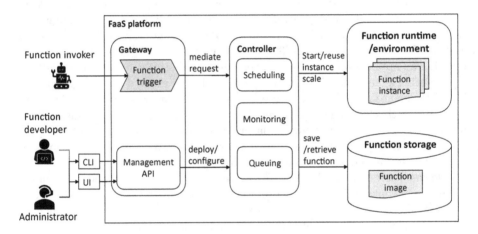

Fig. 1. A generic FaaS platform architecture

2.2   FaaS Platforms

Containerization and container orchestration systems are exploited to build FaaS platforms which offer the ability to transparently execute functions in a scalable and fault-tolerant way as an easy to use service. The most well-known FaaS platforms are hosted by cloud vendors, including platforms such as AWS Lambda[4], Google Cloud Functions[5], or Azure Functions[6]. In addition, installable open source platforms have gained popularity over the last years. Those are in the focus for this work and examples for installable FaaS platforms are the already mentioned Kubeless, OpenFaaS, Fission, Knative, and OpenWhisk.

---

[4] https://aws.amazon.com/lambda/ – accessed 2020-08-18.
[5] https://cloud.google.com/functions – accessed 2020-08-18.
[6] https://azure.microsoft.com/services/functions/ – accessed 2020-08-18.

Although FaaS platforms differ in their implementations, they share the general idea of managing and executing functions transparently. This general idea can be expressed in a generic architecture for FaaS platforms, consisting of distinct components, which is shown in Fig. 1. Specific platform implementations, however, differ in the degree to which components are separated or combined, the degree to which additional artifacts are included instead of platform-specific implementations, and the degree to which aspects are delegated to the underlying infrastructure (e.g. container orchestration systems).

Nevertheless, this generic architecture can be used to explain the important aspects of a FaaS platform. Usually, the platform exposes its functionality via a management application programming interface (API). For the interaction with the management API we differentiate between two roles: administrators and function developers. We assume that administrators have full access to the management API which means they can list, deploy, invoke, update and remove functions, but also access system management functionalities, such as managing of secrets, health checks, logging, user management and more. Function developers actually implement functions but have no or only limited access to the management API depending on the organizational policies and specific use case. This differentiation is necessary to define more precise security threats later. The interaction with the platform API can be established by using a command line interface (CLI) tool that is usually provided by the FaaS vendor. While a CLI tool is available for all platforms, a user interface (UI) that interacts with the platform API is less often. The management functionalities are internally provided by a component that is called *controller*. The controller relies on a function storage where deployed function images, e.g. container images, are stored until needed. The fact that containers are lightweight and can be started up rapidly makes it feasible to run container instances only when needed. In addition, once a function is deployed, also a function trigger is registered through which a function can be invoked by a client. Depending on the use case the client can be an application used by human users, another system or things such as sensors in the IoT use case. The most common trigger is an HTTP request, but most of the FaaS platforms also support cronjob and event-connector patterns where functions are mapped to topics and functions are invoked when specific events occur. Upon a function invocation, the controller deploys a function instance in the function runtime or scales the number of running function instances according to the current load. This is achieved by gathering and analyzing metrics collected by a monitoring component. In case of OpenFaaS, Fission and Knative, Prometheus[7] is used. Some other FaaS platforms implement their own solutions or they use other monitoring systems. To enable asynchronous invocations, a controller can also include a queuing system, such as NATS[8] in the case of OpenFaaS to buffer invocations until execution. The function runtime environment is realized by relying on containerization which means that the functions are deployed within containers. Often, also the FaaS platform components themselves are deployed

---

[7] https://prometheus.io/ – accessed 2020-08-18.
[8] https://github.com/nats-io – accessed 2020-08-18.

as containers and run in the same container orchestration system as the functions. Additionally, some frameworks also have a tight integration with the container orchestration system to provide their functionality. Knative, for example, is built on Kubernetes and provides custom resource definitions to implement and deploy functions [15]. It also does not need a special CLI and relies on the Kubernetes CLI `kubectl`. Functions can be developed with different programming languages, including Java, C#, Go, JavaScript, PHP, Python and Ruby. For all these various programming languages, the FaaS vendors provide function environments/runtimes in form of container images that contain enough binaries and libraries to build and run a function. The function code is packaged within these environment/runtime images during deployment or execution. For instance, the Fission platform uses a *fetcher* container that loads the function and copies the function code into the environment container at runtime[9]. Other FaaS platforms, such as OpenFaaS, build a function container image at deployment time that is based on the original environment image. Such a function container image is usually pushed to an image registry where it can be pulled from.

2.3 Security of FaaS Platforms

When hosting an installable FaaS platform as a private deployment, the underlying infrastructure must also be operated by the respective organization, referred to as the platform provider in the following. Therefore, the platform provider needs to consider security aspects on all layers in contrast to using a hosted FaaS offering from a cloud provider where some concerns can be externalized [13]. Because containerization as a virtualization technique provides the basis for FaaS, security threats specific to virtualization [28, p. 46:5] must be considered in addition to more general security threats. Security threats can be categorized by their *targets* and *sources*. According to the European Union Agency for Network and Information Security (ENISA), the main attack targets in a container-based environment are: applications, containers and the host system [10, p. 38]. The source of an attack describes from where an attack originated [28, p. 46:5], for example another container, the host system or from remote locations. Security threats to container-based environments are similar to hardware-based environments threats, but there are differences. In Fig. 2 well-known threats and defenses for container-based environments in general are shown. For this study, we focus on the layers above of Compute, Hardware, Storage, and Networking because those layers are already investigated in another work [28] and for all virtualization strategies, the security threats for the lower layers are similar. Considering defenses, a distinction is made between hardening and prevention mechanisms. Hardening mechanisms should make the infrastructure more robust and should decrease the attack surface [24]. Prevention mechanisms should protect against several specific threats by closing potential entry points [24].

---

[9] https://docs.fission.io/docs/concepts/components/core/executor/ – accessed 2020-08-18.

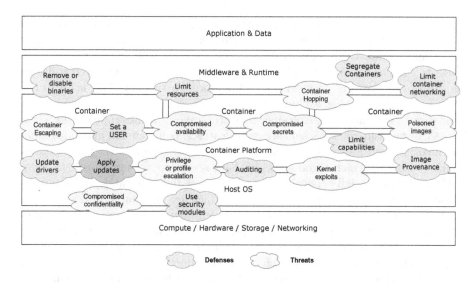

Fig. 2. Security threats and defenses in container-based environments

On the layer of the Host OS an important concept of containerization is to share the kernel between all containers and the host. That means, any kernel vulnerability is also exploitable for containers, provided that the corresponding capabilities are accessible within the container. An important hardening mechanism therefore is to limit the capabilities of containers only to those that are needed. Similar to *VM Escaping*, in container-based environments so-called *Container Breakouts* must be considered where a process of one container gains access to another container or even the host system [1, p. 2]. When breaking out of a container, with some container technologies you will have the same privileges as you had before within the container. Therefore, it is necessary to run containers as non-root user and prevent privilege escalation where a user can get elevated rights, even if you have limited capabilities within the container as root user. Otherwise, a container breakout could lead to a violation of the confidentiality objective for data used within functions or decrease the availability of the FaaS platform depending on the specific aim of the container breakout.

To define specific security threats so-called *threat models* can be used. Although there are different ways to describe threat models, one common approach is using security and trust assumptions [28]. In case of trust assumptions, it must be defined which components and parties of an environment are trustworthy. Based on this, potential attack sources and targets are identified or excluded leading to specific security threats. Because we consider installable FaaS platforms hosted by an organization itself for this study, we assume that the FaaS platform provider is trustworthy. The FaaS platform provider is responsible for the lower layers and the underlying infrastructure including the Host OS. Because we also assume that within the organization there are no malicious insiders, it is reasonable to exclude those layers as attack sources from our threat model. Nevertheless, it should be noted that these layers need to be secured and corresponding threats and defenses for these layers were already discussed in other papers, such as [25]. The platform administrator (see Fig. 1), who has full access to the FaaS platform and container platform, is also considered to be on the side of the platform provider and is therefore trustworthy. This leads to the container platform being excluded from the attack sources and therefore also some threats specific to the container platform are out of the scope of this work. Instead, our considered attackers are remote attackers in general, malicious function invokers, and also malicious function developers (see Fig. 1). The potential attack sources to which those attackers have access to are functions, the FaaS platform and potentially containers in which these functions and platform components are executed. By using attack hops which are introduced in [28, p. 46:7], an attacker who has access to the function container and escaping it, may also have access to the Host OS. Our assumption is that malicious function invokers might be able to inject malicious function input as well as malicious code via the function input and could therefore use the function container as an attack source. The same applies to malicious function developers who could integrate malicious code into function images. Another attack source can be the FaaS platform which is exposed on the Internet and is not correctly hardened or does not support sufficient security mechanisms. Based on our threat model, we therefore narrow our focus from Fig. 2 to only the layers above the Host OS. In Fig. 3, we have detailed this focus by extracting the most important mechanisms and measures for securing an installable FaaS platform which we will then use for our analysis.

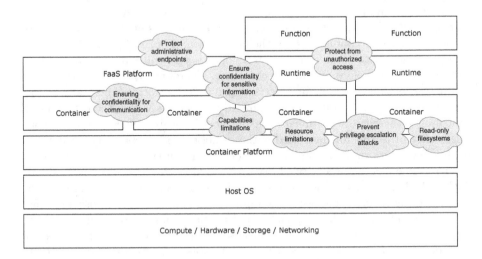

Fig. 3. Securing FaaS platforms and their functions

In the following we present the recommended mechanisms and measures from Fig. 3 more in detail. Privilege escalation attacks can be prevented by running containers with a non-root user [1,31]. In addition, capabilities within function containers can be limited by dropping capabilities that are not required [31]. Providing read-only filesystems to containers, e.g. the container layer, limits the possibilities for injecting malicious code into functions [1]. By also limiting the resources, like CPU and RAM, available to a function container, resource starvation attacks, such as DoS attacks can be avoided [26,31] to ensure availability. For all components shown in Fig. 1 and the functions, confidentiality in transit must be ensured by using protocols such as Transport Layer Security (TLS). This should prevent eavesdropping and tampering of communications between a CLI tool or a UI with the management API of the FaaS platform or a function. The management API should also be protected by using authentication and authorization schemes to ensure confidentiality, authenticity and protecting the respective endpoints for deployed functions. This is of high importance when the management API is accessible within a network where several persons have access to or over the Internet. Sensitive information in the FaaS environment, including API keys, database passwords and ssh keys, should be stored encrypted. Although these security measures are the result of the threat model based on our specific assumptions, they are the most relevant for hosting an installable FaaS platform in production.

3 Methodology

We selected installable platforms to investigate based on which platforms are already mentioned in the literature [16,19,21] and which platforms were recently released in addition. Furthermore, we excluded platforms which do not seem to be in active development anymore. A short overview of the considered FaaS platforms is given in Table 1.

Table 1. Overview of considered installable FaaS platforms

Name	Initial release	Version	Website
Kubeless	2017	1.0.5	https://kubeless.io
OpenFaaS	2017	0.18.2	https://www.openfaas.com/
Fission	2017	1.7.1	https://fission.io
Knative	2018	0.12.1	https://knative.dev
OpenWhisk	2016	0.9.0	https://openwhisk.apache.org/

Based on the considered threat model and trust assumptions we made (see focus of our investigation Subsect. 2.3), the focus of our investigation is on three layers: containers, FaaS platform, and functions (see Fig. 3). For each layer we investigated the selected platforms to find out which mechanisms and measures they support for protecting and hardening the FaaS environment on these layers. Our primary resource for the investigations were the documentations provided for the FaaS platforms. Because all considered platforms are open-source, we also took a look at the source code and opened/closed issues on GitHub. Additional security issues were tested by deploying a specific Python test function to the platforms. This test function is shown in List. 1. It has to be noted that this is only part of the actually deployed function, because for each FaaS platform a platform-specfic wrapper conforming to the required function interface had to be added which then called the shown function upon function execution. The specific functions are also available online[10]. With this function, it was determined if function containers are running with a root-user and if a read-only filesystem is used. Because only OpenFaaS provided some information about read-only filesystems, it was necessary to test the other platforms ourselves.

```
 1  import os
 2  import time
 3  import json
 4
 5  def evaluate(file_folder, filename, file_content):
 6    # check for read—only filesystem
 7    read_only_filesystem = False
 8    try:
 9      with open('{0}/{1}'.format(file_folder, filename), 'w+')
10        as file:
11        file.write(file_content)
12    except IOError:
13      read_only_filesystem = True
14
15    # check container user
16    user = os.popen('whoami').read().rstrip()
17
18    return json.dumps({'whoami': user, 'read—only—fs':
19      read_only_filesystem})
```

List. 1. Test function

We deployed all platforms to a local minikube (v1.7.3) cluster running on a system with Arch Linux 2019-12-01. When installing the platforms we followed the corresponding instructions for the platforms with default settings.

4   Results

The presentation of our investigation results for the various FaaS platforms is organized within three subsections. In each subsection the results are summarized in a table. If a mechanism is directly available/enabled, this is marked with ✓, if a mechanism is not directly available, but can be enabled using the underlying infrastructure, e.g. the container orchestration system, or other plugins/addons this is marked with ∼, and if a mechanism ist not available it is

---

[10] https://github.com/mprechtl/faas-sec-investigation.

marked with -. Nevertheless, a mechanism that is not available can often be enabled/implemented with additional manual effort.

4.1 Security Measures at the Container Level

In this section, we will consider security mechanisms and measures for the container level which were summarized in Fig. 3. Besides general rules and hardening mechanisms, such as keeping the host and the container technology up to date, Table 2 deals with hardening mechanisms that can significantly increase the level of security by minimizing the attack surface. In the following table we will only focus on the functions images.

Table 2. Mechanisms to ensure availability and container security

Threats	Privilege escalation		Compromised availability		Container manipulation
Defenses	Set User	Capabilities limitations	Timeouts	Resource limitations	Read-only filesystems
Kubeless	✓	-	✓	✓	-
OpenFaaS	✓	-	✓	✓	✓
Fission	-	-	✓	✓	-
Knative	✓	-	✓	✓	-
OpenWhisk	-	-	✓	✓	-

The most common way to handle availability issues and prevent Denial of Service (DoS) attacks, is to limit resources, define timeouts and blacklist IPs. All FaaS platforms support timeouts and resource limitations for their functions and in the most cases also for the platform components. Ingress controllers, such as Kong[11], support plugins for rate-limiting that ensure that only a certain number of requests can be made in a given period of seconds, minutes or hours. In addition to rate-limiting plugins, plugins to whitelist and blacklist IPs are usually provided. Running functions with a non-root user can prevent privilege escalation attacks. Almost all FaaS platforms, excluding Fission and OpenWhisk, run their functions with a non-root user. This was investigated by deploying the test function to the various platforms. Fission and OpenWhisk run their functions with a root-user (at least when using the Python environment). For these two FaaS platforms, custom function environments/runtimes must be provided to set a non-root user. This step is connected with much more additional effort. According to the documentation and the test function, only OpenFaaS provides a read-only filesystem. Deploying functions with a read-only filesystem in OpenFaaS requires a property that must be set within the function deployment file (YAML file)[12]. For all the other FaaS platforms no possibility was

---

[11] https://konghq.com/solutions/kubernetes-ingress/ – accessed 2020-08-18.
[12] https://www.openfaas.com/blog/read-only-functions/ – accessed 2020-08-18.

found to configure a read-only filesystem. In Knative, a function developer or administrator has to setup a service configuration file which contains the specification to the function. For each function a security context can be defined, but currently it seems that only the *runAsUser* property is supported within a security context[13],[14]. In general, a security context specification can include besides of the *runAsUser* property also capabilities limitations and enabling of read-only filesystems. None of the FaaS platforms provides possibilities to limit kernel capabilities for function containers. OpenFaaS mentions that they are not allowing the privileged mode for function containers where a container would have extended privileges[15].

In addition to the function containers, the FaaS platform components which are also running in one or several containers must also be secured regarding container security. All FaaS platforms can be installed by using Helm charts or by using the provided Kubernetes resource files. Some of the Helm charts, such as the one for OpenFaaS, are using a security context for their deployments[16]. For other FaaS platforms that do not set a security context, the Kubernetes resource files can be modified to use one. However, this is connected with some effort.

4.2 Security Measures at the Platform Level

The next table (see Table 3) deals with platform security and in which way the management and administration APIs that are exposed by the FaaS platform can be protected. As already mentioned in Subsect. 2.3, this is absolutely necessary when FaaS platforms are exposed on a network or over the Internet.

Only some FaaS platforms, including OpenFaaS and OpenWhisk, support built-in authentication mechanisms for their APIs. OpenFaaS enables basic authentication by default and the OpenFaaS Ltd. also provides an OpenID Connect commercial plugin[17]. In OpenWhisk, besides of basic authentication, client-certificate authentication can be used[18]. All the other FaaS platforms do not support built-in authentication mechanisms. In case of Kubeless, Fission and Knative, the CLI tools that are provided by these platforms are communicating with the `kube-apiserver`. The Kubernetes API can be secured by using authentication strategies, including client certificates, password and plain tokens, but also OpenID Connect[19]. That means, in case of Kubeless, Fission and Knative, authentication schemes can be enabled by using `kubectl` instead of the provided

---

[13] https://knative.dev/docs/serving/spec/knative-api-specification-1.0/.

[14] https://github.com/knative/serving/issues/4130 – accessed 2020-08-18.

[15] https://www.openfaas.com/blog/five-security-tips/ – accessed 2020-08-18.

[16] https://github.com/openfaas/faas-netes/tree/master/chart/openfaas.

[17] https://github.com/alexellis/openfaas-oidc-plugin-pkg – accessed 2020-08-18.

[18] https://github.com/apache/openwhisk/blob/master/docs/cli.md#configure-the-cli-to-use-client-certificate – accessed 2020-08-18.

[19] https://kubernetes.io/docs/reference/access-authn-authz/authentication/ – accessed 2020-08-18.

CLI tool and communicating directly with the `kube-apiserver`. Such an approach is connected with effort, but it would provide a greater level of flexibility
for the administrators and function developers. In general, there seems to be
a lack of access control strategies for all installable FaaS platforms. FaaS platforms that allow the easy usage of `kubectl` can represent an exception, because
Kubernetes supports multiple access control strategies, including attribute-based
access control (ABAC) and role-based access control (RBAC)[20].

Table 3. Mechanisms and protocols for securing the platform level

	Authentication			Authorization	Access control	Transport confidentiality
	Basic	OIDC	Other	OAuth	RBAC,	TLS
Kubeless	~	~	~	~	~	~
OpenFaaS	✓	✓	-	✓	-	~
Fission	~	~	~	~	~	~
Knative	~	~	~	~	~	~
OpenWhisk	✓	-	✓	-	-	~

The communication to management and administration APIs can be secured
by relying on protocols such as Transport Layer Security (TLS) via an ingress
controller. An ingress controller can be deployed on Kubernetes to act as reverse
proxy and enable TLS among other features. In case of Fission, Kubeless and
Knative, where the `kubectl` CLI tool can be used, the Kubernetes API must be
secured which is done by default with self-signed TLS certificates[21].

4.3   Security Measures at the Function Level

In Table 4, protection mechanisms that can be applied to secure the functions
from unauthorized access and ensure confidentiality and integrity for data are
listed. Confidentiality must be ensured for sensitive information, such as passwords, API keys, ssh keys and more, in transit and at rest. This is usually
done by using secret resources within Kubernetes. Functions can be protected
from remote attackers/invokers by using strong authentication and authorization schemes which should guarantee that only authorized invokers have access
to those functions. In addition, access control strategies, like RBAC, should
ensure that invokers have the correct permissions to execute a function. For an
invoker who is communicating with a function, data integrity and authenticity
must be guaranteed. This ensures that a man-in-the-middle is not able to manipulate and eavesdrop sent data. In transit one possible strategy is, relying on an
ingress controller that enables TLS for the functions. On application/function
level, HMACs and digital signatures can be used where a function can evaluate
input data that those data were really sent by a specific function invoker.

---

[20] https://kubernetes.io/docs/reference/access-authn-authz/controlling-access/   –
accessed 2020-08-18.

[21] https://kubernetes.io/docs/reference/access-authn-authz/controlling-access/#
transport-security – accessed 2020-08-18.

Table 4. Mechanisms and protocols to secure serverless functions

	Authentication	Authorization	Access control	Data confidentiality, integrity, authenticity	
	Basic, OIDC, Other	OAuth, JWT,	RBAC,	Secrets	HMAC's & Signatures
Kubeless	~	~	~	~	-
OpenFaaS	✓	✓	~	~	✓
Fission	~	~	~	~	-
Knative	~	~	~	~	-
OpenWhisk	~	~	~	-	-

Because an ingress controller provides features for authentication and authorization, this does not have to be handled by the functions. An ingress controller that supports many authentication mechanisms is the already mentioned Kong ingress controller. Kong supports OIDC, Basic, HMAC, Key and LDAP authentication. It also supports authorization mechanisms and protocols such as JWTs and OAuth[22]. An alternative can be to implement the required authentication and authorization mechanisms directly within, however this is not a recommended approach because it would result in an serious implementation overhead.

Confidentiality in transit can be ensured by using protocols, such as TLS. TLS is not explicitly mentioned in Table 4, but already considered in Table 3 and can be implemented by using an ingress controller and creating a route to the function. API keys, SSH keys, database passwords and other credentials can be stored in encrypted secrets. Kubernetes allows to encrypt resources, including secrets, at rest by using an encryption configuration[23]. For OpenWhisk there are no information provided in which way Kubernetes secrets can be used. TLS already ensures integrity of data in transit, but often it is also desired to ensure integrity in addition to authenticity of data at rest. This can be done with digital signatures and can be of high importance in case of e-Government and e-Business applications, but currently such mechanisms are not supported by the platforms.

5 Discussion

Based on the results of our investigation we answer our research questions and discuss the implications for deploying an installable FaaS platform in an organization in the following. Considering RQ1, overall the investigated platforms do provide necessary security features as it can be seen in the Tables 3, 2, and 4. But there are differences based on the maturity of the platforms. One specific observation in this regard is that OpenFaaS covers most of the recommended security measures with built-in support, such as the possibility to run containers with a read-only filesystem. Also the protection of the management API is supported with built-in mechanisms by OpenFaaS while most of the other platforms do not provide such mechanisms directly.

---

[22] https://docs.konghq.com/hub/ – accessed 2020-08-18.

[23] https://kubernetes.io/docs/tasks/administer-cluster/encrypt-data/ – accessed 2020-08-18.

However, the possibility of enabling authentication and authorization mechanisms for Kubeless, Fission, and Knative via the built-in Kubernetes security features is still a valid option, although leading to an additional overhead to implement them. While it is clear that it should be possible to protect the management API with appropriate authentication mechanisms, it is worth to discuss whether this possibility should be implemented directly within a FaaS platform or provided by another component. For commercial FaaS offerings from cloud vendors the answer to this question is clear. Because they are operated within a larger cloud computing environment, there are specialized services available which take over the responsibilities for authentication and authorization for all different offerings in the environment. An example for this is the IAM[24] service withing AWS. Because there is no such service available for installable FaaS platforms, the question remains where authentication and authorization mechanism should be implemented. An influencing factor is the specific use case for which a FaaS platform should be used. If it is intended as a stand-alone solution, mechanisms for authentication and authorization should rather be built-in. If the platform is used in a larger context together with other components, an independent solution for all components is more appropriate.

This leads to the answer to RQ2: Although the delegation of authentication and authorization mechanisms to Kubernetes is a justifiable approach, there is still room to improve for making this integration with the Kubernetes mechanisms more smooth. For example, tailored commands for the FaaS platform clients could be implemented to make the setup of such authorization and authentication measures more convenient. In addition, the aspect of role-based or attribute-based authorization is not well supported. If function developers are given access to the management API such mechanism could for example enable that function developers only have access to their own functions and not those of others. This security measure is the result of our threat model where malicious function developers have to be considered. An alternative approach would be to deny the access to the management API for function developers and implement an organizational approach to function deployment such that only administrators deploy functions after function developers have provided them. This would however increase the overhead for using a FaaS platform, although a frequently mentioned benefit of FaaS is that functions can be deployed faster because operational concerns are externalized [18].

Considering the protection of functions, all FaaS platforms follow a similar approach by delegating this measure to ingress controllers when the platform is deployed in Kubernetes. An exception hereby is OpenFaaS which provides some protection strategies by default, such as Basic, HMAC and OAuth authentication. However, ingress controllers offer a wide range of available authentication and authorization mechanisms, functions can be effectively protected from external attackers and malicious function invokers. Malicious function invokers who have valid credentials need to be considered as well. Because they have access

---

[24] https://aws.amazon.com/de/iam/ – accessed 2020-08-18.

to the running function instance, the security measures shown in Table 2 are important to stop them from extending their attack.

When protecting functions of a FaaS platform, another aspect to consider is in which context the functions are used. A differentiation can be made between backend use cases where functions are used between internal systems and frontend use cases where functions are invoked by end users. The popularity of both use cases in practice has recently been studied by Leitner et al. [18]. Depending on the use cases different authentication and authorization mechanisms are more appropriate. For backend use cases functions should nevertheless be protected, but a simpler mechanism such as an API key might be sufficient. For frontend use cases more advanced mechanisms like OIDC might be more appropriate. Overall, considering the presented results, it can be stated that the presented FaaS platforms are already sufficiently safe and easy to use for comparatively simple use cases with a limited number of people involved. For more complex use cases, for example as an organizational-wide FaaS offering with many different function developers, the existing FaaS platform still need to be improved.

Some other hardening mechanisms that were included in our overview of security threats and defenses in container-based environments (see Fig. 2), were not covered in detail. This includes general rules, such as updating of drivers, binaries and libraries, but also keeping track on image provenance and segregation of containers with sensitive information from containers with non-sensitive information. All these additional hardening mechanisms can be of high importance in a production environment. It is also necessary to mention that container images can be scanned for vulnerabilities. Container image scans can be performed by using the Docker Trusted Registry[25] or other tools, such as Anchore Engine[26]. An adversary can scan function container images for vulnerable libraries and binaries and then start exploiting them within the function.

While such hardening mechanisms can be applied proactively, the fact that attacks can nevertheless occur should not be neglected. It should therefore be possible to also react on attacks at runtime. One option in this regard is logging and monitoring which should be enabled by a FaaS platform in order to being able to detect suspicious behavior within the platform and to enable forensics investigations after an incident [13]. This is also of importance when considering the mentioned malicious function invokers with valid credentials, in order to discover them and potentially revoke their credentials. Although these possibilities were out of the scope of this work, they should be considered when deploying a FaaS platform. OpenFaaS for example offers the possibility to integrate Grafana[27] dashboards for monitoring and for other platforms existing approaches for Kubernetes could be used.

To conclude our discussion, limitations of our work are highlighted. The scope of our investigation is limited by our considered threat model. Because we

---

[25] https://docs.docker.com/ee/dtr/user/manage-images/scan-images-for-vulnerabilities/ – accessed 2020-08-18.

[26] https://github.com/anchore/anchore-engine – accessed 2020-08-18.

[27] https://grafana.com/ – accessed 2020-08-18.

have limited the types of different attackers, the investigated security measures are focused on these attackers. When deploying an installable FaaS platform, it should be thoroughly evaluated which threat models have to be considered or not. Our methodology for examining the different FaaS platforms is limited in the sense that we relied to a large extent on the documentations provided by the FaaS platform vendors. As there might be deviations between the documentations and the actual implementations, this could have an effect in two ways: measures could be available but not documented, or they could be documented but do not work as expected. However, we tried to verify the documented features wherever possible and are confident that our results are accurate. Finally, attacks on the application layer (see Fig. 2) are out of the scope of this work, because they need to be considered for each specific application. Nevertheless, they should be considered and for example security advises from the Open Web Application Security Project (OWASP) should be followed [30].

6   Related Work

There have already been several comparisons and investigations of installable FaaS platforms similar to this work. Lynn et al. were the earliest to compare different FaaS platforms with a comprehensive set of comparison criteria and comparing both hosted and installable FaaS platforms [19]. Kritikos and Skrzypek have reviewed available FaaS platform and compared their features with a focus on further challenges for FaaS platforms [16]. Mohanty et al. compared FaaS platforms and evaluated their performance [21]. Also focusing on performance, Lee et al. evaluated hosted FaaS platforms from cloud providers [17]. Palade et al. compared installable FaaS platforms according to their suitability for Edge Computing [23]. Kaviani et al. compared installable FaaS platforms, with a special focus on Knative, according to what they call API and runtime contracts in order to arrive at a common API layer for FaaS platforms [15]. And finally Spillner et al. provided a brief overview on available tooling for FaaS, also discussing different platforms [29]. While these works are helpful to make a choice on which FaaS platform to choose for a specific use case, they all had different focuses and none focused specifically on security. Our work is therefore an addition to previous comparisons with a focus not present so far.

Considering FaaS platforms with a special focus on security, there have also been several works already. Although their considered threat models are different, there are nevertheless connecting factors. Alpernas et al. propose a solution based on dynamic information flow control (IFC) which focuses on protecting the confidentiality of data accessible to a function [4]. The threat model is similar in the sense that a function might be compromised and that even in that case the confidentiality of data should be protected. It could therefore be used as an additional approach for increasing the security in an own FaaS deployment but provides a specific solution to a specific problem. Agache et al. discuss the security approaches in a commercial platform (AWS Lambda) where the focus is on isolating functions and their workloads of different customers from each other

[2]. In contrast to our work, their considered platform is shared by many different organizations instead of having a platform deployed privately for a single organization. Therefore, their focus is on the lower layers of the platform stack and how especially isolation of different customers can be guaranteed in a secure way on these levels. They propose to use so-called MicroVMs which are a compromise between containers and virtual machines providing both a very strict isolation while still showing fast start up times and performance. In the future it might be possible also for installable FaaS platforms to adopt the MicroVM approach although the security requirements regarding isolation might not be same, because an installable FaaS platform is typically used by a single organization. Finally, Alder et al. propose a specialized FaaS platform called S-FaaS which enables execution of functions in so-called enclaves based on Intel SGX [3]. They consider the platform provider as an adversary and it is therefore important that the provider cannot access data from the function invoker and the resource usage metrics should be reliable from both the provider and consumer side. The difference to our work therefore is the considered adversary in their threat model as well as the host OS being considered as an attack source.

7   Conclusion and Outlook

We have investigated installable FaaS platforms according to the possibilities they provide for protecting and hardening them in a production deployment. To do so, we derived important security measures and then compared available installable FaaS platforms based on these measures. Our comparison shows that the platforms support the security measures in large parts, although there are differences making platforms more suitable for a production deployment than others. In addition, we point out aspects in which the FaaS platforms could be improved. Our main findings are that the platforms lack support for advanced features such as role-based access control for the management API or possibilities for additional hardening mechanisms at the lower container levels such as capabilities limitations. Thus, the platforms can generally be used in production deployments, but might not be suitable for more complex use cases. A question which could be further investigated is which security measures should be provided by which components. An apparent insight is that FaaS platforms do not directly support authentication and authorization mechanisms for functions, but delegate this to ingress controllers. For authentication and authorization mechanisms for the management API the approaches differ and it remains to be seen whether a common approach establishes.

In summary, it can be stated that security in a FaaS environment is complex and organizations who want to host their own FaaS environments should be aware of several threats, corresponding defenses and protection mechanisms. Our investigation and platform comparison can help organizations in selecting an appropriate platform and deploying it in a secure way.

References

1. Mouat, A.: Docker Security - Using Containers Safely in Production. O'Reilly Media Inc., Beijing (2015). ISBN-13: 978–1491942994
2. Agache, A., et al.: Firecracker: lightweight virtualization for serverless applications. In: Proceedings of the 17th USENIX NSDI, pp. 419–434. USENIX Association, Santa Clara (2020)
3. Alder, F., Asokan, N., Kurnikov, A., Paverd, A., Steiner, M.: S-FaaS: trustworthy and accountable function-as-a-service using Intel SGX. In: Proceedings of the 2019 ACM SIGSAC Conference on Cloud Computing Security Workshop - CCSW 2019, pp. 185–199. ACM Press, New York (2019)
4. Alpernas, K., et al.: Secure serverless computing using dynamic information flow control. Proc. ACM Program. Lang. **2**, 1–26 (2018)
5. Amaral, M., Polo, J., Carrera, D., Mohomed, I., Unuvar, M., Steinder, M.: Performance evaluation of microservices architectures using containers. In: Proceedings of the 14th International Symposium on Network Computing and Applications, pp. 27–34. IEEE (2015)
6. Baldini, I., et al.: Serverless computing: current trends and open problems. In: Chaudhary, S., Somani, G., Buyya, R. (eds.) Research Advances in Cloud Computing, pp. 1–20. Springer, Singapore (2017). https://doi.org/10.1007/978-981-10-5026-8_1
7. Baresi, L., Mendonca, D.F.: Towards a serverless platform for edge computing. In: International Conference on Fog Computing (ICFC). pp. 1–10. IEEE (2019)
8. Burns, B., Grant, B., Oppenheimer, D., Brewer, E., Wilkes, J.: Borg, omega, and kubernetes. Commun. ACM **59**(5), 50–57 (2016)
9. Casalicchio, E.: Container orchestration: a survey. In: Puliafito, A., Trivedi, K.S. (eds.) Systems Modeling: Methodologies and Tools. EICC, pp. 221–235. Springer, Cham (2019). https://doi.org/10.1007/978-3-319-92378-9_14
10. European Union Agency for Network and Information Security (ENISA): Security aspects of virtualization (2017). https://www.enisa.europa.eu/publications/security-aspects-of-virtualization. Accessed 09 Dec 2019
11. Eurostat: Cloud computing services used by more than one out of four enterprises in the EU (2018). https://ec.europa.eu/eurostat/documents/2995521/9447642/9-13122018-BP-EN.pdf
12. van Eyk, E., Iosup, A., Seif, S., Thömmes, M.: The SPEC cloud group's research vision on FaaS and serverless architectures. In: Proceedings of the 2nd International Workshop on Serverless Computing, WoSC 2017, pp. 1–4. ACM, NY (2017)
13. Hellerstein, J.M., et al.: Serverless computing: one step forward, two steps back. In: Proceedings of the 9th Conference on Innovative Data Systems Research (CIDR) (2019)
14. Jawarneh, I.M.A., et al..: Container orchestration engines: a thorough functional and performance comparison. In: International Conference on Communications, pp. 1–6. IEEE (2019)
15. Kaviani, N., Kalinin, D., Maximilien, M.: Towards serverless as commodity. In: Proceedings of the 5th International Workshop on Serverless Computing – WOSC 2019, pp. 13–18. ACM Press, New York (2019)
16. Kritikos, K., Skrzypek, P.: A Review of serverless frameworks. In: Proceedings of the 4th Workshop on Serverless Computing (WoSC), pp. 161–168. IEEE (2018)
17. Lee, H., Satyam, K., Fox, G.C.: Evaluation of production serverless computing environments. In: Proceedings of the IEEE 11th International Conference on Cloud Computing (CLOUD 2018), pp. 442–450. IEEE (2018)

18. Leitner, P., Wittern, E., Spillner, J., Hummer, W.: A mixed-method empirical study of Function-as-a-Service software development in industrial practice. J. Syst. Softw. **149**, 340–359 (2019)
19. Lynn, T., Rosati, P., Lejeune, A., Emeakaroha, V.: A preliminary review of enterprise serverless cloud computing (function-as-a-service) platforms. In: International Conference on Cloud Computing Technology and Science, pp. 162–169. IEEE (2017)
20. McGrath, G., Brenner, P.R.: Serverless computing: design, implementation, and performance. In: Proceedings of the IEEE 37th International Conference on Distributed Computing Systems Workshops (ICDCSW 2017), pp. 405–410. IEEE (2017)
21. Mohanty, S.K., Premsankar, G., di Francesco, M.: An evaluation of open source serverless computing frameworks. In: Proceedings of the IEEE International Conference on Cloud Computing Technology and Science (CloudCom 2018), pp. 115–120. IEEE (2018)
22. Pahl, C.: Containerization and the PaaS cloud. IEEE Cloud Comput. **2**(3), 24–31 (2015)
23. Palade, A., Kazmi, A., Clarke, S.: An evaluation of open source serverless computing frameworks support at the edge. In: Proceedings of the IEEE World Congress on Services (SERVICES 2019), vol. 2642–939X, pp. 206–211. IEEE (2019)
24. Pearce, M., Zeadally, S., Hunt, R.: Virtualization: issues, security threats, and solutions. ACM Comput. Surv. **45**(2), 1–39 (2013)
25. Pék, G., Buttyán, L., Bencsáth, B.: A survey of security issues in hardware virtualization. ACM Comput. Surv. **45**(3), 40:1–40:34 (2013)
26. Reshetova, E., Karhunen, J., Nyman, T., Asokan, N.: Security of OS-level virtualization technologies. In: Bernsmed, K., Fischer-Hübner, S. (eds.) NordSec 2014. LNCS, vol. 8788, pp. 77–93. Springer, Cham (2014). https://doi.org/10.1007/978-3-319-11599-3_5
27. Roberts, M., Chapin, J.: What Is Serverless?. O'Reilly Media, Sebastopol (2017)
28. Sgandurra, D., Lupu, E.: Evolution of attacks, threat models, and solutions for virtualized systems. ACM Comput. Surv. **48**(3), 46:1–46:38 (2016)
29. Spillner, J.: Practical tooling for serverless computing. In: Proceedings of the10th UCC 2017, pp. 185–186. ACM Press (2017)
30. van der Stock, A., Glas, B., Smithline, N., Gigler, T.: OWASP top 10–2017 the ten most critical web application security risks. Technical report, OWASP Foundation (2017)
31. Sultan, S., Ahmad, I., Dimitriou, T.: Container security: issues, challenges, and the road ahead. IEEE Access **7**, 52976–52996 (2019)
32. Turnbull, J.: The Docker Book: Containerization is the New Virtualization. James Turnbull (2014). https://dockerbook.com/
33. Yussupov, V., Breitenbücher, U., Leymann, F., Wurster, M.: A systematic mapping study on engineering function-as-a-service platforms and tools. In: Proceedings of the 12th IEEE/ACM International Conference on Utility and Cloud Computing – UCC 2019, pp. 229–240. ACM Press (2019)

A Quantitative Evaluation Approach for Edge Orchestration Strategies

Sebastian Böhm$^{(\boxtimes)}$ and Guido Wirtz$^{(\boxtimes)}$

Distributed Systems Group, University of Bamberg, Bamberg, Germany
{sebastian.boehm,guido.wirtz}@uni-bamberg.de

Abstract. The continuously rising number of Internet of Things (IoT) devices leads to new challenges in data transportation and processing. Edge computing as an additional layer to the cloud shifts computational resources and applications to edge nodes to provide a better communication quality for those devices. The autonomous management of shifting processes is still an open issue and approached by the field of edge orchestration. Recently, specific strategies for the edge have emerged to face the challenges of dynamically changing conditions in heterogeneous architectures. This work aims to establish a quantitative evaluation approach for edge orchestration strategies. For that, we investigate three selected orchestration strategies and deduce a set of Quality of Service (QoS) measurements. Afterward, we implement the strategies and propose an experimental design that shows the orchestration quality for a CPU-intensive application. All strategies show a better average response time during our experiment. However, the strategies result in different outcomes for other QoS measurements, like resource utilization. This gives first hints for a comprehensible strategy recommendation.

Keywords: Internet of things · Edge computing · Orchestration

1 Introduction

The emergence of IoT has become a significant development in today's information technology. Originally, the term comprises technologies like Radio-Frequency Identification (RFID) for tracing supplies in real-time [1]. IoT devices pervade more and more areas of life, like home automation, production scheduling, and autonomous driving [23]. They are equipped with network capabilities, exchanging messages with other devices, collecting data, and uploading that data to the cloud [6]. According to a case study by Gartner, the number of IoT devices with an own IP stack will grow to 20.4 billion devices by 2020[1].

However, the continuously rising number of IoT devices leads to new challenges in data transportation and processing. Commonly, data generated by those devices is uploaded to the cloud where data processing takes place. The

---

[1] https://www.gartner.com/en/newsroom/press-releases/2017-02-07-gartner-says-8-billion-connected-things-will-be-in-use-in-2017-up-31-percent-from-2016.

© Springer Nature Switzerland AG 2020
S. Dustdar (Ed.): SummerSOC 2020, CCIS 1310, pp. 127–147, 2020.
https://doi.org/10.1007/978-3-030-64846-6_8

cloud offers a centralized high-performance pool of resources that can be used on-demand [3,16]. Unfortunately, uploading and processing all data to the cloud may not be applicable anymore because the amount of data generated by those devices is too large and faced by limited bandwidth [6]. As a result, the cloud can not be fully used anymore and new architectures are needed to deal with the new challenges. Also, the emergence of IoT requires new performance metrics in terms of latency. Typical application areas like autonomous driving and Augmented Reality (AR) require low latency (< 20 ms) for the processing units [4].

Therefore, the edge computing paradigm has been developed to face these issues. It comprises the shifting of applications to devices that are in close proximity to the origin of requests. It is an additional layer to cloud computing that fosters the achievement of low latency, high bandwidth, and reliable communication [24]. A major issue in this area is the autonomous assignment of applications to heterogeneous devices under dynamically changing conditions. Orchestration as a solution approach is concerned with the management of resources in order to guarantee a certain QoS [7]. Besides established platforms for autonomic orchestration, like Docker Swarm[2] and Kubernetes[3], orchestration strategies for the edge have emerged. These strategies challenge the autonomous distribution of applications, achieving low latency, and high response times.

This work aims to provide a quantitative analysis of the edge orchestration strategies Capillary Container Orchestrator (CCO) [28], Boundless Resource Orchestrator (BRO) [33], and Enhanced Container Scheduler (ECSched) [13]. The strategies challenge the problem of autonomous distribution of applications to devices from an architectural and algorithmic perspective. Since there is no widely accepted set of quantitative measurements for edge orchestration, this work wants to contribute a reasonable set for a standardized analysis. Furthermore, there is no standardized evaluation between the formerly mentioned edge orchestration strategies. This leads to the following research questions:

RQ1: What are the specific quality metrics of the edge orchestration strategies CCO, BRO, and ECSched during orchestration?

RQ2: What are domain-specific quantitative metrics that are suitable for the evaluation of edge orchestration strategies?

To perform the required experimental study for *RQ1*, a general understanding of edge orchestration (Sect. 2) and the specific strategies (Subsect. 3.1) is needed. In addition, the analysis requires a comprehensive set of QoS measurements, which are derived from a literature review (Subsect. 3.2). These QoS measurements answer *RQ2* and allow for the implementation of a two-step experiment that compares the achieved orchestration quality for edge-cloud architectures with and without applied orchestration strategies. The experiment is described, conducted, and evaluated in Sect. 4. In Sect. 5, the general- and orchestration-related limitations of our study are outlined. The paper concludes with the related work (Sect. 6) and the conclusion in Sect. 7.

---

[2] https://docs.docker.com/engine/swarm/.

[3] https://kubernetes.io/.

2   Conceptual Foundations of Edge Orchestration

Orchestration for the edge comprises mainly the autonomous distribution of applications under varying conditions such that the QoS measurements are met, and the overall resource utilization is optimized. Most of the orchestration architectures follow a general approach that is stated in Fig. 1. The architecture consists of an autonomic controller, a container registry, and the layers for cloud and edge. A load balancer forwards incoming requests to a cloud or edge node.

At this, the orchestrator continuously receives monitoring data from the cloud and edge devices. Monitoring data comprises, for example, the utilization of nodes in the architecture, like CPU, memory, and disk utilization. The orchestrator uses the received data to analyze the current state of the architecture with a certain strategy (e.g., CCO, BRO, or ECSched). Often the strategies set certain thresholds for resource types, like 80% for CPU utilization [28,33]. If a device exceeds the threshold, the orchestrator initiates the offloading process. This means that the running application on a cloud machine is shifted to an edge device in close proximity to the requesting users. During runtime, all requests of users and other services are initially forwarded to the cloud layer. Thereby, the configured thresholds for resources and the kind of node election process is always dependent on the used strategy [7]. If the election process completes, the orchestrator instructs the elected node to download and execute the application from a so-called container registry. Containers are a lightweight way of virtualization and share the same kernel of a host system. They run on a container engine (e.g., Docker) and contain only the application, the required libraries, and runtime environments. Containerized applications can be executed on any machine that runs a compatible container engine [20]. The elected machine reports the successful startup of the application back to the orchestrator. Afterward, a load balancer reorganizes the routes for requests to discharge the cloud.

In general, orchestration is faced with several challenges. Most of the algorithms are threshold-based. This requires reasonable models for predicting time-series data, like resource utilization [32]. Furthermore, edge architectures consist of heterogeneous devices and continuously varying conditions. Therefore, optimization models are needed that regard a suitable allocation of resources by guaranteeing a reduced latency for requesting users [30].

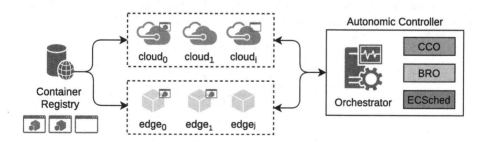

Fig. 1. General orchestration architecture, adapted from [7].

3   Experimental Foundations

This chapter introduces the three orchestration strategies and the required QoS measurements. The two components provide the basis for the experimental study that is the core contribution of this work. In the following, each strategy is analyzed from a theoretical perspective to investigate the mechanisms for application distribution. Thereafter, the required QoS measurements are discussed.

3.1   Orchestration Strategies

Capillary Container Orchestrator. In 2018, TAHERIZADEH ET AL. proposed a Capillary Computing Architecture (CCA) to face the challenges of edge orchestration. This approach uses a multi-tier architecture with cloud and edge layers to enable an effective distribution of applications on the available computational resources [28]. Container technology is typically used for orchestration activities in edge computing to move applications from one location to another. It does also perform the execution and termination of containers. CCO manages the three layers and is responsible for all decisions regarding the distribution of applications. The orchestrator makes use of a comprehensive monitoring system, which provides information about current events, like critical loads on devices. Overall, CCA follows the general edge orchestration architecture, as explained in Sect. 2. CCA focuses on the management of variable workloads by shifting applications across all layers in closer proximity to the origin of requests. The CCA starts the offloading process from bottom-up (i.e., IoT or edge layer). This procedure enables a better response time for all service-requesting devices.

At this point, CCO starts the offloading processes in the architecture based on previously set and fixed thresholds. In the CCA, administrators can define those thresholds for each machine and type of resource (e.g., CPU, memory, and disk utilization) independently [28]. Usually, those limits are set to 80% to ensure a timely reaction of the orchestrator [12,26]. The exceedance of thresholds triggers the CCO to initiate an offloading process from one layer to another in the architecture. To select the most appropriate node, CCO derives the Packet Loss (PL), Network Throughput (NT) from all nodes, which are able to execute the offloaded application. A node is eligible to execute an application if it meets the resource requirements in terms of CPU, memory, and disk capacities of the application. The previously mentioned network-related measurements help to calculate the Node Selection Rank (NSR) (Eq. 1).

$$
\mathrm{NSR} = \frac{\overbrace{\left(1 - \dfrac{\mathrm{PL}}{100}\right) * \mathrm{NT}}^{\text{available bandwidth}}}{\underbrace{\mathrm{ND}}_{\mathrm{RTT}}} \tag{1}
$$

The NSR is the ratio between the Available Bandwidth (AV) and the RTT. NSR declines the NT by multiplying the available share of the PL. For example, if the PL amounts to 5% and the NT amounts to 600 Megabits Per Second (Mbps), the actual AV is 0.95 * 600 Mbps = 570 Mbps. Finally, the reduced bandwidth is divided by the current Network Delay (ND) to express the available bandwidth per millisecond. The higher the AV is and the smaller the ND, the higher is the NSR. Hence, higher NSRs imply more appropriate nodes. After deployment, CCO needs to balance the existing requests between all devices [28].

In conclusion, the strategy is more or less focused on the node election if a certain threshold is exceeded. Thereby, there is no conceptual or mathematical consideration regarding the fit of an application to a machine, based on resource needs and supplies. However, further resource-based criteria can easily be added to the current network-based node election.

Boundless Resource Orchestrator. As the second strategy, we present the BRO. It is introduced by YU ET AL. in 2018 and aims to optimize the distribution of containerized applications in the edge-cloud architecture. BRO uses a master-slave paradigm with a master-cloud and certain edge-cloud systems. In case configured thresholds are exceeded, the orchestrator performs offloading processes from cloud to edge and vice versa. In comparison to CCO, BRO considers resources required by applications and the resources supplied by the architecture. Furthermore, the strategy examines the additional transmission costs for moving a container from the cloud to the edge.

The offloading process starts with the exceedance of a threshold on a certain node, similar to CCO. Of course, also the average application response time can be used to declare a decreasing degree of performance. Afterward, BRO performs the allocation of containers to machines in the architecture, based on a mathematical optimization model. It tries to achieve the best performance for requesting users by reducing the costs of the architecture. This approach is called Best Performance at Least Cost Algorithm (BPLC) and denotes the most important part of the optimization technique, as shown in Eq. 2.

$$\max_{e \epsilon S_a} \alpha \overbrace{\sum_{i=1,2,3} \gamma_i \sum_{e \epsilon S_a} T_e^i}^{\text{available resources}} - \beta \overbrace{\left(\sum_{e_1 \epsilon S_a} \min_{e_2 \epsilon S, e_2 \notin S_a} l_{ce} + \sum_{a \epsilon A} O_a \right)}^{\text{additional transmission costs}} - \theta \overbrace{\sum_{i} \varepsilon_i \sum_{e \epsilon S_a} T_e^i}^{\text{running costs}} \quad (2)$$

The BPLC maximizes the difference between the available resources and the additional transmission costs to make an application available on another node. Furthermore, it includes all running costs in the architecture. The following paragraph explains the symbols and calculations of all three components.

Available Resources. At first, BPLC sums up all theoretically available resources of all nodes e in the current edge-cloud S_a. In this case, the available resource types are computational capacity, memory, and storage expressed by $i = 1, 2, 3$ in the first sum. The symbol T_e^i implies the total available resources i on node e. The resource types can be weighted with the factor γ_i, such that $\sum_{i=1}^{3} \gamma_i = 1$.

Additional Transmission Costs. Secondly, the costs for application transmission are calculated. The first addend l_{ce} represents the minimum latency between the cloud c and a potential node e. The average transmission overhead O_a as second addend denotes the size of the container image for an application $a \in A$.

Running Costs. Lastly, the optimization problem must consider the running costs. The calculation is quite similar to the computation of the available resources except for the weighting parameter ε_i. BPLC sums up again the available amount of provided resources by all nodes. Then, the sum is weighted by ε_i, which describes the average resource utilization of an application for a resource type i. Finally, the algorithm allows to define the weight parameters $\alpha + \beta + \theta = 1$ to influence the respective components of the optimization model [33].

BRO uses an optimization model for managing the distribution of containerized apps within the architecture. The applied BPLC approach undertakes the optimization by considering available resources, costs for the offloading process, and the running costs. Nevertheless, the computation time is quite higher than for CCO because BRO runs a complex optimization model. Also, resources like CPU utilization (%), the obtained latency (ms), and the transmission overhead (MB) must be normalized before a calculation, e.g., with ratio normalization.

Enhanced Container Scheduler. The last strategy, ECSched, also challenges the distribution of containers to a set of heterogeneous nodes. HU ET AL. propose this orchestration strategy. In contrast to CCO and BRO, ECSched supports concurrent container scheduling. If a certain threshold exceeds, ECSched can distribute a set of container instances to the set of available nodes. Also, ECSched supports multi-resource constraints in terms of resources required by an application and resources provided by available machines [13]. The strategy uses a flow network, a special type of directed graph $G = (V, E)$ that consists of a set of vertices $v \in V$ and edges $e \in E$. The set of edges E can be used to connect the vertices V in order to represent the relation as unique arc $(u, v) \in E$. Each edge $e_{u,v} \in E$ holds as primary attribute a capacity $c_{u,v} > 0$ and as secondary attribute the transportation costs $w_{u,v}$. The goal is to send a flow $f_{u,v}$ from the

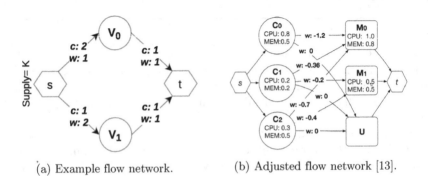

(a) Example flow network.   (b) Adjusted flow network [13].

Fig. 2. Flow networks.

source node s to the sink node t by finding an optimal way that minimizes the costs in adherence to flow network restrictions (Fig. 2a).

HU ET AL. adapt the general idea of flow networks to build its orchestration architecture that deals with the concurrent distribution of applications to machines. Figure 2b shows the architecture of the adapted flow network with additional components. The source node s generates the initial flow K. ECSched interprets K as the number of container instances that should be scheduled concurrently. For example, system administrators can define the number arbitrarily. The container nodes c_i with c_0, c_1, c_2 represent the requested container instances. The values between 0 and 1 for CPU and MEM are the normalized resource needs of a container c_i. The authors use ratio normalization where each value of a resource type is divided by the maximum of the resource. For example, if the maximum resource demand amounts to 2 CPU cores and the need for a container is 1 CPU, the normalized CPU value amounts to $\frac{1}{2} = 0.5$. Finally, the resource demands of a container c_i can be described by a vector $D_i = \{d_i^1, d_i^2, ..., d_i^R\}$, where R denotes the type of resource and d_i^j the demand of container c_i. The same applies accordingly to the resource supplies of machines with the vector $V_i = \{v_i^1, v_i^2, ..., v_i^R\}$. As a third layer, the set of machines M with m_1, m_2 denotes the entities used for application offloading. They also show the currently available amount of resources in a normalized manner [13]. The unscheduled node U enables dealing with containers that could not be assigned to a machine m_i. Hence, each container node c_i is always connected to the unscheduled node to drain off the flow [14]. All machines m_i and the unscheduled node U are connected to the sink node to drain off the flow regardless of whether the assignments of containers to machines are successful.

The scheduler starts the construction of the flow network if a certain threshold (e.g., 80% CPU utilization) is exceeded. Firstly, the container requests with the normalized resource vector are connected to the source node s. The scheduler checks afterward if a machine is basically able to run the application based on a comparison between the normalized resource vectors d_i and v_i. If a machine m_i is able to execute the container, the container nodes are connected via edges to the respective machines. Finally, all machine nodes are connected to the sink node t. ECSched analyzes the degree of alignment between the needed resources of containers and provided resources of machines. For this, the dot-product heuristic can be used, which is already shown in Fig. 2b as symbol w on each edge [13]. It is calculated by the sum of products between resource needs and demands over all resources $(dp_{ij} = \sum_{r_k \in \mathcal{R}} d_i^k v_j^k)$. For example, the alignment between c_0 and m_0 amounts to $dp_{c_0 m_0} = 0.8 * 1.0 + 0.5 * 0.8 = 1.2$. Higher values imply a better alignment. In order to be prepared for solving the Minimum Cost Flow Problem (MCFP) by selected algorithms, all weights are inverted. Therefore, the calculated degree of alignment $dp_{c_0 m_0}$ is just transformed to $w = -dp_{c_0 m_0} = -1.2$. Costs for connecting containers with the unscheduled node U are the highest with $w = 0$. After the complete construction of the flow network, the scheduler executes an algorithm for solving the MCFP [13]. The optimal path through the network shows the placement decisions. According to this, the machines are instructed to pull and execute the containers.

ECSched is a complex orchestration strategy for managing the allocation of containers to applications. The approach maps the architecture on a special kind of graph. The scheduler supports concurrent container scheduling to a set of nodes and is adherent to multi-resource constraints of containers and machines. However, ECSched might require a higher computation time because of its high complexity for constructing the flow network and executing the MCFP.

3.2 Quality of Service Measurements.

Load shifting from the cloud to edge or IoT layer needs a strong foundation for analyzing the overall performance. Gathering information about the current state of each node is one key component in all orchestration activities. CPU measurements, like the current CPU utilization or average response time for requesting users, can describe the state of nodes and the current state of the entire orchestration. Those measurements help judge the quality of orchestration strategies. Furthermore, autonomous orchestrators must obtain comprehensive data in the form of QoS measurements to perform reasonable decision making. Finding a set of suitable QoS parameters for edge orchestration is an essential requirement to enable the empirical study.

TAHERIZADEH ET AL. provide a comprehensive overview of metrics in monitoring systems for Virtual Machine (VM), container, link, and application management systems [27]. We adopt this general structure, add further parameters, and focus on three important QoS levels, namely system-, link-, and application-level measurements. Finally, we extend the structure by orchestration-level measurements that are especially suitable for an evaluation of the orchestration strategies. This chapter presents the most important QoS measurements.

System-Level Measurements. The first kind of measurement represents all important physical resources of the used machines, like VMs, edge, or IoT devices. The parameters are shown in Table 1. CPU utilization and memory usage are often in focus to observe the current state of machines [2,5,19,28]. The values are measured in percent and taken as PC and PM in the qualitative evaluation framework.

Table 1. Selected system-level measurements

QoS parameter	Name	Abbreviation	Unit
CPU usage	Percentage CPU	PC	%
Memory usage	Percentage memory	PM	%
Disk usage	Free disk percentage	FDP	%
	Read bytes disk	RBD	Byte
	Write bytes disk	WBD	Byte
	I/O Operations	IOPS	#/sec.
	I/O service time	IOST	%

Disk-related parameters like Free Disk Percentage (FDP) consider only the percentage of free or used space in a static way [2,33]. This is only useful if there is constant access to the disk, and this access does never exceed the device's storage performance limit. Otherwise, the system can be considered as overloaded, which might lead to lower performance. Indeed, measuring I/O utilization is still an open issue because it relies on many assumptions and uncertainties. Especially in the area of edge computing, where devices only have limited resources, disk utilization may be an undetected point of computational overload. The system-level measurements include Input/Output Operations Per Second (IOPS) and Input/Output Service Time (IOST) as additional parameters to enable an analysis of I/O activities during orchestration. IOPS measure the number of input and output operations per second. The parameter IOST states the average operation time [17]. Operation time means the time a device was busy during a certain interval, e.g., by performing read or write operations. For example, if a storage device remains 0.5 s in I/O during a period of one second, the IOST amounts to 50%. IOST implies I/O utilization. Hence, the unit is in percent.

Both values should not be exclusively used because their isolated meaningfulness is restricted to some extent. IOPS and IOST only make a statement about the number of operations in a certain time interval. They do not consider any amount of read or written bytes [22]. Therefore, the system-level measurements should include Read Byte Disk (RBD) and Write Byte Disk (WBD) to establish the derivation of adequate threshold techniques for disk utilization.

Link-Level Measurements. Link-level measurements map all QoS parameters that are concerned with in and outgoing communication within and between all components in a edge-cloud architecture. The measurements refer to network usage, where received and transmitted traffic is continuously measured. Like before, an overview of the considered parameters is shown in Table 2. In general, three different communication-channels could be considered for an evaluation of the orchestration quality.

Data center ⇄ Edge. The network quality to large and powerful data-centers has a strong influence on the edge orchestration. In the case of low or high network activities, it is possible to adjust the size of network functionalities (e.g., routers, switches, and gateways) by automatic scaling [27].

Edge ⇄ Edge. The main goal of edge computing is performance enhancement by reducing the physical distance between requesting users and service-providing machines. By using containerization, applications may be distributed on multiple edge nodes. Therefore, it is required that those edge nodes have a common standard measuring network-quality between them. This is helpful if container shifting is necessary among edge nodes [33].

Edge ⇄ User. The reason for all deliberations in edge computing is always the perceived performance on the user's side. Therefore, QoS parameters must consider the user's perspective and circumstances in terms of network-related measurements for time-critical applications [10].

Table 2. Selected Link-level measurements

QoS parameter	Name	Abbreviation	Unit
Network	Network throughput	NT	Mbps
	Network delay	ND	ms
	Packet loss	PL	%
	Received bytes network	RBN	Byte
	Transmitted bytes network	TBN	Byte
	Received packets	RP	#
	Transmitted packets	TP	#

Over the years, standards in measuring network activities have been established in the field of cloud computing. Monitoring systems for cloud and edge computing systems often follows the three metrics NT, ND, and PL. The parameter NT comprises the average amount of data, which is sent through the network in a certain amount of time. ND is also an important measurement that undermines the importance of locality, thus, the proximity between computational resources. It denotes the time interval that is needed to send a package to a certain endpoint and receiving it back subsequently. The ND gets larger if the distance between the two nodes increases. Network quality between two stations in regard to the reliability of the connection can be measured with the PL. The parameter is the ratio between lost packets and the total amount of packets sent. It is used to get a comparable impression of a connection's quality [8,18,29].

None of these parameters should be taken as a single aspect for analyzing network activities. It is more difficult to draw conclusions when the network bandwidth is exceeded because no meaningful parameters are available, like IOPS and IOST for disk utilization that might lead to an assumption about over-utilization. The assessment of network congestion may be worth investigating in order to derive reasonable thresholds for edge orchestration. It may for example include the Received Bytes Network (RBN), Transmitted Bytes Network (TBN), Received Packets (RP), and Transmitted Packets (TP) to provide a combined approach.

Application-Level Measurements. Application-level measurements depend on the particular application that is running on the architecture. Basically, there are two goals stated in the literature for the execution of applications. The first one is the average Response Time (RT). It denotes the time a request needs to be processed by the service on the infrastructure and subsequently sent back to the user. The average RT is measured from the client's perspective. This measurement is often used, especially for managing the performance of applications that are deployed on cloud computing architectures [11,15,25]. Its usage emerged in 2011, where RT takes a fundamental place in optimizing cloud orchestration [21]. EMEAKAROHA ET AL. state that the performance measurement of applications should also be done from the server-side. They introduce the Application Throughput (AT) that measures the average application RT.

Table 3. Selected application-level measurements

QoS parameter	Name	Abbreviation	Unit
Application	Response time	RT	s
	Application throughput	AT	s

Therefore, the AT does not include the transmission overhead of receiving and sending messages [11]. RT and AT can not always be used with the same semantics because they are often used interchangeably. The average RT must be measured from the client's side, since the processing server-side can not be aware of the message transmission times. Therefore, it is necessary to place monitoring dummy clients at places where a concentration of requests can be measured [31]. This increases the data quality because realistic values on the client-side are returned to the schedulers without any approximation.

Orchestration-Level Measurements. The last type of measurement refers to all parameters that are involved in the orchestration process (Table 4). The presented orchestration strategies are partially threshold-based and perform several operations like node election and instructing nodes to download and run containers. This implies the possibility to derive statistical data during the orchestration for further evaluation. The Number of Exchanged Messages (NEM) reveals the overhead that is caused by shifting containers among the edge. Furthermore, the Node Election Time (NET) and Number of Node Elections (NNE) give an impression of how many and how long a strategy needs to decide which nodes should be used for offloading. The parameters Number of Offloaded Nodes (NON), Number of Exceeded Thresholds (NETH), and Number of Exceeded Thresholds after Container Shifting (NETHAS) are used to analyze the resource efficiency of the strategies before and after the application offloading. The higher

Table 4. Selected orchestration-level measurements

QoS parameter	Name	Abbreviation	Unit
Node	Number of exchanged messages	NEM	#
	Node election time	NET	s
	Number of node elections	NNE	#
	Number of offloaded nodes	NON	#
	Number of exceeded thresholds	NETH	#
	Number of exceeded thresholds after container shifting	NETHAS	#

the NETH and NETHAS is, the less the perceived RT by the user, because exceeding thresholds imply over-utilization of nodes and perhaps lower response times. Similar to the former QoS measurements, no parameter should be used exclusively. To enhance the meaningfulness, all orchestration-level measurements are set in relation to the RT to establish a fair comparison.

4   Evaluation of Edge Orchestration Strategies.

After the introduction of the principles of the edge orchestration strategies and QoS measurements, the empirical evaluation is examined in this chapter.

4.1   Experimental Design and Setup

Figure 3 shows the experimental design that is separated in a baseline and orchestration phase. The baseline phase investigates the basic behavior of an application without any orchestration mechanism. The respective application is just deployed on a particular layer in the edge-cloud architecture. After the deployment on a certain machine, a pseudo-randomized simulation agent requests the application with a reproducible behavior. The simulation agent causes a high load on the application and leads the machines to exhausting capacities. This approach represents the outcomes if a service is requested by too many devices. It helps to measure the actual performance without the usage of dynamic deployment capabilities and allows a comparison of the orchestration strategies later on. During the simulation, the derived QoS measurements like system-, link-, application-, and orchestration-level metrics are stored into a SQL database.

In contrast to the baseline phase, the orchestration phase applies an orchestration strategy opposing the simulated requests. All layers are used by the access control of the respective orchestrator that is in charge of managing the edge-cloud architecture. The orchestration phase evaluates the overall quality of orchestration and the differences to the baseline phase. In this phase, the same

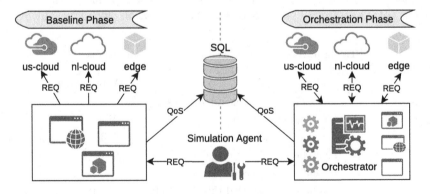

Fig. 3. Experimental design and setup – baseline and orchestration phase.

simulation model is requesting the architecture with the same amount and order of executions. Each machine and layer will run out of the available resources. Exceeding resources lead to the initialization of scheduling processes. These processes perform all necessary actions of the respective orchestration strategy and result in the shifting of computational resources across the remaining devices. Because the overall performance of the orchestration process is in focus, all QoS measurements are considered as it is done in the baseline phase.

Figure 3 also shows the experimental setup. In general, the entire experiment is designed for the execution of different types of applications. Often, applications have certain performance requirements, like resource needs for CPU, memory, or network resources. To test all orchestration strategies based on the former derived QoS metrics, we implement a prototypical CPU-intensive application, the so-called *knnapp*. This application runs a Machine Learning (ML) web service accessible over HTTP that classifies customers based on the attributes age and income as creditworthy. We approach this CPU-intensive classification with the k-Nearest-Neighbor (kNN) algorithm that assigns new customers to a predefined number of classes. The algorithm calculates the class membership such that the within-group similarities are high, and the between-group similarities are small [9]. We use this kind of application, to evaluate the ability of orchestration strategies to enhance the perceived QoS by requesting users.

We use a three-layer architecture with a heterogeneous device structure for all simulations. The *us-cloud0* machine is located in US-Virgina, around 7000 km away from Bamberg, where the simulation agent is requesting the service. This machine is a B2S VM from Microsoft Azure with 2 vCPU, 4 GB memory, and 8 GB of fast SSD storage. As a secondary machine (*nl-cloud0*), we set up a B1S VM with 1 vCPU, 1 GB of memory, and 4 GB of fast SSD storage, located in the Netherlands around 600 km away. The last layer is located in Germany (Bamberg) and comprises dedicated desktop machines (*edge0* and *edge1*) with 4 CPU cores, 16 GB memory, and 1000 GB of slow HDD storage. All machines communicate using HTTP via a client application, which sends monitoring data to the orchestrator every 5 s. The orchestrator runs on a B2S VM in US-Virgina. If a machine needs to download a container, the download time always amounts to 60 s because we use a geo-replicated container registry.

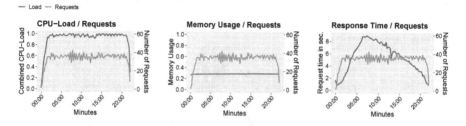

Fig. 4. Selected QoS measurements for the baseline phase on *nl-cloud0*.

Figure 4 shows the performance profile of the *knnapp* on *nl-cloud0* during the baseline phase. Whereas the memory utilization stays nearly constant, the increasing number of requests and exhausting CPU load have a strong influence on the RT. It increases from 1 s to around 9 s. At the end of the simulation, the CPU utilization is still high although the RT is decreasing. The reason for this is that requests are queued at the beginning because they can not be fulfilled immediately. During the baseline phase, the average CPU utilization amounts to 76%, the memory utilization to 28%, and the RT to 4.334 s.

4.2   Quantitative Comparison of Orchestration Strategies

At the beginning of the simulation, we initially deployed the *knnapp* on the topmost layer (*us-cloud0*). Then, we started the pseudo-randomized simulation to analyze the orchestration behavior of each strategy during runtime by measuring all QoS parameters that were in focus in Subsect. 3.2. We executed each simulation three times and took the average of the QoS values. The following chapter aims to evaluate the core characteristics of the orchestration strategies. For that, we analyze how system-, link-, application-, and orchestration-level measurements are reflected by the performance of the orchestration strategies.

The evaluation starts with the analysis of system-level measurements to get a first overview of the performance (Fig. 5). The *knnapp* is a CPU-intensive application. On average, the CPU utilization over all orchestration strategies amounts to 39.4%. The QoS parameters for PM and IOPS are nearly constant and not really high. For example, the overall memory usage amounts only to 17.1%, and the average IOPS with 8.20 is far away from the theoretical maximum range of 120–150 IOPS. PC is the only parameter that shows major differences between the strategies.

CCO shows the smallest PC, whereas BRO and ECSched exhibit a slightly higher CPU utilization. The reason for that is the scheduling order and the complexity of the orchestration strategies. In terms of node election, CCO schedules in the order edge0→edge1→nl-cloud0. BRO and ECSched take at first the node *nl-cloud0* and subsequently *edge0* and *edge1*. As mentioned in the previous chapter, the architecture of edge computing typically consists of a heterogeneous device structure. The node *nl-cloud0* runs only on 1 vCPU core, and the edge nodes have dedicated CPUs with 4 cores each. After container offloading, the

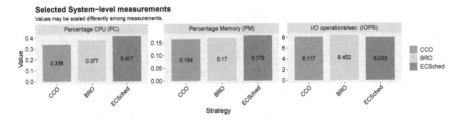

Fig. 5. Selected system-level measurements.

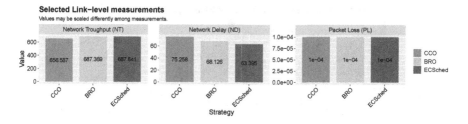

Fig. 6. Selected link-level measurements.

orchestrator distributes new incoming requests uniformly. That results in a probably higher resource utilization if schedulers decide to offload containers on nodes with worse specifications. This is the case for BRO and ECSched because they take *nl-cloud0* as a first selection. Strong edge devices, like *edge0* and *edge1* run into under-utilization, whereas slow *nl-cloud0* machine is completely exhausted. Of course, this is not a recommended way to set up the architecture because usually the cloud is equipped with high-performance devices. However, it shows the node election results of the strategies for a heterogeneous device structure.

The link-level measurements also show a relatively uniform distribution for almost all QoS parameters (Fig. 6). Only ND is a bit lower for BRO and ECSched. The reason for this is again the scheduling order of both strategies. For example, ECSched schedules *nl-cloud0* and *edge0* at first concurrently. Afterward, *edge1* is charged with new requests. Concurrent scheduling helps to reduce the latency again because the load balancer distributes incoming requests uniformly. BRO uses *edge0* and then *edge1*, which results in less network delay since the devices are in closer proximity to the requesting simulation agent. The very small PL of 0.001%, and the high NT of 677.27 Mbps on average imply a stable network connection.

In regards to the application response time, it is not clear which strategy should be favored. Especially CCO and BRO show similar and nearly symmetric distributions (Fig. 7). The Interquartile Range (IQR) is nearly equal, and there are only a few outliers at BRO's distribution. However, ECSched achieves the worst performance from a distribution's perspective because the IQR is broader and the maximum value and outlier are larger than at CCO or BRO. The average response times amounts to 0.694 s for CCO and BRO, and 0.937 s for ECSched. All strategies perform better than the baseline phase. CCO and BRO show the best results. Thus, the application of edge orchestration strategies leads to major benefits on the user's side.

The quantitative evaluation concludes with the orchestration-level measurements, which are shown in Fig. 8. All parameters show different results for all strategies except for NON. Recall that all parameters are expressed as a ratio to the AT. As an example, the execution of CCO results in 1728.821 exchanged messages per perceived sec. of average response time (from client's perspective). BRO creates the largest NEM and exhibits the highest node election time. The reason for that is the effortful optimization algorithm of BRO. To achieve the

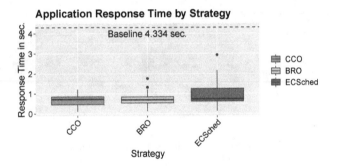

Fig. 7. Selected application-level measurements *knnapp*.

best performance at least cost, BRO is required to check the latency between nodes and the current resource utilization. CCO is faster because it only regards network-related measurements. Even ECSched can provide a faster NET despite its runtime intensive optimization model that consists of the construction of the flow network and finding an optimal solution subsequently. For the NNE, ECSched provides the best performance since it performs less scheduling in comparison to CCO and BRO. ECSched can perform fewer node elections because it applies concurrent container scheduling. In this case, K was set to 2. Hence, ECSched tries to allocate two containers simultaneously. All strategies use all available nodes during the orchestration process (NON). Overall, the orchestration with CCO causes the smallest NETH. That means that the set threshold exceeded 91.547 times during orchestration. BRO and ECSched realize higher values. This result depends mainly on the already introduced scheduling order and the time of scheduling processes. As the last measurement, the NETHAS is in focus. It comprises all node election processes as a consequence of exceed-

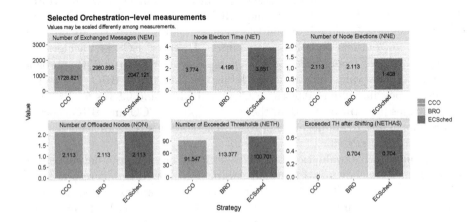

Fig. 8. Selected orchestration-level measurements.

ing thresholds, which are ending in no further shifting processes because the affected nodes have already been scheduled. The NETHAS does not consider the lowermost layer if all other machines are exhausted. A rising number of thresholds increases the NETH. Only BRO and ECSched realize exceeding thresholds. Because the number is very small, the NON should be revised wisely. This implies that the available machines in the architecture were not sufficient to fulfill all requests. As a consequence, there is a high amount of NETH on the lowest layer.

5 Discussion

In the previous chapter, we conducted an experiment with all considered orchestration strategies by the usage of the derived QoS measurements. Also, we showed a first approach, how the results could be interpreted. However, our study shows a few limitations, which are discussed in this chapter.

General Limitations. As described in Sect. 3, we only used a CPU-intensive application for the evaluation. Indeed, the strategies may behave differently for applications with other performance profiles. Furthermore, the orchestrations do not define a potential location of the necessary container registry for container offloading. Hence, this work uses a geo-replicated container registry on Microsoft Azure at the locations Germany, Netherlands, and US-Iowa. This decreases the average container download time. The next limitation refers to the resource availability. Limited resources denote the specification of the orchestration architecture. In each layer, there are only a small number of devices subject to the orchestration process to show the orchestration strategies' fundamental characteristics. In total, we used only 4 machines without any subsequent extension of resources. The dimension of the architecture was chosen such that offloading processes have a high likelihood during the simulation. Furthermore, the request profile (time and count of requests) of the simulation agent was previously known and pseudo-randomized. However, this serves as a quality attribute of the empirical evaluation because it allows a genuine comparison between orchestration strategies. In real environments, the expected load underlies stochastic progress.

Orchestration Limitations. Since the strategies lack a detailed description of essential parts of the orchestration like the concrete value of thresholds, forecast methods for time-series, and the right amount of measuring intervals, this work assumes reasonable values. Firstly, we applied ratio normalization to the strategies CCO, BRO, and ECSched to offer a comparable and comprehensible calculation basis for all orchestration strategies. It is still an open question of which perspective should be used to initiate an offloading process. Often, measurements on the system-side, like resource utilization and average response time of an application, are used. However, the inclusion of measurements like RT on the user's side may also be a possible option. In this work, the average application response time was measured from a user's perspective by the simulation agent. In real environments, this might not always be possible. Resource utilization plays an important role in container shifting besides the average response time. The definition of predicting the development of load progresses to enable container shifting on time without risking an under-provisioning of computational resources was not specified by the orchestration strategies. Therefore, this work proposes first-order exponential smoothing with $\alpha = 0.3$ and $\beta = 0.7$ as a method for smoothing load curves. We applied it to all strategies. Indeed, other approaches may lead to deviating results for the orchestration strategies. Thresholds are a further limitation of this work. The strategies do not recommend any concrete threshold value. Therefore, the value must be assumed. We assumed a value of 80% as a critical level for the CPU utilization and initiated the offloading process.

6   Related Work

The considered edge orchestration strategies in this work have already been evaluated by the respective authors. We selected the three orchestration strategies because they are following the generic orchestration architecture, as stated in Sect. 2. However, an overall evaluation between different orchestration strategies has not yet been in focus of the current research. Often, the evaluation is only done by the usage of state-of-the-art orchestration, like Docker Swarm and Kubernetes, as introduced in Sect. 1. Furthermore, all evaluations conducted by the authors use different environments, applications, and measurements.

For example, TAHERIZADEH ET AL. evaluate the performance of CCO for cloud and edge-cloud architectures. They collect different measurements like the NSR, measures of central tendencies (i.e., mean and percentiles), and measures of dispersion (i.e., standard deviation and IQR) of the average application response time over a certain amount of time [28].

YU ET AL. provide a performance evaluation of BRO by the usage of Kubernetes. Furthermore, they take a random allocation of containers to a VM, native, and a centralized cloud environment. For the evaluation, they deploy a set of applications with different performance profiles to a VM, native, and centralized cloud environment. They take the average job completion time for a new task as a measurement for the performance evaluation [33].

HU ET AL. take Docker Swarm and Kubernetes as a foundation for the evaluation. Concerning architecture, they use a set of homogeneous and heterogeneous machines for all experiments. They measured the average CPU utilization and memory utilization and the container completion time and compared the results to the orchestration with Kubernetes [13].

7   Conclusion

This work introduced a prototypical study for the quantitative evaluation of edge orchestration strategies. Firstly, we derived a set of quantitative metrics from the current research. We extended this set based on a detailed investigation of already established orchestration strategies. Finally, we implemented all strategies and proposed an experimental study to evaluate the quality of orchestrations. For this, we used a CPU-intensive application for all simulations. The orchestration strategies showed different results for all QoS levels and also differences in the scheduling behavior. Hence, there is no general recommendation for an orchestration strategy. Our study is limited to some extent, especially with respect to the used architecture, sample application, set of thresholds and load prediction mechanisms, and normalization methods. Indeed, the generic framework can help to select an orchestration strategy for a given set of requirements.

For our future work, we plan to focus on the extension of QoS measurements by regarding further orchestration strategies and also measurements from established cloud computing providers like Microsoft Azure, Amazon Web Services, and others. Moreover, we want to establish a qualitative framework to enrich the quantitative analysis with an additional dimension. In the end, we pursue a recommendation system for orchestration strategies that suggest a certain orchestration strategy based on the performance profiles of applications, type of available machines, and agreed QoS.

References

1. Ahmed, A., Ahmed, E.: A survey on mobile edge computing. In: 2016 10th International Conference on Intelligent Systems and Control (ISCO) (January 2016)
2. Al-Hazmi, Y., Campowsky, K., Magedanz, T.: A monitoring system for federated clouds. In: 2012 IEEE 1st International Conference on Cloud Networking (CLOUD-NET) (November 2012)
3. Ali, S., Kumar, V., Laghari, A., Karim, S., Brohi, A.: Comparison of fog computing and cloud computing. Int. J. Math. Sci. Comput. 5(1), 31–41 (2019)
4. Babou, C.S.M., Fall, D., Kashihara, S., Niang, I., Kadobayashi, Y.: Home edge computing (HEC): design of a new edge computing technology for achieving ultra-low latency. In: Liu, S., Tekinerdogan, B., Aoyama, M., Zhang, L.-J. (eds.) EDGE 2018. LNCS, vol. 10973, pp. 3–17. Springer, Cham (2018). https://doi.org/10.1007/978-3-319-94340-4_1
5. Caglar, F., Gokhale, A.: iOverbook: intelligent resource-overbooking to support soft real-time applications in the cloud. In: 2014 IEEE 7th International Conference on Cloud Computing (June 2014)
6. Cao, J., Zhang, Q., Shi, W.: Challenges and opportunities in edge computing. Edge Computing: A Primer. SCS, pp. 59–70. Springer, Cham (2018). https://doi.org/10.1007/978-3-030-02083-5_5
7. Casalicchio, E.: Autonomic orchestration of containers: problem definition and research challenges. In: Proceedings of the 10th EAI International Conference on Performance Evaluation Methodologies and Tools (2017)
8. Cervino, J., Rodriguez, P., Trajkovska, I., Mozo, A., Salvachua, J.: Testing a cloud provider network for hybrid p2p and cloud streaming architectures. In: 2011 IEEE 4th International Conference on Cloud Computing (July 2011)
9. Das, T.K.: A customer classification prediction model based on machine learning techniques. In: 2015 International Conference on Applied and Theoretical Computing and Communication Technology (iCATccT) (October 2015)
10. Dusia, A., Yang, Y., Taufer, M.: Network quality of service in docker containers. In: 2015 IEEE International Conference on Cluster Computing (September 2015)

11. Emeakaroha, V.C., Ferreto, T.C., Netto, M.A.S., Brandic, I., Rose, C.A.F.D.: CASViD: application level monitoring for SLA violation detection in clouds. In: 2012 IEEE 36th Annual Computer Software and Applications Conference (July 2012)

12. Han, R., Guo, L., Ghanem, M.M., Guo, Y.: Lightweight resource scaling for cloud applications. In: 2012 12th IEEE/ACM International Symposium on Cluster, Cloud and Grid Computing (ccgrid 2012) (May 2012)

13. Hu, Y., Zhou, H., de Laat, C., Zhao, Z.: Concurrent container scheduling on heterogeneous clusters with multi-resource constraints. Future Gener. Comput. Syst. **102**, 562–573 (2020)

14. Isard, M., Prabhakaran, V., Currey, J., Wieder, U., Talwar, K., Goldberg, A.: Quincy: fair scheduling for distributed computing clusters. In: Proceedings of the ACM SIGOPS 22nd Symposium on Operating Systems Principles, pp. 261–276. New York (2009)

15. Islam, S., Keung, J., Lee, K., Liu, A.: Empirical prediction models for adaptive resource provisioning in the cloud. Future Gener. Comput. Syst. **28**(1), 155–162 (2012)

16. Laghari, A., He, H.: Analysis of quality of experience frameworks for cloud computing. IJCSNS Int. J. Comput. Sci. Netw. Secur. **12**, 228–233 (2017)

17. Lee, L.W., Scheuermann, P., Vingralek, R.: File assignment in parallel i/o systems with minimal variance of service time. IEEE Trans. Comput. **49**(2), 127–140 (2000)

18. Mathur, M.: A comprehensive solution to cloud traffic tribulations. IJWSC 2230–7702 vol. I (12 2010)

19. Meera, A., Swamynathan, S.: Agent based resource monitoring system in IaaS cloud environment. Procedia Technol. **10**, 200–207 (2013)

20. Pahl, C., Lee, B.: Containers and clusters for edge cloud architectures - a technology review. In: 2015 3rd International Conference on Future Internet of Things and Cloud (August 2015)

21. Rao, J., Bu, X., Xu, C.Z., Wang, K.: A distributed self-learning approach for elastic provisioning of virtualized cloud resources. In: 2011 IEEE 19th Annual International Symposium on Modelling, Analysis, and Simulation of Computer and Telecommunication Systems (July 2011)

22. Riska, A., Riedel, E., Iren, S.: Adaptive disk scheduling for overload management. In: First International Conference on the Quantitative Evaluation of Systems, 2004. QEST 2004. Proceedings (2004)

23. Satyanarayanan, M., Bahl, P., Caceres, R., Davies, N.: The case for VM-based cloudlets in mobile computing. IEEE Pervasive Comput. **8**(4), 14–23 (2009)

24. Satyanarayanan, M.: Edge computing. Computer **50**(10), 36–38 (2017)

25. Shao, J., Wang, Q.: A performance guarantee approach for cloud applications based on monitoring. In: 2011 IEEE 35th Annual Computer Software and Applications Conference Workshops (July 2011)

26. Subramanian, S., Krishna, N., Kumar, K., Sreesh, P., Karpagam, G.: An adaptive algorithm for dynamic priority based virtual machine scheduling in cloud. Int. J. Comput. Sci. Issues(IJCSI) **9**, 397 (2012)

27. Taherizadeh, S., Jones, A.C., Taylor, I., Zhao, Z., Stankovski, V.: Monitoring self-adaptive applications within edge computing frameworks: a state-of-the-art review. J. Syst. Softw. **136**, 19–38 (2018)

28. Taherizadeh, S., Stankovski, V., Grobelnik, M.: A capillary computing architecture for dynamic internet of things: orchestration of microservices from edge devices to fog and cloud providers. Sensors **18**(9), 2938 (2018)

29. Taherizadeh, S., Taylor, I., Jones, A., Zhao, Z., Stankovski, V.: A network edge monitoring approach for real-time data streaming applications. In: Economics of Grids, Clouds, Systems, and Services, pp. 293–303 (2017)

30. Varshney, P., Simmhan, Y.: Demystifying fog computing: characterizing architectures, applications and abstractions. In: 2017 IEEE 1st International Conference on Fog and Edge Computing (ICFEC) (May 2017)

31. Wamser, F., Loh, F., Seufert, M., Tran-Gia, P., Bruschi, R., Lago, P.: Dynamic cloud service placement for live video streaming with a remote-controlled drone. In: 2017 IFIP/IEEE Symposium on Integrated Network and Service Management (IM) (May 2017)

32. Wen, Z., Yang, R., Garraghan, P., Lin, T., Xu, J., Rovatsos, M.: Fog orchestration for internet of things services. IEEE Int. Comput. **21**(2), 16–24 (2017)

33. Yu, Z., Wang, J., Qi, Q., Liao, J., Xu, J.: Boundless application and resource based on container technology. In: Liu, S., Tekinerdogan, B., Aoyama, M., Zhang, L.-J. (eds.) EDGE 2018. LNCS, vol. 10973, pp. 34–48. Springer, Cham (2018). https://doi.org/10.1007/978-3-319-94340-4_3

Service-Based Applications

A Qualitative Literature Review on Microservices Identification Approaches

Christoph Schröer$^{(\boxtimes)}$ ⓘ, Felix Kruse ⓘ, and Jorge Marx Gómez

Department Very Large Business Applications, University of Oldenburg,
26129 Oldenburg, Germany
{christoph.schroeer,felix.kruse,jorge.marx.gomez}@uol.de

Abstract. Microservices has become a widely used and discussed architectural style for designing modern applications due to advantages like granular scalability and maintainability. However, it is still a complex task decomposing an application into microservices. Software architects often design architectures manually. In this paper we give a state-of-the-art overview of current approaches to identifying microservices. Therefore we use a literature review and classify the content based on the software development process.

The main results are that mostly monolithic artifacts are used for starting with microservice decomposition. Data-intensive applications are less focused. Rule-based and clustering algorithms are suitable ways to find microservice candidates. Both researchers and software architects profit from this overview. Practically it supports choosing suitable approaches considering aspects like cohesion, coupling, workload, deployment and further quality criteria for each phase during the software development process.

Keywords: Microservices · Literature review · Software architecture · Identification · Decomposition

1 Introduction

Microservices become a popular architectural style for designing modern applications and deploying these on cloud platforms [7]. They are defined as small services which are independently and continuously deployable and communicating through lightweight mechanisms. Specific characteristics are their high cohesion and loose coupling [18]. This kind of architecture addresses beneficial quality attributes like scalability and maintainability, but also has drawbacks and can end-up in higher complexity [7,10]. In contrast, monolithic applications are the traditional architectural style. Monoliths are usually limited to only one technology and require higher effort on maintenance, but are less complex [18].

Architecting microservices has several perspectives. Besides infrastructural and organizational aspects, designing the services itself has become increasing attention in research. For example, research focuses on finding a suitable size,

© Springer Nature Switzerland AG 2020
S. Dustdar (Ed.): SummerSOC 2020, CCIS 1310, pp. 151–168, 2020.
https://doi.org/10.1007/978-3-030-64846-6_9

granularity and number of microservices. This is a complex challenge because several criteria like cohesion, coupling and quality attributes influence design decisions. Furthermore, there is a runtime uncertainty. Too much microservices can result in communication overhead, whereas too less microservices can retain the drawbacks of monoliths [3,14]. Figure 1 shows a visual example of the influence of the number of microservices on the costs of deployment and quality assurance.

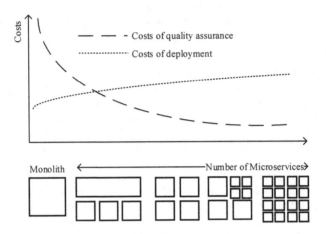

Fig. 1. Influence of the number of microservices on cost criteria [12].

Domain-driven design is an often mentioned approach for designing microservices [24]. However, more approaches exist. The approaches differ in focused criteria, different algorithms and evaluation methods. Due to these many and manifolds approaches, it is challenging to choose an appropriate method. Therefore, this study aims to conduct a literature review of existing approaches for identifying microservices. The approaches are classified into the phases of the software development process: requirements analysis, design phase, implementation phase and test phase. Microservices can be developed within the software development process [7] so that our new classification approach helps to find methods for each phase during the development and evaluation of microservices. This study has practical and theoretical implications. Practically, software architects can select appropriate methods from literature. Theoretically, researchers profit from a recent overview of existing approaches.

The study is structured as follows. Section 2 gives an overview of related work that can be compared to our literature review. Section 3 explains the research methodology and defines the research questions. Section 4 presents the results. Section 5 discusses the results and Sect. 6 sums up and gives an outlook of further research.

2   Related Work: Literature Reviews on Approaches for Identifying Microservices

Architecting microservices means to decompose a software application into a set of small services. The topic of software decomposition is not new to microservices and are also related to identifying modules and components in (monolithic) application in general. Different approaches like weighted-clustering approaches can support the software decomposition process [1]. However, further criteria need to be integrated into microservices architecture [21]. There are existing literature reviews for microservices architectures. These reviews focus on infrastructure, architectures and target problems and do not research the design phase of microservices in detail [8,26].

Cojocaru [6] conducted a literature review and evaluated specific quality criteria on static and dynamic source code analysis. However, they focused on decomposition of monoliths alone, whereas we extend our search query and are not limited to monoliths.

The study of Kazanavicius [16] summarized an authors selection of different approaches for migrating legacy monolithic applications to microservices architecture. The authors assessed quality, benefits and drawbacks of the approaches. However, they only compared and summarized a small number of studies.

Fritzsch [11] selected studies by a search query focused on refactoring monolithic applications. The classification framework was developed from the selected studies inductively and focused on different strategies. However, the classification framework of this paper considers the software development process and is not limited on refactoring.

3   Methodology: Qualitative Content Analysis

For this study, we choose the method of qualitative content analysis based on research literature. Qualitative content analysis is an appropriate research method in design science research [27]. The qualitative content analysis considering scientific publications and studies is a literature review. Mayring [20] defines the qualitative content analysis as a "mixed methods approach: assignment of categories to text as qualitative step, working through many text passages and analysis of frequencies of categories as quantitative step" [20]. Following its exploratory research design, the steps are (1) defining the research questions, (2) searching the data, (3) formulating categories inductively and (4) proofing them after approx. 15% of the data. Following steps are (5) the processing of the full study and (6) discussing the results [5,20].

In general, we would like to answer the main research question:

– Which approaches do exist to support the identification of microservices along the software development process considering several criteria?

Therefore, we concretize the research questions along the software development process:

- RQ1: Which starting points can be used for microservices identification approaches during requirements analysis?
- RQ2: Which microservices identification approaches do exist at design phase?
- RQ3: How can identified microservices be evaluated?

To operationalize the research questions, we formulate a search strategy based on the research questions. The different terms of writing microservice are based on DiFrancesco [8]. Furthermore, we find synonyms for "identification" in the basic literature book written by Richardson [24] and adjust or extend terms after 15% of the data. Finally, we applied the following search strategy in relevant scientific data sources ScienceDirect, IEEE and ACM Digital Library in the beginning of 2020:

ALL = ((microservice OR microservices) AND (identif* OR extract* OR migrati* OR decompos* OR refactor*)) AND PY >= (2014)

We have chosen to limit the results regarding the publication year to 2014 since the concept of microservices has established since 2014 [18]. We define the inclusion criteria according to which the studies must describe concrete approaches for identification and be written in English. We exclude papers that are out of scope, are grey literature and have no abstracts. The method of snow-balling (see [23]) results in four additional paper. The number of resulted studies are shown in Fig. 2. Appendix A lists the selected paper. Totally, we have read 81 abstracts of all found paper and 31 full texts of relevant paper.

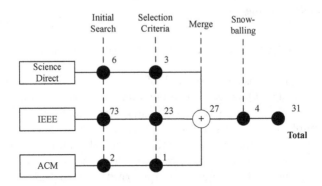

Fig. 2. Search results.

For the classification framework, we developed three main categories inductively that follow the software development process: requirement analysis, design phase and implementation/evaluation phase. We exclude the operation phase because the identification of microservices is mainly a design than an opreational topic. For answering the research question, this phase is out of scope. During reading the full texts, we continuously develop sub-categories deductively from the papers [20].

4   State-of-the-Art Identification Approaches for Microservices

The number of publications grouped by publication year are shown in Fig. 3. There is a higher number since 2017, but a trend for increasing number of studies is not observable.

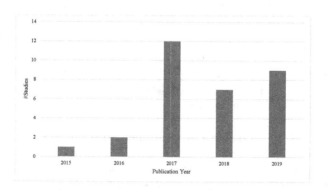

Fig. 3. Number of the selected papers grouped by publication year.

4.1   RQ1: Requirements Analysis of Microservice Identification Approaches

Accordingly to [7], we also identified that the main research focus is migration from monoliths to microservices architecture. Therefore, 21 of the 31 papers start with artifacts from monoliths. For static artifacts, 17 studies deal with source code, API documentation, domain models or data from version control systems. For dynamic analysis, four studies start with execution logs of the monolith. Table 1 lists further results.

Table 2 shows that there is a focus on *general, transactional-oriented applications* like web and mobile applications. For *data-intensive applications*, three papers propose a method for decomposition in microservices.

4.2   RQ2: Microservice Identification Approaches for Design Phase

The design phase is crucial in software development process in general. In this phase, the architecture of a system is structured in several components and their dependencies [25].

Di Francesco [7] have found out that the main research focus on architecting microservices is design phase. The following findings go into detail regarding the decomposition approaches.

Extending the idea of Fritzsch [11], we also consider atomar units. We define an atomar unit as the smallest unit on that a decomposition approach begins.

Table 1. Starting points for identification.

Starting points for identification	Details	#	Studies
Monolith (static)	e.g. source code, migration, API specification, domain model	17	P27, P26, P25, P24, P23, P22, P19, P15, P14, P12, P9, P8, P7, P5, P4, P3, P1
Greenfield	e.g. list of requirements	9	P30, P29, P28, P21, P17, P13, P6, P4, P2
Business processes	e.g. BPMN	5	P24, P18, P16, P11, P6
Monolith (dynamic)	e.g. execution logs	4	P31, P25, P20, P10
Monolith first	like greenfield, but designing a monolith first	2	P21, P20

Table 2. Type of application.

Type of application	Details	#	Studies
General applications	e.g. web or mobile applications, transaction-oriented applications	26	P31, P30, P27, P25, P24, P23, P22, P21, P20, P19, P18, P16, P15, P14, P12, P11, P10, P9, P8, P7, P6, P5, P4, P3, P2, P1
Data-intensive applications	e. g. IoT, machine learning, stream	3	P29, P28, P17
Telecommunication/Network		2	P26, P13

We identified seven types of atomar units, as Table 3 shows. Plain *functions* are the most frequent atomar units. For example, function calls can be logged. Such logs of function executions can be used to group microservices (see P20).

Modeling the Application. During the design phase, the application has to be modeled with suitable approaches and modeling techniques. These models are the basis for processes or algorithms for finding microservice candidates. We differ between modeling approaches, the algorithms and the criteria that influence the service decomposition. The Tables 4, 5, 6 and 7 contain these topics.

Table 3. Atomar units.

Atomar unit	Details	#	Studies
Function	e.g. public methods of service classes, functions or properties	8	P29, P28, P27, P26, P21, P20, P10, P8
Business capability	e. g. business activity in BPMN, business vocabulary based on nouns	7	P30, P18, P16, P14, P11, P9, P6
Interface	e. g. facades, entry points, URI resources	6	P31, P22, P19, P15, P4, P1
Entity	e.g. also database tables	4	P12, P9, P3, P1
Functionality	set of functions; functional units, atoms, modules	3	P25, P13, P7
With one mention		2	requirement (P2), software tier (P17)
n.a./not clear		3	P24, P23, P5

Table 4 lists the identified modeling approaches. We defined a category called *decomposition through atomar units* (six studies). That means that the prior identified atomar units are used for decomposition. For example, Tserpes (2019) defines functions as atomar units and develops each of these functions as an own microservice (see P29). Further, the *domain-driven design approach* is also part of research in this context. For example, Knoche et al. (2019) describe a process of defining bounded context focused on microservices (see P22).

Graph-based approaches are used to model atomar units and their dependencies as directed graphs. For example, Kamimura et al. (2018) model functions and function-calls as a graph (see P19). Similarly, *data-flow driven approaches* represent applications through data flow diagrams to model data dependencies. For example, Li et al. (2019) model data exchange of a ticket booking system with data-flow diagrams (see P30).

The *black-box approach* uses interfaces (not specific classes or entities) as the entry point of applications. For example, Baresi et al. (2017) use OpenAPI specifications and calculate semantic similarities to group interfaces into microservices (see P15). *Performance models* are used to consider workload criteria. For example, Klock et al. (2017) model a M/M/1 queuing network for a microservice performance model (see P10).

The *manual nominal/ordinal estimation model* evaluates specific requirements of an application regarding their importance manually. For example, Shimoda et al. (2018) evaluate the possibility to change of functions on a scale between 0 and 5 (see P21).

Table 4. Approaches/models.

Approach/models	#	Studies
Modeling through atomar units	6	P29, P27, P24, P13, P7, P2
Scenario analysis	5	P24, P18, P14, P5, P1
Graph-based approach	5	P19, P10, P8, P3, P1
Domain-driven design	4	P24, P22, P14, P12
Dataflow-driven approach	4	P30, P16, P11, P9
Black-box-approach	3	P31, P15, P4
Tier-based approach	3	P17, P7, P1
Performance model	3	P28, P26, P10
Execution-trace modeling	3	P25, P20, P1
Manual nominal/ordinal estimation model	2	P21, P2
With one mention	2	probabilistically (P6), interview (P23)

Identifying Microservice Candidates. After modeling the application, specific algorithms and methods are used to identify microservices candidates (see Table 5). *Rule-based algorithms* are the most popular method, followed by *clustering algorithms*. One example for a rule-based approach is presented in P22 where deterministic rules are used from defining services facades covering functionalities to their mapping to microservices. Based on a graph model, the authors of P8 use a minimum spanning tree based on weights of the edges and build then clusters with deleting remaining edges by depth-first-search. Three studies define the identification of microservices as a multi-criteria optimization problem and use *genetic algorithms* for solving.

One finding is that eight studies give hints on microservice identification *informally*, but not in form of a particular method or algorithm. We have not classified them as irrelevant because these studies also give valuable support for microservice identification. For example, Gouigoux et al. (2017) explain in their experience report relationships of costs of service deployments and service granularity (see P14).

Table 5. Algorithms and methods.

Algorithm/Method	#	Studies
Rule-based algorithm	13	P30, P29, P28, P27, P22, P21, P19, P18, P17, P9, P4, P2, P1
Unsupervised learning/clustering	9	P31, P25, P20, P19, P16, P10, P8, P6, P3
Genetic algorithm	3	P26, P25, P10
Natural language processing	1	P15
n.a./manually/informal	8	P24, P23, P14, P13, P12, P11, P7, P5

Criteria for Identification of Approaches. The proposed approaches and algorithms from all 31 studies differ in the criteria used for decomposition. Accordingly to the qualitative study of Carvalho et al. (2019), we also identified criteria like cohesion, coupling, workload and quality attributes [4]. Further, we have quantified the occurrence.

Table 6 shows *cohesion* and *coupling* criteria. Seventeen of the research papers includes cohesion and coupling criteria in their approaches. Following the definition by Richardson [24] it matters "[...] that each service has a focused, cohesive set of responsibilities.". Cohesive criteria can be characterized by the atomar units itself (see Table 3), by specific metrics, by business capabilities or by interface similarity.

Table 6. Cohesion and coupling criteria.

Cohesion	Details	#	Studies
Atomar unit oriented	e.g. ServiceClass public methods of service classes, functions or properties in general	6	P29, P28, P27, P24, P13, P9
Cohesion metric	Relational cohesion, Cohesion at domain level/message level, resource count	4	P30, P25, P20, P4
Business capabilities	e. g. facades, entry points, URI resources	4	P24, P18, P5, P1
Semantic or reference similarity		3	P24, P15, P3
Qualitative		6	P15, P13, P12, P11, P9, P3
Coupling	Details	#	Studies
Dependencies between atomar units	Foreign keys, intra/inter-connectivity	10	P25, P19, P16, P12, P10, P8, P7, P3, P2, P1
Coupling metric	Afferent/efferent coupling, instability, interactions, structural/ conceptual modularity quality	4	P30, P25, P20, P4
TF/IDF		1	P8
Qualitative		5	P15, P13, P12, P11, P9, P3

Coupling criteria consider the dependencies of the atomar units. For example, Kamimura et al. (2018) use source code dependencies of classes to extract microservices (see P19). Further, concrete metrics can measure coupling. The *qualitative* row means that cohesion and coupling are taken into consideration, but the authors have not described that precisely that it can be classified here.

Table 7. Further criteria adopted in the selected studies.

Criteria	Sub-criteria	#	#Studies
Deployment and infrastructure		8	P31, P28, P26, P21, P17, P14, P13, P7
Workload		5	P31, P26, P10, P7, P3
Compatibility		2	P7, P3
Quality attributes	Change frequency	6	P25, P21, P8, P7, P6, P3
	Scalability	4	P21, P6, P5, P2
	Data coordination effort	3	P21, P19, P3
	Organisation	2	P8, P5
	Suitable technologies	2	P7, P6
	With one mention	4	Cost (P14), Variability (P23), Security (P2), Reliability (P5)

Table 7 lists non-functional criteria for decomposition into microservices. *Deployment criteria* mean that the automation of deployment (like in P14) or deployment on different computing instances (like in P28) influence the decomposition into microservices. *Workload criteria* consider expected response times, count of requests or document sizes. *Compatibility* (like P3) defines a microservice with compatible criteria, like compatible technologies. *Quality attributes* are divided into further sub-criteria like common changes, scalability, data coordination effort, team organization and suitable technologies. The table aggregates criteria that have been mentioned one time.

Finally, we will give one example, how to connect the categories of the design phase. Giving the paper P25. the tables show that the approach includes coupling criteria. Further, the approach models the application on execution-trace modeling based on the atomar unit of functionality. To find optimal microservice candidates, the authors propose a genetic algorithm.

4.3   RQ3: Testing and Evaluation of Microservice Identification Approaches

It is crucial that authors evaluate their proposed approaches. Primarily, we differ between *runtime* evaluation and *case study* evaluation, whereas the latter is a theoretical evaluation without implemented microservices (see Table 8). The latter occurred 18 times, the former seven times. We classified four papers as an *experience report* since the authors evaluated the decomposition in a real-world application. Only two papers do not describe an evaluation of their approaches in the published study.

Runtime evaluation concentrates on performance metrics like:

- throughput (P31, P29, P17, P13, P10),
- response time (P31, P26, P17, P10),
- CPU utilization (P31, P26, P13),
- data communication over network (P28, P17),
- runtime costs (P31, P29),
- memory usage (P13),
- allocated virtual machines (P31) and
- total execution time over all microservices (P28).

Table 8. Evaluation methods.

Evaluation methods	#	Studies
Case study	18	P30, P27, P25, P21, P20, P19, P18, P16, P15, P12, P11, P9, P8, P6, P4, P3, P2, P1
Experiments	7	P31, P29, P28, P26, P17, P13, P10
Experience report	4	P24, P22, P14, P5
n.a	2	P23, P7

The case studies identify microservices candidates and evaluate resulted architectures with:

- experts (P19, P16, P15, P3),
- with required time for decomposition process (P27, P8, P3) or
- compare the number of resulted number of microservice candidates (P27, P19, P2, P1).

A further finding is that the application code used for evaluation are mostly *non-public or own developed* (Table 9). Eleven papers use *public available* source code basis. For example, the authors of P30 use the Cargo Tracking System (https://github.com/citerus/dddsample-core) that initially was developed for illustrating domain-driven design by Evans [9].

Table 9. Applications for evaluation.

Evaluation application	#	Studies
own developed/not public	22	P29, P28, P27, P26, P24, P23, P22, P19, P18, P17, P16, P14, P12, P10, P9, P8, P7, P6, P5, P4, P2, P1
Public available	11	P31, P30, P25, P21, P20, P19, P15, P13, P11, P8, P3

Third, we also investigate how the resulted microservice architectures are compared (Table 10). Twelve papers compare their microservice architectures with *alternative microservice architectures* decomposed by another approach. Four papers compare a microservice architecture with the monolithic application as *baseline*. The majority of the paper do not compare any decomposed architectures.

5   Interpretation of the Results and the Derived Future Research Topics

The purpose of the literature review is to give the current state-of-the-art methods of microservice identification approaches. Decomposing an application into smaller parts is a challenging task in software development in general. However, microservice development adds more complexity due to new aspects like runtime processes and team organization. Finally, we identified the following four main findings.

Table 10. Comparisons.

Comparison	#	Studies
Between microservice architectures	12	P31, P30, P26, P25, P20, P19, P17, P16, P15, P10, P9, P8
Compared with monolith	4	P29, P26, P24, P15
No comparison	16	P28, P27, P23, P22, P21, P18, P14, P13, P12, P11, P7, P6, P5, P4, P2, P1

1. Focus on Monoliths: Our results show that for the identification of microservices mostly monolithic artifacts are the standard starting point. One reason could be that monoliths have already existing artifacts like source code or runtime logs. Starting from greenfield development directly could also have limitations like higher complexity at the beginning. However, approaches for greenfield development regarding microservices identification have still less attention in research, as Table 1 shows.

As the identification of microservice is a non-trivial challenge, approaches considering also the new development of applications, can facilitate the usage of microservice architectures. Potential artifacts can be lists of requirements, business oriented documents or also interviews. However, the potential of usage such artifacts should be part of further research.

2. Formal and Informal Methods Exist: Table 5 also shows that eight papers have proposed a non-structural way of finding microservice candidates. Further research should be done regarding structured algorithms and non-informal, comparable processes to support software architects in a more formally way. The Tables 6 and 7 show the manifold criteria catalog that could be considered during the development of microservices.

If the methods for the identification are not sufficient, the perspective of service-oriented architectures (SOA) can be included, as microservices are a kind of SOA. In this field, existing approaches like Web Services Development Lifecycle (SDLC) and Service-Oriented Modeling and Architecture (SOMA) integrates a service modeling and service identification phase. These phases can support the design of microservices, as the services from SOA have to be mapped to microservices [2, 15, 22, 28].

3. Experimental Evaluations are Underrepresented: The results of RQ3 shows further that only seven times papers conducted experiments, although the granularity of services has a significant impact regarding the performance of the whole system. We think, that experiments could strengthen the evaluation of microservice identification approaches. The evaluation with case studies and with experts seems that manual effort is further necessary.

4. Data-Intensive Applications Mostly Out of Scope: We also observed that identification approaches were developed mostly for general, transaction-oriented applications (such as web or mobile applications), as Table 2 shows. Data-intensive applications have not been considered yet, although data science, artificial intelligence and big data applications are strongly in the scientific and economic focus.

Microservices could be a suitable architecture for data-intensive application to integrate different technologies, algorithms and applications. Data-intensive applications are analytical-oriented. Mostly, they implement so-called data pipe"-lines. The requirements of such applications differ from those of transactional applications due to the characteristics of Big Data (5 Vs). With further research in this direction, software architects could be significantly supported in the development of data-intensive applications based on microservice architecture.

Existing architectural patterns for implementing data-intensive applications are batch, stream and lambda architecture pattern [19]. These patterns are a modular approach, that could be combined with the microservice architecture style. First approaches for using service-oriented approaches or microservices in data-intensive context exist for the processing of large geospatial data in the cloud [17] or for entity matching approaches for data integration [13]. However, those approaches concentrate on specific tasks, domains or technologies. Further research should also focus on how microservices can be identified.

6   Conclusion

This paper explores the recent microservice identification approaches. These approaches are necessary to find suitable microservices considering several criteria like cohesion, coupling and quality attributes. However, one limitation is that we have not evaluated the classification framework in practice yet. We can only assume the practical implications, although we think that the results could support software architects in the choice of appropriate approaches. Furthermore, the deductive derivation of the categories and the selection of relevant papers are based on our assertions or other publications.

Based on a comprehensive qualitative literature review, an overview of the state-of-the-art approaches is presented. A total of 31 papers were selected as relevant. We have classified the microservice development into the phases of the software development process. We derived further categories deductively. The results are structured into the initially phrases research questions. Answering RQ1, mostly monolithic artifacts are used for starting with microservice decomposition. Answering RQ2, formal and informal approaches exist. Following formal approaches, modern algorithms like clustering algorithms could also an appropriate way finding microservice candidates. Answering RQ3, experimental evaluations for measuring performance metrics of microservice architecture are underrepresented.

The practical implication is that software architects could select a suitable approach regarding pre-defined criteria. The theoretical implication is the state-of-the-art overview for researchers. One result is that microservice identification approaches for data-intensive and analytical applications are underrepresented. We want to deal with this problem in the future and make recommendations for finding suitable microservices in a data-intensive context.

A   Selected Studies

The selected studies are listed below and in reverse chronological order.

Key	Study
P31	Abdullah, M., Iqbal, W., Erradi, A.: Unsupervised learning approach for web application auto-decomposition into microservices. Journal of Systems and Software (2019)
P30	Li, S., Zhang, H., Jia, Z., Li, Z., Zhang, C., Li, J., Gao, Q., Ge, J., Shan, Z.: A dataflow-driven approach to identifying microservices from monolithic applications. Journal of Systems and Software (2019)
P29	Tserpes, K.: stream-MSA: A microservices' methodology for the creation of short, fast-paced, stream processing pipelines. ICT Express (2019)
P28	Alturki, B., Reiff-Marganiec, S., Perera, C., De, S.: Exploring the Effectiveness of Service Decomposition in Fog Computing Architecture for the Internet of Things. IEEE Transactions on Sustainable Computing (2019)
P27	Kaplunovich, A.: ToLambda-Automatic Path to Serverless Architectures. In: 2019 IEEE/ACM 3rd International Workshop on Refactoring (IWoR), pp. 1–8 (2019)

(continued)

Table 1. *(continued)*

Key	Study
P26	Sharma, S., Uniyal, N., Tola, B., Jiang, Y.: On Monolithic and Microservice Deployment of Network Functions. In: 2019 IEEE Conference on Network Softwarization (NetSoft), pp. 387–395 (2019)
P25	Jin, W., Liu, T., Cai, Y., Kazman, R., Mo, R., Zheng, Q.: Service Candidate Identification from Monolithic Systems based on Execution Traces. IEEE Transactions on Software Engineering (2019)
P24	Gouigoux, J.; Tamzalit, D.: "Functional-First" Recommendations for Beneficial Microservices Migration and Integration Lessons Learned from an Industrial Experience. In: 2019 IEEE International Conference on Software Architecture Companion (ICSA-C), pp. 182–186 (2019)
P23	Carvalho, L., Garcia, A., Assunção, W.K.G., Bonifácio, R., Tizzei, L.P., Colanzi, T.E.: Extraction of Configurable and Reusable Microservices from Legacy Systems: An Exploratory Study. In: Proceedings of the 23rd International Systems and Software Product Line Conference - Volume A, pp. 26–31. Association for Computing Machinery, New York, NY, USA (2019)
P22	Knoche, H., Hasselbring, W.: Using Microservices for Legacy Software Modernization. IEEE Softw. (2018)
P21	Shimoda, A., Sunada, T.: Priority Order Determination Method for Extracting Services Stepwise from Monolithic System. In: 2018 7th International Congress on Advanced Applied Informatics (IIAI-AAI), pp. 805–810 (2018)
P20	Jin, W., Liu, T., Zheng, Q., Cui, D., Cai, Y.: Functionality-Oriented Microservice Extraction Based on Execution Trace Clustering. In: 2018 IEEE International Conference on Web Services (ICWS), pp. 211–218 (2018)
P19	Kamimura, M., Yano, K., Hatano, T., Matsuo, A.: Extracting Candidates of Microservices from Monolithic Application Code. In: 2018 25th Asia-Pacific Software Engineering Conference (APSEC), pp. 571–580 (2018)
P18	Tusjunt, M., Vatanawood, W.: Refactoring Orchestrated Web Services into Microservices Using Decomposition Pattern. In: 2018 IEEE 4th International Conference on Computer and Communications (ICCC), pp. 609–613 (2018)
P17	Sriraman, A., Wenisch, T.F.: μ Suite: A Benchmark Suite for Microservices. In: 2018 IEEE International Symposium on Workload Characterization (IISWC), pp. 1–12 (2018)
P16	Amiri, M.J.: Object-Aware Identification of Microservices. In: 2018 IEEE International Conference on Services Computing (SCC), pp. 253–256 (2018)
P15	Baresi, L., Garriga, M., Renzis, A. de: Microservices Identification Through Interface Analysis. In: Paoli, F. de, Schulte, S., Broch Johnsen, E. (eds.) Service-Oriented and Cloud Computing. European Conference, ESOCC 2017, Oslo, Norway, September 27–29, 2017 (2017)
P14	Gouigoux, J.; Tamzalit, D.: From Monolith to Microservices: Lessons Learned on an Industrial Migration to a Web Oriented Architecture. In: 2017 IEEE International Conference on Software Architecture Workshops (ICSAW), pp. 62–65 (2017)

(continued)

Table 1. *(continued)*

Key	Study
P13	Boubendir, A., Bertin, E., Simoni, N.: A VNF-as-a-service design through micro-services disassembling the IMS. In: 2017 20th Conference on Innovations in Clouds, Internet and Networks (ICIN), pp. 203–210 (2017)
P12	Fan, C., Ma, S.: Migrating Monolithic Mobile Application to Microservice Architecture: An Experiment Report. In: 2017 IEEE International Conference on AI Mobile Services (AIMS), pp. 109–112 (2017)
P11	Hausotter, A., Koschel, A., Zuch, M., Busch, J., Kreczik, A.: Process and Service Modelling of Insurance Use Cases. In: 2017 IEEE 10th Conference on Service-Oriented Computing and Applications (SOCA), pp. 116–124 (2017)
P10	Klock, S., van der Werf, J.M.E.M., Guelen, J.P., Jansen, S.: Workload-Based Clustering of Coherent Feature Sets in Microservice Architectures. In: 2017 IEEE International Conference on Software Architecture (ICSA), pp. 11–20 (2017)
P9	Chen, R., Li, S., Li, Z.: From Monolith to Microservices: A Dataflow-Driven Approach. In: 2017 24th Asia-Pacific Software Engineering Conference (APSEC), pp. 466–475 (2017)
P8	Mazlami, G., Cito, J., Leitner, P.: Extraction of Microservices from Monolithic Software Architectures. In: 2017 IEEE International Conference on Web Services (ICWS), pp. 524–531 (2017)
P7	Sarita, Sebastian, S.: Transform Monolith into Microservices using Docker. In: 2017 International Conference on Computing, Communication, Control and Automation (ICCUBEA), pp. 1–5 (2017)
P6	Sayara, A., Towhid, M.S., Hossain, M.S.: A probabilistic approach for obtaining an optimized number of services using weighted matrix and multidimensional scaling. In: 2017 20th International Conference of Computer and Information Technology (ICCIT), pp. 1–6 (2017)
P5	Hasselbring, W., Steinacker, G.: Microservice Architectures for Scalability, Agility and Reliability in E-Commerce. In: 2017 IEEE International Conference on Software Architecture Workshops (ICSAW), pp. 243–246 (2017)
P4	Asik, T., Selcuk, Y.E.: Policy enforcement upon software based on microservice architecture. In: 2017 IEEE 15th International Conference on Software Engineering Research, Management and Applications (SERA), pp. 283–287 (2017)
P3	Gysel, M., Kölbener, L., Giersche, W., Zimmermann, O.: Service Cutter: A Systematic Approach to Service Decomposition. In: Aiello, M., Johnsen, E.B., Dustdar, S., Georgievski, I. (eds.) Service-Oriented and Cloud Computing. 5th IFIP WG 2.14 European Conference, ESOCC 2016, Vienna, Austria, September 5-7, 2016, Proceedings, pp. 185–200 (2016)
P2	Ahmadvand, M., Ibrahim, A.: Requirements Reconciliation for Scalable and Secure Microservice (De)composition. In: 2016 IEEE 24th International Requirements Engineering Conference Workshops (REW), pp. 68–73 (2016)
P1	Levcovitz, A., Terra, R., Valente, M.T.: Towards a Technique for Extracting Microservices from Monolithic Enterprise Systems. 3rd Brazilian Workshop on Software Visualization, Evolution and Maintenance (VEM), 97–104 (2015)

References

1. Andritsos, P., Tzerpos, V.: Information-theoretic software clustering. IEEE Trans. Softw. Eng. **31**(2) (2005)
2. Arsanjani, A., Ghosh, S., Allam, A., Abdollah, T., Ganapathy, S., Holley, K.: SOMA: a method for developing service-oriented solutions. IBM Syst. J. **47**(3), 377–396 (2008)
3. Carrasco, A., van Bladel, B., Demeyer, S.: Migrating towards microservices: migration and architecture smells. In: Proceedings of the 2nd International Workshop on Refactoring, IWoR 2018, pp. 1–6. Association for Computing Machinery, New York (2018)
4. Carvalho, L., Garcia, A., Assunção, W.K.G., Mello, R.d., Lima, M.J.d.: Analysis of the criteria adopted in industry to extract microservices. In: 2019 IEEE/ACM Joint 7th International Workshop on Conducting Empirical Studies in Industry (CESI) and 6th International Workshop on Software Engineering Research and Industrial Practice (SER IP), pp. 22–29 (2019)
5. Cato, P.: Einflüsse auf den Implementierungserfolg von Big Data Systemen: Ergebnisse einer inhalts- und kausalanalytischen Untersuchung. Dissertation, Friedrich-Alexander-Universität Erlangen-Nürnberg, Erlangen-Nürnberg (2016)
6. Cojocaru, M., Uta, A., Oprescu, A.: Attributes assessing the quality of microservices automatically decomposed from monolithic applications. In: 2019 18th International Symposium on Parallel and Distributed Computing (ISPDC), pp. 84–93 (2019)
7. Di Francesco, P., Lago, P., Malavolta, I.: Architecting with microservices: a systematic mapping study. J. Syst. Softw. **150**, 77–97 (2019)
8. Di Francesco, P., Malavolta, I., Lago, P.: Research on architecting microservices: trends, focus, and potential for industrial adoption. In: IEEE International Conference on Software Architecture, pp. 21–30 (2017)
9. Evans, E.: Domain-Driven Design: Tackling Complexity in the Heart of Software. Addison-Wesley, Upper Saddle River (2011)
10. Fritzsch, J., Bogner, J., Wagner, S., Zimmermann, A.: Microservices migration in industry: intentions, strategies, and challenges. In: IEEE International Conference on Software Maintenance and Evolution (ICSME), pp. 481–490 (2019)
11. Bruel, J.-M., Mazzara, M., Meyer, B. (eds.): DEVOPS 2018. LNCS, vol. 11350. Springer, Cham (2019). https://doi.org/10.1007/978-3-030-06019-0
12. Gouigoux, J., Tamzalit, D.: From monolith to microservices: lessons learned on an industrial migration to a web oriented architecture. In: 2017 IEEE International Conference on Software Architecture Workshops (ICSAW), pp. 62–65 (2017)
13. Govind, Y., et al.: Entity matching meets data science. In: SIGMOD 2019: Proceedings of the 2019 International Conference on Management of Data, pp. 389–403 (2019)
14. Hassan, S., Bahsoon, R.: Microservices and their design trade-offs: a self-adaptive roadmap. In: IEEE International Conference on Services Computing, pp. 813–818 (2016)
15. Johnston, S.: RUP Plug-In for SOA V1.0. IBM developerWorks (2005)
16. Kazanavičius, J., Mažeika, D.: Migrating legacy software to microservices architecture. In: 2019 Open Conference of Electrical, Electronic and Information Sciences (eStream),pp. 1–5 (2019)
17. Krämer, M.: A microservice architecture for the processing of large geospatial data in the cloud. Dissertation, Technische Universität Darmstadt, Darmstadt (2017)

18. Lewis, J., Fowler, M.: Microservices: a definition of this new architectural term (2014). https://martinfowler.com/articles/microservices.html
19. Marz, N., Warren, J.: Big Data: Principles and Best Practices of Scalable Real-time Data Systems, 1. aufl. edn. Manning, Shelter Island (2015)
20. Mayring, P.: Qualitative content analysis: theoretical foundation, basic procedures and software solution. Klagenfurt (2014)
21. Mazlami, G., Cito, J., Leitner, P.: Extraction of microservices from monolithic software architectures. In: 2017 IEEE International Conference on Web Services (ICWS), pp. 524–531 (2017)
22. Papazoglou, M.: Web Services: Principles and Technology. Pearson, Prentice Hall, Upper Saddle River (2008)
23. Petersen, K., Vakkalanka, S., Kuzniarz, L.: Guidelines for conducting systematic mapping studies in software engineering: an update. Inf. Softw. Technol. **64**, 1–18 (2015)
24. Richardson, C.: Microservice Patterns: With Examples in Java. Manning, Shelter Island (2019)
25. Starke, G.: Effektive Softwarearchitekturen: Ein praktischer Leitfaden, 7 edn. Hanser eLibrary, Hanser, München (2015)
26. Taibi, D., Lenarduzzi, V., Pahl, C.: Architectural patterns for microservices: a systematic mapping study. In: Proceedings of the 8th International Conference on Cloud Computing and Services Science, vol. 1, pp. 221–232 (2018)
27. Wilde, T., Hess, T.: Forschungsmethoden der Wirtschaftsinformatik: Eine empirische Untersuchung. WIRTSCHAFTSINFORMATIK **49**(4), 280–287 (2007)
28. Zimmermann, O.: An architectural decision modeling framework for service-oriented architecture design. Dissertation@Stuttgart, University (2009)

Navigational Support for Non HATEOAS-Compliant Web-Based APIs

Sebastian Kotstein[(✉)] and Christian Decker

Herman Hollerith Zentrum, Reutlingen University, 71034 Böblingen, Germany
{sebastian.kotstein,christian.decker}@reutlingen-university.de

Abstract. Hypermedia as the Engine of Application State (HATEOAS) is one of the core constraints of REST. It refers to the concept of embedding hyperlinks into the response of a queried or manipulated resource to show a client possible follow-up actions and transitions to related resources. Thus, this concept aims to provide a client with a navigational support when interacting with a Web-based application. Although HATEOAS should be implemented by any Web-based API claiming to be RESTful, API providers tend to offer service descriptions in place of embedding hyperlinks into responses. Instead of relying on a navigational support, a client developer has to read the service description and has to identify resources and their URIs that are relevant for the interaction with the API. In this paper, we introduce an approach that aims to identify transitions between resources of a Web-based API by systematically analyzing the service description only. We devise an algorithm that automatically derives a URI Model from the service description and then analyzes the payload schemas to identify feasible values for the substitution of path parameters in URI Templates. We implement this approach as a proxy application, which injects hyperlinks representing transitions into the response payload of a queried or manipulated resource. The result is a HATEOAS-like navigational support through an API. Our first prototype operates on service descriptions in the OpenAPI format. We evaluate our approach using ten real-world APIs from different domains. Furthermore, we discuss the results as well as the observations captured in these tests.

Keywords: HATEOAS · REST · OpenAPI

1 Introduction

Hypermedia as the Engine of Application State (HATEOAS) is one of the core constraints of the architectural style Representational State Transfer (REST) [5]. It should be fulfilled by any Web-based API claiming to be RESTful. HATEOAS refers to the concept of embedding hyperlinks and forms into the response of a queried or manipulated resource to advertise follow-up actions. More precisely, these hyperlinks and forms address either related resources, which the client can query in course of the next interaction step, or describe actions for manipulating

© Springer Nature Switzerland AG 2020
S. Dustdar (Ed.): SummerSOC 2020, CCIS 1310, pp. 169–188, 2020.
https://doi.org/10.1007/978-3-030-64846-6_10

the current or related resources. By choosing and executing one advertised action (e.g. querying a related resource), the current application state changes. Therefore, these hyperlinks and forms represent legitimate state transitions. On the one hand, this concept simplifies the navigation through Web-based APIs, since the application tells a client possible actions and legitimate state transitions in the given application state. On the other hand, the embedding of hyperlinks also frees a client of having to know all URIs addressing resources that are relevant for the interaction. Given that all resources are linked to each other through hyperlinks, a client can discover the whole application and its resources with just one well-known entry point URI [22].

However, HATEOAS is often not implemented by Web-based APIs [19][16]. Instead of embedding hyperlinks and forms into responses, providers of Web-based APIs tend to offer API documentations, so-called service descriptions. They define the set of resources of an API, URIs for addressing them, as well as the list of operations and their respective input and output parameters. Common formats for service descriptions are OpenAPI, RAML, API Blueprint, and WADL [11].

Although both concepts have the objective to instruct a client about how to interact with an API, they use URIs in different ways: HATEOAS uses a URI as a connector linking two resources with each other to show a possible state transition. In contrast, service descriptions list URIs as pointers addressing resource endpoints. However, these pointers have no source and, therefore, the relations between resources are lost.

Moreover, in many APIs, the list of valid URIs changes as the set of resources changes at run time. As a result, new URIs are added and existing URIs become invalid. A HATEOAS-compliant API maintains the current application state and exposes only valid URIs. A service description, however, is static and stateless. It must describe all possible application states in a comprehensible way. For that purpose, service descriptions use URI Templates, which contain path parameters and describe ranges of possible URIs [8]. To create stable URIs from a URI Template at run time, a client has to substitute these path parameters of the URI Template with identity-based values [14].

With URI Templates, there seems to be a feasible solution for documenting this interface dynamism in a static way. Moreover, RFC6570 [8] specifies the rules for substituting path parameters in URI Templates. However, this form of documentation lacks in telling a reader *where* these values required for the substitution of path parameters can be obtained from. According to our experience, many Web-based APIs offer these missing values within the boundaries of their own application. In practice, a client has just to query a specific resource (e.g. a collection) to obtain a list of values that are feasible for the substitution of a specific path parameter. The client is expected to extract these values from the response payload and to plug them into that specific path parameter in order to create stable URIs. However, these relations between properties that hold these values embedded into the response payloads of queried resources and path parameters are often not clearly evident from an API's service description.

Only two of the aforementioned service descriptions formats, namely WADL and OpenAPI, offer a feature for linking path parameters with resources. Interestingly, in case of OpenAPI this feature called *Links* is barely used in practice. In preparation of this work, we conducted a systematical analysis of OpenAPI documentations obtained from *APIs.guru*[1] revealing that only three out of 1611 OpenAPI documentations use this feature. At the same time, WADL is no longer relevant for today's APIs [11].

To sum it up, the following two issues emerge when using service descriptions: Firstly, the client is not able to systematically derive stable URIs in order to address resources being relevant for the interaction, since the sources providing feasible values for the substitution of path parameters are unknown. Secondly, the client cannot automatically discover resources, because transitions between resources are not obvious. All in all, service descriptions provide very weak support to enable an automated client to interact with an API autonomously. Instead, a developer has to interpret the given service description in order to identify the resources that are relevant for the interaction. Furthermore, he or she has to identify the resources providing required values for creating stable URIs for addressing these relevant resources. Finally, he or she has to define an interaction sequence and implement this sequence as well as the procedures for creating stable URIs into the client's logic. In contrast to HATEOAS, which frees a client from creating URIs and gives navigational support, this is a disadvantage and increases the coupling between client and API.

Nevertheless, we are convinced that a service description still offers sufficient information for creating stable URIs from URI Templates and to recover knowledge about possible transitions between resources automatically. In this paper, we introduce an approach that aims to identify transitions between resources of an API by systematically analyzing a service description. Our approach consists of two steps: In the first step, we parse a given service description and convert the listed URI Templates into a *URI Model* reflecting the hierarchical URI structure of the API. In the second step, an algorithm identifies possible transitions between resources from this model. Finally, we pass the identified transitions and the URI Model to a proxy application acting as intermediary between a client and the respective API. The proxy creates and injects the corresponding hyperlinks, which represent the identified transitions, into the response payload as soon as a client requests a resource. All steps from the analysis till the proxy generation utilize the service description as the only external input and do not require any additional manual modeling. The final result is a HATEOAS-like navigational support through an API, which frees the client from knowing and creating URIs. Our first prototype implementation operates on service descriptions in the OpenAPI format, which has the highest relevance in the field of Web-based APIs [11].

---

[1] https://apis.guru.

The implementation of the proxy application including the procedures for converting an OpenAPI documentation into a URI Model and for identifying transitions is publicly available on GitHub[2].

The remaining paper is organized as follows: In Sect. 2, we introduce an exemplary Web-based API, which we use to illustrate our approach throughout the paper. Section 3 discusses related work. In Sect. 4, we explain our approach in detail. In Sect. 5, we evaluate our approach using ten real-world APIs and discuss our findings as well as the next steps. Finally, we give a conclusion in Sect. 6.

2   Example

In order to explain our approach, we consider a fictive Web-based API, called *ContactManager*. The API provides functionality for creating, modifying, and deleting contacts. Additionally, a client can assign multiple contacts to a group. Groups and contacts are assigned to a specific user profile such that many clients/users can use the API in parallel and have their own realm.

We expose the entities contact, group, and user profile as resources. Furthermore, for each user profile there exists two resources (so-called collections) listing all contacts and groups, respectively, belonging to this user profile. Apart from this, there exists a resource listing all available user profile resources. Figure 1 illustrates the mentioned resources of the ContactManager API, their supported operations (i.e. HTTP Methods), and their relations. Furthermore, Fig. 1 shows the URIs and URI Templates for addressing them as well as the data model (so-called schema) of the response payload a client can expect when querying (i.e. issue an HTTP GET on) a specific resource.

A client is expected to substitute the path parameters of a URI Template with identity-based values in order to create a stable URI addressing a specific resource. These path parameters are indicated by an enclosing pair of curly brackets (e.g. {userId}). Moreover, feasible values for substituting these path parameters can be found in the response payloads of specific resources. For instance, by querying a group collection of a specific user profile (e.g. GET on /0/groups/all), the client receives a collection of group entities, where each entity encloses a property with the name groupId. The value of a groupId property can be plugged into the path parameter {groupId} in order to address a single group resource (e.g. /0/groups/1). Here, the relation between the property groupId and the path parameter {groupId} is obvious due to identical naming. However, for real-world APIs, we cannot always assume that an identical naming is given. According to our experience, besides an identical naming, APIs tend to use short forms for the property name (e.g. id) and long forms for the parameter name (e.g. {deviceId}) and vice versa. Therefore, we have incorporated these cases into our ContactManager API as well. Moreover, you may have noticed an inconsequent URI structure in our API. More precisely, /{userId}/groups/all addresses a collection of groups whereas a collection of

---

[2] https://github.com/SebastianKotstein/HATEOAS-Proxy.

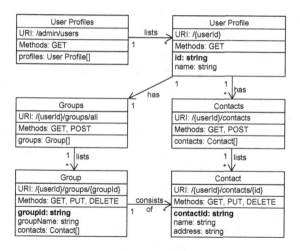

Fig. 1. Resource model of the ContactManager API

contacts is fetched using /{userId}/contacts. This also reflects the, unfortunate, common practice in the field of Web-based APIs. We use this exemplary API and its URI structure to explain our approach throughout the paper.

3   Related Work

The principles and core constraints of REST including HATEOAS have been originally described in [6] and [5]. Although the community often complains about the absence of HATEOAS compliance in Web-based APIs, efforts targeting tools and solutions for simplifying the realization of HATEOAS-compliant APIs are quite limited.

In [9], Haupt et al. introduce a model-driven approach for the design of REST-compliant applications. This approach enforces REST compliance by distributing the modelling of different aspects and artifacts of a REST application on separate meta-models. For instance, the Resource Model allows a designer to model the resources of the application. Moreover, the designer has to specify all relations between these resources in this model. A separated URI Model defines the URIs for these resources. Finally, an automatism maps these relations between resources to links and enables HATEOAS compliance.

Liskin et al. [13] present an approach enabling HATEOAS support for a non HATEOAS-compliant API as an afterthought. In detail, they place a HATEOAS-compliant layer as a wrapper between a client and the respective API and inject hyperlinks into the API's response. The architecture of this approach is quite similar to the architecture of our proxy application. However, in contrast to our approach, the wrapper requires a manually created model describing the possible states the wrapped application may have. Based on the returned API response and the state model, the wrapper determines the current application state and injects hyperlinks into the response headers as defined in the state model. Moreover, the state model has to specify XPath2 expressions pointing to values in the response payload, which might be required for the substitution of URI Templates in order to create these hyperlinks. We estimate the effort for creating such a state model as quite high and, therefore, as less practicable compared to our approach. Moreover, we assume that it is more likely that the respective API provides a service description rather than a state model. Nevertheless, we consider the approach of Liskin et al. as a foundation of our work, since we seize the idea of placing a separate layer between client and API that injects hyperlinks in the API's response.

The second aspect of our approach is the systematic and automated analysis of the API's service description in order to gain insights into a Web-based API. This aspect is not completely new, but, to the best of our knowledge, have only been covered by the following work so far: In [10], Haupt et al. introduce a framework that aims to provide insights about the structure of a REST API by analyzing its service description systematically. Moreover, Bogner et al. [3] propose a modular approach called *RESTful API Metric Analyzer (RAMA)*, which calculates maintainability metrics from service descriptions and, therefore, enables the automatic analysis of RESTful APIs. Similar to our approach, both the framework from Haupt et al. and the approach from Bogner et al. convert the content of a service description into a canonical meta-model. However, while our approach processes information derived from the meta-model with the goal to enhance the API's capabilities (namely to add a HATEOAS-like navigational support), their solutions focus on the pure acquisition of metrics for evaluating the structure and maintainability of APIs.

4   Approach

Our approach has the objective to inject hyperlinks into the response payload of a queried or manipulated resource in order to show a client possible transitions to other resources and the URIs for addressing them. Moreover, we decided to implement the approach as a proxy application that acts as an intermediary between a client and the respective API. This has the advantage that we neither have to modify a client nor the given API to enable this HATEOAS-like navigational support. Furthermore, the proxy application should operate stateless, which means that the context of a queried or manipulated resource (i.e. the request issued by the client as well as the response coming back from the API) must hold all information required to create these hyperlinks. More precisely, the context must contain all values that are required for the substitution of path parameters of a URI Template to create hyperlinks that represents transitions to these other resources. Conversely, if the context contains all required values for creating a hyperlink for addressing a particular resource, we consider a transition to this particular resource as given. Thus, we define a transition as follow:

Definition 1 (Transition). *A transition from a resource c to a resource r is given, if r is reachable from the context of c. This means that the context of c must contain the values that are required to substitute all path parameters of a specific URI Template in order to create a stable URI addressing r.*

In order to inject hyperlinks into the response payload of a queried or manipulated resource, the proxy application must know the transitions from this queried or manipulated resource to other resources and how to create the respective hyperlinks. One option would be that the proxy application scans the context, which the client and the API exchange (i.e. the request URI and the response payload), for values and checks which hyperlinks could be created from the URI Templates listed in the OpenAPI documentation based on these values at run time. However, we assume that this identification of possible transitions at run time would slow down the overall processing of through-going requests and responses, especially in case of large APIs with many URI Templates, path parameters, and complex response payload structures. Instead, possible transitions between resources should be already identified in the course of a preliminary offline analysis.

Therefore, before the proxy application is ready to act as an intermediary between a client and the API, it has to conduct the following two steps: The first step is to parse a given OpenAPI documentation and to convert the listed URI Templates into a URI Model reflecting the URI structure of the API.

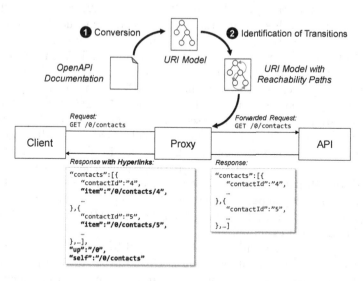

Fig. 2. The proxy application: Before the proxy is ready to inject hyperlinks, the application converts the OpenAPI documentation into a URI Model and identifies transitions in the course of an offline analysis.

In the second step, based on this URI Model, an algorithm tries to identify transitions between resources by analyzing the URI structure and the documented response payload schemas. The algorithm adds the identified transitions as reachability paths to the URI Model. Finally, the proxy application takes the URI Model together with the added reachability paths as input and is able to create and inject hyperlinks based on these identified transitions. Figure 2 illustrates this described process from a high-level perspective. In the following, we present the details of the application: First, we describe the characteristics of the URI Model and how to convert a given OpenAPI documentation into such a URI Model. Then, we present the algorithm for identifying transitions. Finally, we explain how the proxy application creates and injects hyperlinks.

4.1   URI Model

The URI Model is a tree structure consisting of nodes and edges. The URI Model should reflect the hierarchical URI structure of the respective API. More precisely, a node of the URI Model represents either a static or variable path segment of a URI path. An edge connects to path segments adjacent to a slash.

Our parsing algorithm iterates over the list of URI paths documented in the OpenAPI documentation, splits each path into its path segments, and adds them as nodes to the URI Model. Furthermore, the algorithm flags a path segment in the URI Model as variable, if its name contains at least one path parameter indicated by an enclosing pair of curly brackets (e.g. {id}). Our approach supports only APIs with variable path segments having exactly one path parameter (We will explain the reason for this limitation in Sect. 4.2). Since an API might have multiple root path segments (i.e. multiple path segments having different names on the first level), we insert a virtual root node that represents the API itself and is the parent of the actual root path segments. This virtual root node will be ignored when composing the path segments to a URI path later.

Furthermore, for each URI path, the OpenAPI documentation specifies the set of allowed operations (e.g. GET, PUT, POST, and DELETE) as well as their input and output parameters (e.g. payload schemas). We add them as node attributes to the respective path segments in the URI Model. More specifically, the parsing algorithm attaches each operation including all details about input and output parameters as an attribute to the node that represents the last path segment of the respective URI path to which the operation can be applied (e.g. the GET operation on /{userId}/groups/all is attached to the path segment all). Figure 3 illustrates the final URI Model derived from the OpenAPI documentation of our ContactManager API example.

Since a client interacts with an Web-based API by querying or manipulating resources [5], we consider a path segment having at least one operation attribute as a single resource or a set of resources. More precisely, a path segment represents a single resource, if the URI path composed of all path segments on the tree path from the root to this path segment consists only of static path segments. Conversely, a path segment represents a set of resources, if the composed URI path contains at least one variable path segment. These variable path segments must be substituted with identity-based values in order to address a specific resource in the represented set of resources at run time.

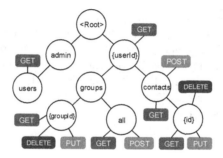

Fig. 3. The URI model of the ContactManager API

4.2 Identification of Transitions

In the second step of the offline analysis, an algorithm tries to identify possible transitions between resources. Consider that the actual number of resources at run time is still unknown in the current stage. Nevertheless, the URI Model defines the magnitude of resources. More precisely, the URI Model specifies whether a path segment represents a single or multiple resources. Furthermore, all resources that are represented by the same path segment share the same context structure (i.e. the same request URI structure as well as the same response payload schemas). This implies that all resources represented by the same path segment also share the same set of potential transitions to other resources, since whether a transition is given depends on the exchanged context. Therefore, for each path segment p in the URI Model, which represents one or a set of resources, we check which other path segments representing resources are potentially reachable from the context of a resource represented by p by analyzing the context structure of p.

In detail, we use the following procedure: For each path segment p in the URI Model, which represents one or a set of resources, we choose a hypothetical resource c that is represented by p. By choosing this hypothetical resource c, we simulate the situation when a client queries or manipulates a resource represented by p. For this resource c and, representatively, for all resources represented by p, we verify which other resources, or more specifically, path segments are reachable from the context of c.

Furthermore, since c represents the queried or manipulated resource, we can assume that the client knows the stable URI for addressing c. Moreover, since the client specifies this URI in the HTTP request, the client automatically sets the values for all path parameters on the tree path from the root to p. Hence, the first step is to substitute all variable path segments on the tree path from the root to p with values set by the client. Since we do not know the actual values set by the client in the current stage (consider that this is still a simulation) and, anyway, the actual values would not be relevant for the analysis, we substitute the variable path segments with random values. We call this process a *pre-allocation*.

Let us consider the following example applied to the URI Model of the *ContactManager API* to amplify this: In this example, we choose a hypothetical resource c of the path segment {groupId}. Moreover, we pre-allocate all variable path segments on the tree path from the root to {groupId} with randomly chosen values, e.g. 0 for {userId} and 1 for {groupId} such that the resulting stable URI for addressing c is /0/groups/1. Figure 4 illustrates the URI Model resulting from the pre-allocation.

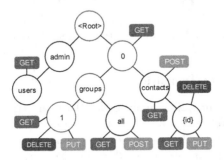

Fig. 4. The URI model of the ContactManager API after pre-allocation

You may have noticed that this pre-allocation has affected p as well as further path segments regarding their magnitude of represented resources. Figure 4 shows that the path segment p = {groupId} but also the path segments {userId}, all, and contacts represent only a single resource instead of a set of resources after the pre-allocation.

The next step is to determine path segments that represent resources and are reachable from the context of c. Here, we distinguish between path segments, which represent exactly one resource, and path segments, which represent a set of resources, after pre-allocation.

Path Segments Representing One Resource after pre-allocation are reachable from the context of c without requiring any further values from the response payload. They are reachable from the context of c, since the URI path for addressing them either consists only of static path segments or the client will set the values of all variable path segments on the tree path to the respective path segment by specifying them in the request URI at run time, which we have simulated by pre-allocating them in the previous step. For the previous example, this means that the resources represented by the path segments users, {userId}, all, and contacts would be reachable from c by merely taking values from the request URI.

However, especially in complex APIs, there would be hundreds of path segments that represent exactly one resource and, therefore, would be reachable from c. We would overwhelm a client with hyperlinks and possible navigational paths the client can follow. Hence, the response payload should only contain as few hyperlinks as necessary so that the client can merely reach the "next hop". Therefore, in case of path segments representing one resource, we limit the reachability from the context of c to path segments that are *descendants* or *ancestors* of p in the tree of the URI Model. More precisely, they must be the *next* (i.e. closest) *descendants* or *ancestor* of p. This means that the tree path between the respective next descendant or ancestor path segment and p cannot be blocked by another path segment that represents resources (otherwise this blocking path segment would be the next descendant or ancestor on the specific path). Note that due to the structure of a tree, p can have only one next ancestor (but multiple next descendants).

For example, the next ancestor of {groupId} (i.e. the path segment p from our previous example) is {userId}. Since {groupId} has no next descendants, we have to construct another case to give an example for a next descendant: Let us consider the case where p is the path segment {userId} in the URI Model and c is the resource addressed by the URI /0. For that case, all and contacts are next descendants of p.

Our algorithm iterates over all path segments in the URI Model that represent one resource after the pre-allocation and verifies whether they are a next ancestor or a next descendant of p. If so, the algorithm adds a directed, *one-to-one reachability path* to the URI Model, which starts at p and ends at the respective path segment q. We interpret this reachability path as follows: For any resource c represented by p, there exists one resource r represented by q that is reachable from the context of c.

Path Segments Representing a Set of Resources. after the pre-allocation are only reachable from the context of c, if the response payload of c contains feasible values for the substitution of all remaining variable path segments on the tree path from the root to the respective path segment. Concerning our previous example (i.e. p is the path segment {groupId} and c is represented by p), this means that the resources represented by the path segment {id} are only reachable from c, if the response payload of c contains feasible values for the substitution of {id}.

Of course, the actual content of the response payload of c can only be determined at run time. Nevertheless, an OpenAPI documentation specifies the data model, so-called payload schema, for the case that the response payload will contain structured data, e.g. JSON or XML. In detail, a payload schema describes the properties that are embedded into the payload, their names, their data types, and how these properties are nested into each other in case of complex data types such as objects or arrays. Consider that a resource may have multiple representations, supports multiple operations, and these operations may lead to different outcomes reflected by different HTTP status codes. Therefore, an OpenAPI documentation typically does not only specify one response payload schema per resource but multiple schemas for different media types, operations, and status codes. While parsing the OpenAPI documentation (see Sect. 4.1), we have attached these response payload schemas as part of the operation attribute to the path segments in the URI Model.

Based on these documented payload schemas, we use the following procedure to check whether the response payload of c may provide feasible values for the substitution of a specific variable path segment:

The algorithm iterates over all payload schemas (i.e. for all operations) that are attached to the path segment p in the URI Model and searches each schema for properties matching the path parameter name of the specific variable path segment. However, we limit this search on response payload schemas that can be expected in case of a positive operation outcome (i.e. having a status code 2XX), since we assume that an error response does not include any useful data. A path parameter name matches a property name, if (regardless of case sensitivity) both names are equal, the name of the path parameter contains the name of the property, or vice versa. We limit our search on primitive, so-called basic, types, although [8] and the OpenAPI specification supports the substitution of path parameters with complex data types. However, this feature is barely used in practice.

For each identified property matching the given path parameter name, we create a so-called *Link*. This Link should document the identified property. More precisely, it specifies the property name, the XPath/JSONPath for querying the property within a given data structure, and the matching variable path segment. For the case that the identified property is nested in an array, we add a flag indicating that multiple values can be expected. Furthermore, we add the operation, the response status code, and the media type to the Link in order to specify when this payload schema can be expected. After completing the search process for all payload schemas, the procedure returns the list of created Links.

Actually, we have to repeat this procedure for all variable path segments on the tree path from the root to the specific path segment. However, consider that the response payload of c may contain multiple values for the substitution of a specific variable path segment at run time. In detail, for n values n different hyperlinks addressing n different resources can be created. With any further variable path segment on the tree path from the root to the specific path segment, the number of possible hyperlinks is multiplied by the number of feasible values for this variable path segment, and so further, leading to an explosion of created hyperlinks.

Therefore, we limit the reachability from the context of c to path segments that represent a set of resources as follows: The URI path of that respective path segment q, which is composed of all path segments from the root to q, must have only one remaining variable path segment v after the pre-allocation. For the same reason, our approach supports only variable path segments that have exactly one path parameter, since if a variable path segment has multiple path parameters, the same explosion of different combinations and hyperlinks, respectively, would arise. Moreover, this respective path segment q must be either a next descendant of v or the variable path segment itself (i.e. $v = q$). This second limitation is comparable to the limitation when processing a path segment representing only one resource. It should enable a client to reach the next hop, instead of all possible resources lying beyond this variable path segment.

Our algorithm iterates over all path segments in the URI Model that represent a set of resource after the pre-allocation and verifies whether there is only one variable path segment v on the tree path from the root to the respective path segment q. Moreover, as stated before, q must be a next descendant of v. If this is the case, the algorithm searches the payload schemas in p for properties matching the path parameter name of v by applying the previously described procedure. Furthermore, if the procedure returns at least one Link, the algorithm adds a directed, *one-to-many reachability path* to the URI Model, which starts at p and ends at the respective path segment q. The algorithm adds these Links to that reachability path. We interpret this reachability path as follows: For any resource c represented by p, there exists an unknown number of resources represented by q that are reachable from the context of c. The actual number of reachable resources in q depends on the set of feasible values that are embedded into the response payload of c at run time.

4.3 Proxy Application

After we have created the URI Model and have identified possible transitions between path segments representing resources, the application is ready to act as an intermediary between client and API. Moreover, the proxy application takes the created URI Model together with the added reachability paths as input. For each request of the client, the proxy application performs the following procedure:

The proxy application forwards the HTTP request of the client to the API without any modifications. Nevertheless, it stores a copy of the request including the URI and the HTTP Method. As soon as the response of the API arrives, the proxy application tries to determine the resource c and the operation o the client has addressed with the request. Moreover, it has to determine the path segment p representing c. For that purpose, it splits the stored URI into its path segments and maps them as well as the HTTP Method to the path segments and operations in the URI Model. For instance, for a GET request on /0/contacts, the proxy application determines contacts as the path segment p representing the addressed resource c and GET as the executed operation o.

In the next step, the proxy application loads the reachability paths from p. First of all, the proxy application iterates over all one-to-one reachability paths. For each one-to-one reachability path, the proxy application creates exactly one hyperlink addressing a single resource. The required values for substituting all variable path segments on the tree path from the root to p can be taken from the URI of the request (e.g. 0 for substituting {userId}).

Then, the proxy application iterates over the list of one-to-many reachability paths. For each one-to-many reachability path, the proxy application loads the variable path segment v, which must be substituted, and the stored set of Links. Based on these Links, especially the documented XPath/JSONPath, the proxy application tries to extract values from the given response payload. Consider, that not every Link is applicable to the given response payload because the operation o, the returned status code, or the requested media type differ. For each extracted value, the proxy application creates a hyperlink by substituting variable path segments on the tree path from the root to p with values taken from the URI of the request and the remaining variable path segment v with the extracted value. In our example, there is a one-to-many reachability path between contacts and {id}, since the response payload schema of contacts contains a property named contactId (see Fig. 1) matching {id}. For each extracted value for the property contactId (we may extract multiple values, since the property is nested in an array), the proxy application creates a hyperlink by substituting {userId} with 0 taken from the request URI and {id} with the extracted value.

Finally, the proxy application embeds all created hyperlinks into the response payload and forwards the response back to the client. Figure 2 illustrates an exemplary response with embedded hyperlinks for this example where the client queries a contacts resource.

5   Evaluation

We implemented the proxy application including the procedures for converting an OpenAPI documentation into a URI Model and the analysis process for identifying transitions as a C# .NET application. Moreover, we tested this implementation and analyzed our approach regarding its practicability using ten real-world APIs. These tests revealed that our approach is indeed able to identify semantically valid transitions between resources and to convert these transitions into hyperlinks, but only if the respective API fulfills several criteria. Besides presenting the results of the analysis in this section, we, therefore, will discuss these criteria an API has to fulfill such that our approach works reliably. Nevertheless, as we noticed that only a minority of the tested APIs fulfills these criteria, we will also discuss possible options to revise and extend the process of identifying transitions such that the approach is also applicable to APIs that do not fulfill these criteria.

5.1   Analysis and Observations

To test and evaluate our approach, we chose ten real-world APIs from different domains. Table 1 lists these chosen APIs and the observations that we captured while applying our approach on the respective APIs. We will discuss these observations in the following. All chosen APIs have a dynamic resource model and, therefore, at least one variable path segment and one path parameter, respectively, in their URI structure.

For two APIs (1 and 4), we noticed that the documented response payload schemas differ from the actual response payloads, which are returned when querying a particular resource. For these cases, the analysis process was able to identify transitions based on the given OpenAPI documentation, however, the proxy application could not extract the required values from the response payloads, since the documented XPaths/JSONPaths could not be applied. For the remaining eight APIs, the approach was at least able to identify transitions based on one-to-one reachability that were all semantically valid. However, the identification of transitions based on one-to-many reachability paths - i.e. transitions that require the substitution of path parameters with identity-based values from response payloads - was quite error-prone:

In case of the SwaggerHub Registry API (9), we observed that values for substituting the path parameters {owner}, {domain}, and {api} are not provided within the boundaries of this application and must be queried from an external source. Therefore, as expected, the approach was not able to identify any transition requiring the substitution of these path parameters, since the algorithm could not determine any source providing feasible values. Similarly, the algorithm could not identify any transition that requires the substitution of the path parameter {version}. In contrast to the aforementioned path parameters, the API indeed provides values for substituting this path parameter. However, these values are not contained within a single property (e.g. "version":"v1") but nested into an object having the structure {"type":"X-Version", "value":"1.1"}. As a consequence, the approach could not identify a Link between this nested value property and the path parameter {version} and, therefore, any transition relying on this Link. In general, we call this case when the algorithm does not identify a Link between a property and a path parameter although there is a semantic relation and, therefore, misses a valid transition a *false negative*. Fortunately, the SwaggerHub Registry API is the only API where we observed these false negatives.

For five APIs (2, 3, 6, 8, and 10), we noticed that for each path parameter the approach was able to identify at least one Link between a property and the respective path parameter, which is semantically valid, and which is the basis for a valid transition. However, in addition to these valid Links and transitions, we observed that the approach also identified Links between properties and path parameters that are semantically not related to each other. As a consequence, the approach exposed multiple invalid transitions. In contrast to a false negative, we call this erroneously identified Link and the transition relying on this Link a *false positive*. The reason for these false positives is the fact that our approach identifies a Link between a path parameter and a property by merely comparing the names of both artifacts. In detail, both names must be either equal or one name must contain the other name such that the algorithm links these two artifacts. APIs, however, tend to use same or similar names for path parameters and properties although these artifacts address different semantic concepts. In detail, on the one hand, we noticed that the tested APIs either use distinct names for path parameters addressing different entity types, like {userId} and {meetingId}, but use generic names like id for properties embedded in all response payloads regardless of the entity type. This naming pattern is adopted by the APIs 3, 5, 6, and 10. On the other hand, there are APIs (2 and 8) that use generic names for both path parameters and properties like {code} and code, respectively, although these artifacts are associated with different entity types. This inexpressive naming of properties and path parameters hampers the identification of semantically correct Links and leads to a high degree of invalid transitions. As we observed this issue of false positives with half of all tested APIs, we will discuss possible options for eliminating false positives in the following section.

Table 1. List of real-world APIs tested with our approach and the captured observations.

#	API	Ref.	Observation
1	Adafruit IO 2.0.0	[1]	Response payloads differ from documented schemas
2	API Géo 1.0	[2]	**False positives:** API uses generic path parameter and property names {code} and code for different entity types
3	Canada Holidays API 1.0	[17]	**False positives:** API uses distinct path parameter names, e.g. {provinceId} and {holidayId}, however, all properties containing identity-based values are named id regardless of the entity type
4	Deutsche Bahn Fahrplan-Free v1	[4]	Response payloads differ from documented schemas
5	Giphy API 1.0	[7]	Only one path parameter {gifId} and the property name id. Match is semantically correct
6	Home Connect API 1.0	[12]	**False positives:** API uses distinct path parameter names, e.g. {imagekey} and {statuskey}, however, the properties containing identity-based values are named key regardless of the entity type
7	Mercedes-Benz Car Configurator API 1.0	[15]	API uses distinct path parameter and property names. Therefore, our approach works reliably with this API
8	Spotify API v1	[21]	**False positives:** API uses the generic path name {id} for many path parameters as well as the property name id regardless of the entity type
9	SwaggerHub Registry API 1.0.47	[20]	Values for the path parameters {owner} and {api} are not provided by the API. **False negatives:** Values for substituting {version} are embedded into an object having the structure: {"type":"X-Version", "value":"1.1"}
10	Zoom API 2.0.0	[23]	**False positives:** API uses distinct path parameter names, e.g. {userId} and {meetingId}, however, all properties containing identity-based values are named id regardless of the entity type

Only for two APIs (5 and 7), the set of identified transitions was satisfactory, which means that this set is complete (i.e. it does not contain any false negative), and all identified transitions and their Links are semantically valid (i.e. the set does not contain any false positive). However, the results of the application of the approach to the Giphy API (5) need to be interpreted with caution, since this API uses the same inexpressive naming of properties and path parameters that potentially leads to false positives. Nevertheless, the API exposes only one entity type (namely a *GIF*) and, therefore, there exists only one path parameter named {`gifId`} and a related property named `id`. Thus, invalid Links and transitions relying on these Links (i.e. false positives) could be avoided, since there exists no further path parameters or properties that could be erroneously linked with each other.

In contrast, the Car Configurator API of Mercedes-Benz (7) uses distinct names for properties and path parameters addressing different semantic concept and, conversely, identical names for identical concepts. Moreover, the API avoids to use generic names like `id` for properties containing identity-based values. Hence, our approach was able to identify all Links between properties and path parameters reliably without any errors. We estimate the API Design of the Car Configurator, especially its naming convention, as a foundation for achieving reliable results with our approach. Thus, we will use this API as a reference to derive the criteria that an API must fulfill such that our approach could identify transitions reliably.

5.2 Recommended Naming Convention

The analysis has shown that the half of all tested real-world APIs uses an inexpressive naming for properties containing identity-based values or for both path parameters and properties by giving them generic names like `id` or `code` leading to a high number of false positives when applying our approach. However, the application of our approach to the Mercedes-Benz Car Configurator API has shown that a consistent naming with distinct names for different concepts enables a reliable identification of transitions and avoids false positives as well as false negatives. Thus, we define the following criteria that an API must fulfill such that our approach is able to identify transitions reliably: (1) The API must use identical names for properties and path parameters that are related to each other (e.g. {`meetingId`} and `meetingId`). Conversely, (2) the API must use different names for properties and path parameters that are not related to each other and address different concepts, respectively. Nevertheless, even if an API fulfills both criteria, there is still a minimal risk of false positives, since the second criterion does not prevent one name from being a substring of another name (e.g. {`name`} and `surname`). This case would lead to false positives again, since we have defined that a match between a property and a path parameter is given, if both names are equal or one name contains the other name (i.e. is a substring of the other name). However, with the fulfillment of both criteria, this second condition saying that a property name can be a substring of a path parameter name, or vice versa, becomes obsolete. For the case that both criteria are fulfilled by an API, we can tighten the matching condition to equal names only in order to achieve reliable transitions.

5.3 Further Options for Improvement and Next Steps

In the course of the analysis in Sect. 5.1, we experienced that the half of all tested APIs does not fulfill these two criteria defined in Sect. 5.2. Therefore, we cannot assume that a wide range of real-world APIs fulfills these two criteria, too.

Hence, we plan to incorporate further metrics and techniques into the process of identifying Links between properties and path parameters such that these Links are valid even with APIs using inexpressive names.

On the one hand, we plan to incorporate natural language processing (NLP) techniques like embeddings (e.g. based on GloVe [18]) to calculate the distance between two names rather than merely comparing the name of a property and a path parameter character by character. This should improve the accuracy of the results and, therefore, reduce the number of false positives as well as false negatives. On the other hand, besides the examination of names, further metrics like the tree path distance in the URI Model between the resource providing a property and the respective path parameter could also be interesting and serve as criterion for deciding whether an identified Link is plausible or not. We assume that the shorter the distance the higher is the probability of a semantically valid Link. Additionally, some APIs like the Home Connect API (6) uses a strict hierarchy in their data and URI structure. In this case, we observed that the resource providing values for a respective path parameter is always the parent of this path parameter in the URI structure. For instance, by fetching /homeappliances the client obtains feasible values for substituting the path parameter {haid} in /homeappliances/{haid}.

Similar to the hierarchical URI structure, the hierarchical position of a property within the structured data could also be relevant and should be compared with the URI Template structure containing the respective path parameter. For instance, there might be a plausible relation between the path parameter {id} and the property groupId, if the URI Template containing this path parameter is /groups/{id} and the property groupId is nested within an array having the name groups.

A further option would be to test each created hyperlink before embedding it into the response payload by sending an HTTP HEAD or HTTP GET "pre-flight" request to the API. This request checks whether a resource can be addressed and whether the created hyperlink is valid. We have already tested this option. However, with many APIs, we experienced that we exceeded the number of allowed API calls for a certain time period with these additional requests.

6   Conclusion

In this paper, we introduced an approach that aims to identify transitions between resources of a Web-based API by analyzing a given service description systematically. We implemented this approach as a proxy application that injects hyperlinks into the response of a queried or manipulated resource in order to show a client possible transitions to other resources. Our first prototype operates on service descriptions in the OpenAPI format, since this format has the highest relevance in the field of Web-based API. We tested this approach with ten real-world APIs from different domains. These tests showed that there is a high risk of false positives, which means that the approach identifies transitions that are semantically incorrect. The causes for these false positives are, on the one hand, an inexpressive naming of path parameter and properties with generic names like `id` or `code` in many APIs, but also, on the other hand, the fact that we merely compare the strings of two names with each other in order to identify a relation between a path parameter and a property. Nevertheless, the tests also revealed that if an API uses distinct names for properties and path parameters, the approach is able to identify reliable transitions. However, as the majority of tested APIs use inexpressive names, we also discussed further improvements of the identification process in order to support these types of APIs as well.

References

1. Adafruit: Adafruit IO HTTP API 2.0.0. https://io.adafruit.com/api/docs/. Accessed 1 Oct 2020
2. api.gouv.fr: API Géo 1.0. https://api.gouv.fr/documentation/api-geo. Accessed 1 Oct 2020
3. Bogner, J., Wagner, S., Zimmermann, A.: Collecting service-based maintainability metrics from RESTful API descriptions: static analysis and threshold derivation. In: Muccini, H., et al. (eds.) ECSA 2020. CCIS, vol. 1269, pp. 215–227. Springer, Cham (2020). https://doi.org/10.1007/978-3-030-59155-7_16
4. Deutsche Bahn AG: Fahrplan-Free v1. https://developer.deutschebahn.com/store/apis/info?name=Fahrplan-Free&version=v1&provider=DBOpenData. Accessed 1 Oct 2020
5. Fielding, R.T., Taylor, R.N.: Principled design of the modern web architecture. ACM Trans. Internet Technol. **2**(2), 115–150 (2002). https://doi.org/10.1145/514183.514185
6. Fielding, R.T.: Architectural styles and the design of network-based software architectures. Ph.D. thesis, University of California, Irvine, USA (2000)
7. Giphy Inc.: Giphy API 1.0. https://developers.giphy.com/docs/api/. Accessed 1 Oct 2020
8. Gregorio, J., Fielding, R., Hadley, M., Nottingham, M., Orchard, D.: URI Template. RFC 6570, RFC Editor (2012)
9. Haupt, F., Karastoyanova, D., Leymann, F., Schroth, B.: A model-driven approach for REST compliant services. In: 2014 IEEE International Conference on Web Services (ICWS), pp. 129–136. IEEE, Anchorage (2014). https://doi.org/10.1109/ICWS.2014.30
10. Haupt, F., Leymann, F., Scherer, A., Vukojevic-Haupt, K.: A framework for the structural analysis of REST APIs. In: 2017 IEEE International Conference on Software Architecture (ICSA), pp. 55–58. IEEE, Gothenburg (2017). https://doi.org/10.1109/ICSA.2017.40
11. Haupt, F., Leymann, F., Vukojevic-Haupt, K.: API governance support through the structural analysis of REST APIs. In: Computer Science - Research and Development, pp. 291–303 (2017). https://doi.org/10.1007/s00450-017-0384-1
12. Home Connect GmbH: Home Connect API 1.0. https://apiclient.home-connect.com. Accessed 1 Oct 2020
13. Liskin, O., Singer, L., Schneider, K.: Teaching old services new tricks: adding HATEOAS support as an afterthought. In: Proceedings of the 2nd International Workshop on RESTful Design, pp. 3–10. Association for Computing Machinery, New York (2011). https://doi.org/10.1145/1967428.1967432

14. Masse, M.: REST API Design Rulebook, 1st edn. O'Reilly Media Inc., Sebastopol (2011)
15. Mercedes-Benz Connectivity Services GmbH: Car Configurator API 1.0. https:// developer.mercedes-benz.com/products/car_configurator/specification. Accessed 1 Oct 2020
16. Neumann, A., Laranjeiro, N., Bernardino, J.: An analysis of public REST web service APIs. IEEE Trans. Serv. Comput.(2018)
17. Craig, P.: Canada Holidays API 1.0. https://canada-holidays.ca/api. Accessed 1 Oct 2020
18. Pennington, J., Socher, R., Manning, C.D.: GloVe: global vectors for word representation. In: Proceedings of the 2014 Conference on Empirical Methods in Natural Language Processing (EMNLP), pp. 1532–1543. Association for Computational Linguistics, Doha (2014). https://doi.org/10.3115/v1/D14-1162
19. Renzel, D., Schlebusch, P., Klamma, R.: Today's top "RESTful" services and why they are not RESTful. In: Wang, X.S., Cruz, I., Delis, A., Huang, G. (eds.) WISE 2012. LNCS, vol. 7651, pp. 354–367. Springer, Heidelberg (2012). https://doi.org/ 10.1007/978-3-642-35063-4_26
20. SmartBear Software: SwaggerHub Registry API 1.0.47. https://app.swaggerhub. com/apis/swagger-hub/registry-api/1.0.47. Accessed 1 Oct 2020
21. Spotify, A.B.: Web API v1. https://developer.spotify.com/documentation/web-api/. Accessed 1 Oct 2020
22. Webber, J., Parastatidis, S., Robinson, I.: REST in Practice: Hypermedia and Systems Architecture, 1st edn. O'Reilly Media Inc., Sebastopol (2010)
23. Zoom Video Communications Inc.: Zoom API 2.0.0. https://marketplace.zoom.us/ docs/api-reference/zoom-api. Accessed 1 Oct 2020

Domain-Driven Service Design
Context Modeling, Model Refactoring and Contract Generation

Stefan Kapferer$^{(\boxtimes)}$ and Olaf Zimmermann

University of Applied Sciences of Eastern Switzerland (HSR/OST),
Oberseestrasse 10, 8640 Rapperswil, Switzerland
{stefan.kapferer,olaf.zimmermann}@ost.ch

Abstract. Service-oriented architectures and microservices have gained much attention in recent years; companies adopt these concepts and supporting technologies in order to increase agility, scalability, and maintainability of their systems. Decomposing an application into multiple independently deployable, appropriately sized services and then integrating them is challenging. Domain-driven Design (DDD) is a popular approach to identify (micro-)services by modeling so-called Bounded Contexts and Context Maps. In our previous work, we proposed a Domain-specific Language (DSL) that leverages the DDD patterns to support service modeling and decomposition. The DSL is implemented in Context Mapper, a tool that allows software architects and system integrators to create domain-driven designs that are both human- and machine-readable. However, we have not covered the tool architecture, the iterative and incremental refinement of such maps, and the transition from DDD pattern-based models to (micro-)service-oriented architectures yet. In this paper, we introduce the architectural concepts of Context Mapper and seven model refactorings supporting decomposition criteria that we distilled from the literature and own industry experience; they are grouped and serve as part of a service design elaboration method. We also introduce a novel service contract generation approach that leverages a new, technology-independent Microservice Domain-Specific Language (MDSL). These research contributions are implemented in Context Mapper and being validated using empirical methods.

Keywords: Domain-driven Design · Domain-Specific Language · Microservices · Model-driven software engineering · Service-oriented architecture · Architectural Refactorings

1 Introduction

Domain-driven Design (DDD) was introduced in a practitioner book in 2003 [8]. Tactical DDD patterns such as Aggregate, Entity, Value Object, Factory, and Repository have been used in software engineering to model complex domains in an object-oriented way since then. While these tactical patterns focus on the

© Springer Nature Switzerland AG 2020
S. Dustdar (Ed.): SummerSOC 2020, CCIS 1310, pp. 189–208, 2020.
https://doi.org/10.1007/978-3-030-64846-6_11

domain model of an application, strategic ones such as Bounded Context and Context Map establish domain model scopes as well as the relationships between such scopes. The strategic DDD patterns have gained attention through the popularity of microservices recently [33].

The tactical part within a Bounded Context can be modeled with UML or existing Domain-Specific Languages (DSLs) for DDD such as Sculptor[1]. Existing modeling tools have not supported the strategic patterns explicitly; Context Maps that use these relationships have had to be created manually so far. Hence, Context Mapper[2] [18] proposes and implements a DSL that allows business analysts, software architects, and system integrators to describe such models in a precise and expressive way.

The identification of Bounded Contexts is still a difficult task. Conflicting criteria have to be applied when splitting a domain into Bounded Contexts or monolithic systems into services. Many such criteria have been proposed by practitioners and researchers. However, not many concrete practices and systematic approaches how to decompose the models exist to date. Thus, we researched the criteria to be used for service decomposition and derived a series of Architectural Refactorings (ARs) [34] to decompose DDD-based models written in the Context Mapper DSL (CML) iteratively and incrementally.

Furthermore, the DDD patterns do not define how to realize the modeled contexts in (micro-)service-oriented architectures. We propose a mapping from the DDD patterns to Microservice API patterns (MAP) concepts[3] and Microservice Domain-Specific Language (MDSL)[4], a novel, technology-independent service contract and API description language.

In summary, the contributions of this paper are: a) a novel, layered and extensible tool architecture for DDD-based architecture modeling and discovery, b) a model refactoring catalog, tool, and method and c) a meta-model mapping (from DDD to service-oriented architectures) that allows Context Mapper to generate technology-independent service contracts (MDSL).

The remainder of this paper is structured as follows. Section 2 introduces key DDD concepts and patterns, and explains them in a fictitious insurance example. The section also establishes the context and vision of our work. Section 3 introduces our three research contributions: the modular and extensible tool architecture, a model refactoring catalog and method, and a service contract generation approach for DDD Context Maps. In Sect. 4 we outline our validation activities including prototyping, action research and case studies. Section 5 covers related work. Finally, Sect. 6 summarizes the paper and outlines future work. Appendix A introduces MDSL.

---

[1] http://sculptorgenerator.org/.

[2] https://contextmapper.org/.

[3] https://microservice-api-patterns.org/.

[4] https://microservice-api-patterns.github.io/MDSL-Specification/.

2   Context, Vision, and Previous Work

2.1   Domain-Driven Design (DDD) Pattern Essentials

Since the publication of the first DDD book by Evans [8], other – mostly gray –
literature has been published [33]. Our interpretation of the patterns primarily
follows the guidelines from Evans and Vernon. The CML language [18] supports
the strategic as well as the tactical patterns based on these books. Strategic
DDD is used to decompose a domain into Subdomains and so-called Bounded
Contexts (i.e., abstractions of (sub-)systems and teams). A Bounded Context
establishes a boundary within which a particular domain model applies. The
domain model has to be consistent within this boundary and the terms of the
domain have to be clearly defined to build a *ubiquitous language*. The Context Map describes the relationships between these Bounded Contexts. Figure 1
illustrates a Context Map of the fictitious insurance application called Lakeside
Mutual[5]. The strategic patterns Partnership and Shared Kernel describe symmetric relationships where two Bounded Contexts have organizational or domain
model related interdependencies. In Upstream-Downstream relationships on the
other hand only one Bounded Context is dependent on the other. The upstream-
downstream metaphor indicates the *influence flow* between teams and systems
as discussed by Plöd [26].

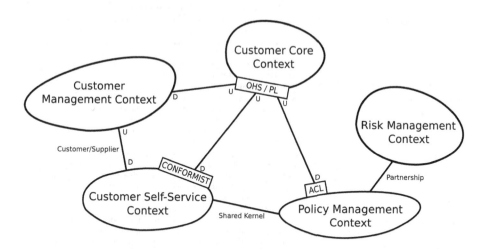

Fig. 1. Context map: lakeside mutual microservice project

The patterns Open Host Service (OHS), Published Language (PL),
Anticorruption-Layer (ACL) and Conformist allow the modelers to specify the
roles of the upstream and downstream Bounded Contexts. Table 1 introduces
the strategic DDD patterns relevant for this paper and depicted in Fig. 1.

---

[5] https://github.com/Microservice-API-Patterns/LakesideMutual/.

Table 1. Strategic Domain-driven Design (DDD) pattern overview

Pattern	Description
Subdomain	A subdomain is a part(ition) of the functional domain that is analyzed and designed. DDD differentiates between *core domains*, *supporting subdomains*, and *generic subdomains* [8]. Subdomains (or parts of them) are realized by one or more Bounded Contexts.
Bounded Context	A Bounded Context establishes a boundary within which a particular domain model is valid. The concepts of the domain must be defined clearly and distinctively within this boundary, constituting a *ubiquitous language* [8] for it. As abstractions of (sub-)systems and teams, Bounded Contexts realize parts of one or more subdomains.
Context Map	A Context Map specifies the relationships between the Bounded Contexts and how they interact with each other.
Customer/Supplier (C/S)	A Customer/Supplier (C/S) relationship is an Upstream-Downstream relationship in which the downstream Bounded Context influences the upstream a lot. The upstream supplier respects the requirements of its downstream customer and adjusts its planning accordingly.
Open Host Service (OHS)	If an upstream team has to provide the same functionality to multiple downstreams, it can implement a unified and open API, an Open Host Service (OHS).
Published Language (PL)	A context which offers functionalities to other contexts has to expose some parts of its own domain model. Direct translations and exposing internals of the domain model impose coupling. Industry standards or organization-internal specifications establish a well-documented and agreed-upon model subset, a Published Language (PL). This allows providers to guarantee language stability.
Anticorruption Layer (ACL)	A downstream Bounded Context has to integrate with the exposed model of the upstream which may not harmonize with its own domain model. In this case the downstream team can decide to implement an Anticorruption Layer (ACL) that translates between the two models and provides the upstream's functionality in terms of the downstream's own domain model to reduce coupling.
Conformist (CF)	A downstream may decide to simply run with the domain model of the upstream (and not implement an ACL). Rather than translating between two different domain models, the downstream adjusts its own design so that it fits to the upstream domain model (tight coupling).
Partnership (P)	A Partnership is a cooperative, symmetric relationship in which the two Bounded Contexts can only succeed or fail together. The pattern advises to establish a process for coordinated planning of development and joint management of integration in case two contexts are mutually dependent subsystems or teams.
Shared Kernel (SK)	A Shared Kernel is a very intimate relationship between two Bounded Contexts that share a part of their domain models. Shared Kernel is a symmetric relationship that is typically implemented as a shared library maintained by the two teams in charge of the two contexts

The tactical DDD patterns are used to design the domain model within a Bounded Context. An Aggregate is a cluster of domain objects which is kept consistent with respect to invariants. It typically represents a unit of work regarding system (database) transactions. Each Bounded Context consists of a set of Aggregates that cluster Entities, Value Objects, Services, and Domain Events.

Entities have an identity and a life cycle (mutable state); Value Objects are immutable and faceless. Both Entities and Value Objects may define attributes and methods; Services expose methods only. Domain Events record things that have happened and are worth reporting (for instance, changes to an Entity's state).

2.2   Vision, Goals, and Our Previous Work

Decomposing a software system into modules, components or services has long been an open research question and challenging problem in practice. In 1972 Parnas wrote a seminal paper [24] on the criteria to be used for decomposing systems. Since then, many other researchers and practitioners proposed criteria and approaches to tackle the challenge. Many practitioners, especially in the microservice community, suggest to use the strategic DDD patterns to answer the decomposition question. Systems shall be modeled in terms of Bounded Contexts in order to implement one (micro-)service per Bounded Context later. Context Maps and *context mapping* as a practice shall support the DDD adopters in identifying Bounded Contexts and in modeling the relationships between them. However, the identification of the contexts is still challenging. A clear understanding of how the DDD patterns can be combined is often missing, and the hand-drawn models do not offer the possibility to apply concrete refactoring steps or systematic decomposition approaches. Hence, our first hypothesis is:

Software architects and system integrators can benefit from a modeling language that lets them describe Context Maps in a precise manner and offers the possibility to apply systematic decompositions and model transformations. The language can further support business analysts describing a problem domain and its subdomains in a natural, yet precise and ubiquitous language.

Motivated by this hypothesis we realized the Context Mapper open source tool and proposed the CML Domain-specific Language (DSL) [18] to describe such models. Software architectures evolve and Context Maps must emerge iteratively. Brandolini [4] has shown how Context Maps can evolve and how Bounded Contexts can be identified step by step. A precise, machine-readable modeling approach allows us to offer transformations to improve the architecture in an agile way and generate other representations such as (micro-) service contracts out of the models. Our second hypothesis captures this vision:

Adopters of DDD who model Context Maps in a precise manner benefit from tools that allow them to evolve the architecture semi-automatically (i.e., supported by service decomposition heuristics and model refactorings), document the architecture, and generate other representations of the models such as Unified Modeling Language (UML) diagrams and service API contracts.

In our previous work [18] we introduced the CML language. Listing 2.1 illustrates the Lakeside Mutual Context Map modeled in CML. The symbol ->

depicts directed Upstream-Downstream relationships; <-> depicts symmetric relationships. The relationship patterns from Table 1 appear in square brackets [ ] (this is optional). The language reference can be found online[6].

Listing 2.1. Context Map Syntax in CML

```
ContextMap LakesideMutualSubsystemsAndTeams {
  contains CustomerCore, CustomerManagement, CustomerSelfService
  contains PolicyManagement, RiskManagement

  CustomerCore [OHS,PL] -> CustomerManagement // influence flow: left to right

  CustomerSelfService [C ] <- [S] CustomerManagement // flow: right to left

  CustomerCore [OHS, PL] -> [CF] CustomerSelfService

  CustomerCore [OHS, PL] -> [ACL] PolicyManagement

  PolicyManagement [P] <-> [P] RiskManagement // Partnership (symmetric)

  CustomerSelfService [SK] <-> [SK] PolicyManagement // Shared Kernel
}
```

We also proposed a meta-model for the strategic DDD patterns previously [18]. It clarifies how the patterns can be combined in Context Maps. We also presented a set of semantic rules that outline pattern combinations that do not make sense according to our interpretation. The Context Mapper tool implements these semantic rules to enforce that they are met by CML models.

3   Context Mapper Concepts

In this section, we first introduce the Context Mapper tool architecture, which combines elements from language tool design (editors, linters) with a layered organization of refactorings and transformations. Next we establish a method for the stepwise refinement of DDD models via model refactoring, which supports common decomposition criteria from the literature and is implemented in Context Mapper. Finally, we specify how to map DDD models to service contracts; this mapping is also implemented in Context Mapper.

3.1   Modular and Extensible Tool Architecture

The Context Mapper framework architecture illustrated in Figure 2 includes multiple components that allow users to *discover, systematically decompose*, and *refactor* DDD Context Maps. In addition, the generators support transforming the models into other representations. The Context Mapper DSL (CML) grammar and tool constitute the hub of the three-stage architecture; all other components are integrated as spokes.

The Discovery Library shall support users in brownfield projects to reverse engineer Context Maps and Bounded Contexts from source code. The design of the library supports the users in implementing arbitrary discovery mechanisms

---

[6] https://contextmapper.org/docs/language-reference/.

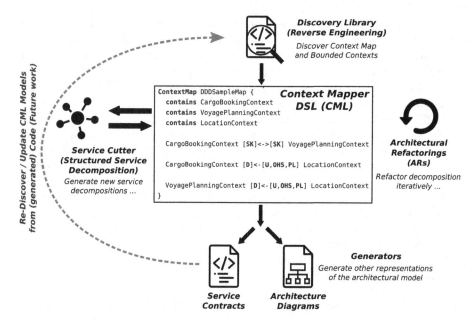

Fig. 2. Context mapper framework architecture: three stages, DSL as Hub

by applying the Strategy pattern [14]. The Architectural Refactorings (ARs) [34] (a.k.a. model refactorings) represent one component of the architecture and shall assist the users in decomposing a system step by step. In Sect. 3.2 we will present the AR component in detail. The Structured Service Decomposition component integrates Service Cutter [10] to derive completely new Context Maps by using coupling criteria and graph clustering algorithms. In addition, it is possible to generate PlantUML diagrams, graphical Context Maps (.svg, .png), or technology-independent service contracts (MDSL) with the generators. Discovery Library and Service Cutter integration are out of scope of this paper.

All black arrows in Fig. 2 are implemented and open sourced. In the future we plan to close the "model-code" gap indicated by the dashed arrow in Fig. 2. Through an enhanced Discovery Library it shall be possible to update the CML model if generated artifacts such as contracts or code are changed manually.

3.2   Model Refactoring: Catalog, Tool Integration, and Method

In this section we propose a series of model refactorings that allow modelers to decompose DDD Context Maps, written in CML, in an iterative manner. They allow to improve the modeled architectures and/or decompose a monolithic system by splitting up Bounded Contexts and Aggregates step by step. The ARs are derived from decomposition criteria (DCs) researched in mostly gray literature and our own practical experience. They are implemented as model transformations for the CML language in the Context Mapper tool.

A) Distillation of Decomposition Criteria. The refactorings proposed in this paper are based on criteria to be used for service decomposition. We researched such criteria from literature, the already existing coupling criteria catalog of Gysel et al. [10], and our own professional experience [3,17]. The conducted literature covered research papers such as the one of Parnas [24] and practitioners articles and online posts from DDD experts such as Brandolini [4], Plöd [27], Tune and Millet [32] or Tigges [31].

We describe our decomposition criteria and how we derived them in [16]. We selected a set of five DCs in order to derive and implement prototypical ARs from the collected criteria. To do so, we applied the following selection criteria:

- *Relevance in practice*: We chose criteria that are relevant for all software projects and not only in specific contexts.
- *Representativeness*: Criteria which are mentioned by multiple sources were preferred in our selection process.
- *Generality*: The set of criteria and derived ARs was chosen so that others could be implemented in a similar way.

Applying the above criteria yielded the following DCs (details appear in [16]):

- *DC-1: Business entities*: It is common to group attributes and entities which belong to the same part of the domain. These areas or parts of the domain form *linguistic* or *domain expert* boundaries [32].
- *DC-2: Use cases*: It is often recommended to group domain objects which are used by the same use cases together.
- *DC-3: Code owners/development teams*: Bounded Contexts are often built around the owners of the code (development teams).
- *DC-4: Likelihood for change*: According to Parnas [24], one should isolate things that change often from things that do not.
- *DC-5: Generalized Non-functional Requirement (NFR)*: NFRs often differ by subsystem or component. In Context Mapper, model elements that are similar with respect to an NFR can be grouped. Such NFRs could be *mutability*, *storage similarity*, *availability*, or *security*.

From the DCs listed above we then derived ARs that allow refactoring DDD Context Maps. For the prototypical implementation in our Context Mapper tool[7] we focused on Aggregates and Bounded Contexts. To be able to (de-)compose these objects, we realized ARs that are able to *split* or *merge* Aggregates or Bounded Contexts. Other ARs offer the possibility to *extract* Aggregates from a Bounded Context and build a new context based on them. Figure 3 illustrates the resulting ARs derived.

In our technical report [16] we elaborated *context*, *motivation*, and *solution and effect* for all ARs presented in this paper. Figure 3 exhibits this template structure for one exemplary refactoring (AR-3).

---

[7] https://contextmapper.org/.

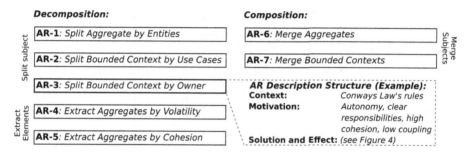

Fig. 3. Architectural/model refactorings by operation and element

B) Realization of Refactorings as Model Transformations for CML.

The CML language leverages Xtext[8], a DSL framework building on the Eclipse Modeling Framework (EMF) [30]. As described in [15], we implemented the ARs presented above as model transformations for CML. ARs are applied to a CML model in three steps:

1. DSL Text $\xrightarrow{parsing}$ Abstract Syntax Tree (AST) $\rightarrow$ EMF Model
2. EMF Model $\xrightarrow{transformation}$ EMF Model
3. EMF Model $\rightarrow$ Abstract Syntax Tree (AST) $\xrightarrow{unparsing}$ DSL Text

Figure 4 shows an example Bounded Context, written in CML, on which the refactoring *Split Bounded Context by Owner* can be applied. The illustrated Bounded Context contains two Aggregates which are owned by different teams.

```
BoundedContext CustomerSelfServiceContext {
  type APPLICATION
  domainVisionStatement "This context shall manage ..."
  responsibilities "Address changes", "Claim submissions"

  Aggregate CustomerFrontend {
  owner CustomerFrontendTeam

    Entity CustomerAddressChange {
    aggregateRoot

    -UserAccount issuer
    Address changedAddress
    }
  }
Aggregate Accounts {
owner CustomerBackendTeam

  Entity UserAccount {
  aggregateRoot

    String username
    Customer accountCustomer
    }
  }
}

BoundedContext CustomerFrontendTeam { type TEAM }
BoundedContext CustomerBackendTeam { type TEAM }
```

Split Bounded Context by Owner ➡

```
BoundedContext CustomerSelfServiceContext {
  type APPLICATION
  domainVisionStatement "This context shall manage ..."
  responsibilities "Address changes", "Claim submissions"

  Aggregate CustomerFrontend {
  owner CustomerFrontendTeam

    Entity CustomerAddressChange {
    aggregateRoot

    -UserAccount issuer
    Address changedAddress
    }
  }
}

BoundedContext NewBoundedContext1 {
  Aggregate Accounts {
  owner CustomerBackendTeam

    Entity UserAccount {
    aggregateRoot

      String username
      Customer accountCustomer
      }
    }
}

BoundedContext CustomerFrontendTeam { type TEAM }
BoundedContext CustomerBackendTeam { type TEAM }
```

Fig. 4. Example refactoring: split bounded context by owner (team)

---

[8] https://www.eclipse.org/Xtext/.

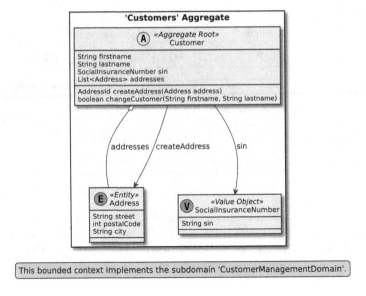

Fig. 5. Generated PlantUML diagram for an aggregate

Striving for autonomous teams with clear responsibilities, an application of this AR ensures that only one team works on a Bounded Context. Applied to this example, the AR creates a new Bounded Context for one of the Aggregates.

Once the architecture model has been refactored, one can use our generators to transform the Context Map into other representations. In previous work [18] we introduced our PlantUML[9] generator. Figure 5 illustrates an example of a PlantUML diagram generated with Context Mapper. It shows another simple Aggregate of our fictitious insurance scenario (two Entities, one Value Object).

C) Stepwise Application of the Refactorings. The ARs presented above are designed to decompose an application incrementally. Figure 6 outlines a logical process to decompose a system including a suggested order of AR applications. Note that the logical order does not mandate a strict, one-time chronological execution of the steps; other decomposition strategies can be applied as well. The process might be repeated multiple times.

One has to analyze the domain and identify an initial set of subdomains early in a(ny) project. Context Mapper allows the users to model the entities that a subdomain contains. From use cases, user stories, or techniques such as Event Storming [5], a set of initial Bounded Contexts has to be identified.

The given contexts can then be decomposed iteratively. As indicated in Fig. 6, Bounded Contexts are typically formed around the features or use cases (AR-2). If teams are getting too big during the project the contexts might be split accordingly (AR-3). During the implementation and maintenance of the software it may

---

[9] https://plantuml.com/.

become clear which parts of the software exhibit increased volatility. This may lead to additional decompositions (AR-4). AR-5 can then be further adapt the decomposition according to quality attributes (QAs) and non-functional requirements (NFRs). AR-7 allows inverting the mentioned operations and merging split Bounded Contexts.

Figure 6 further illustrates that a Bounded Context is defined by one or multiple Aggregates that can be decomposed by Entities (AR-1). They can be merged again with AR-6, similar to Bounded Contexts. The Context Map relationship definitions and their knowledge which Aggregates are exposed in such relationships finally allow us to generate MDSL (micro-)service contracts.

3.3   Metamodel-Based Service Contract Generation

As another contribution, we developed a service contract generator that maps the DDD patterns to MAP patterns, and therefore specifies how such Context Map models can be transformed into a (micro-)service-oriented architecture.

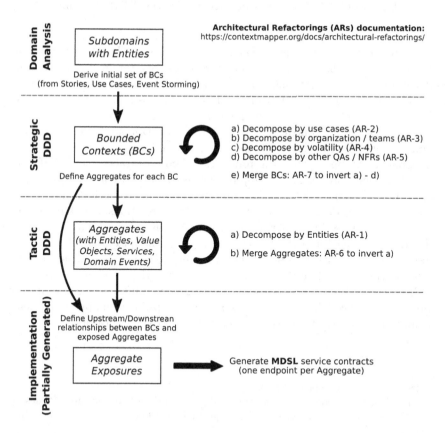

Fig. 6. Incremental, stepwise Architectural Refactoring (AR) application process

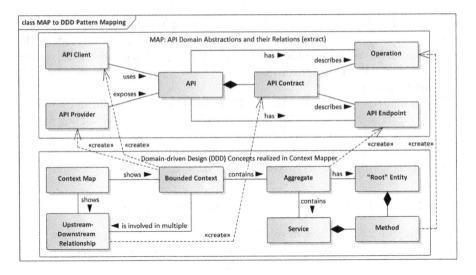

Fig. 7. MAP API domain model [20] to strategic DDD Mapping

The architecture models using Domain-driven Design (DDD) patterns allow users to describe the decomposition of a software system. However, these models do not indicate how such a system shall be implemented as microservices. The Microservice API Patterns (MAP)[10] discuss how such microservices shall be implemented and offer corresponding design patterns. As a DSL to denote (micro-)service contracts[11], the Microservice Domain-Specific Language (MDSL)[12] supports the *API Description*[13] pattern.

A Context Mapper generator produces MDSL contracts from CML Context Maps, hence proposing a mapping between the two concepts that specifies how DDD-based models can be implemented as microservices. Lübke et al. [20] presented the domain abstractions and their relationships that are part of such microservice API descriptions. Figure 7 illustrates a simplified version of this domain model and the mapping. An API description [20] describes the exposed endpoints with its operations. An operation expects and delivers specific data types. The described API is used by an API client and exposed by an API provider. Table reftab:dddspstospsmdslspsmappingspstable describes the mappings introduced in Figure reffigspsmapspstospsdddspsmapping in detail; Appendix A then introduces MDSL including its MAP decorators.

---

[10] https://microservice-api-patterns.org/.

[11] A *contract* is not a pair of *precondition and postcondition* here, but an *API description* that specifies and governs the message exchange between two services or subsystems.

[12] https://microservice-api-patterns.github.io/MDSL-Specification/.

[13] https://microservice-api-patterns.org/patterns/foundation/APIDescription.

Table 2. DDD context map to service contract mapping

DDD concept	MAP concept	Description
Bounded Contexts (that are upstream in a relationship)	API contract	As many DDD experts we suggest to implement one microservice per Bounded Context. Therefore, we create one API contract per context.
Aggregates exposed by Upstream	API endpoint	We suggest to create a separate endpoint for every Aggregate.
Methods in Aggregate root Entities or Services	Operation	From methods defined in root Entities or Services that are part of the Aggregate we derive operations.
Parameters and return types of the methods mentioned above	Data type definitions (referenced in request and response messages of operations)	The methods that are mapped to API operations as described above declare parameters and return types. From these types we derive corresponding data type definitions.
Upstream Bounded Context	API provider	The upstream context in an Upstream-Downstream relationship exposes parts of his domain model to be used by the downstream. It is therefore the API provider.
Downstream Bounded Context	API client	The downstream context uses parts of the domain model that are exposed by the upstream. It is therefore mapped to the API client

The MDSL generator in Context Mapper is documented online[14]. The following Listing 3.1 shows an excerpt of an example MDSL contract generated from the Lakeside Mutual insurance project we modeled in CML.

---

[14] https://contextmapper.org/docs/mdsl/.

Listing 3.1. MDSL Example Contract

```
API description CustomerCoreAPI // a.k.a. service contract
usage context PUBLIC_API for BACKEND_INTEGRATION and FRONTEND_INTEGRATION

data type Customer { "firstname":D<string>, "lastname":D<string>,
                     "sin":SocialInsuranceNumber, "addresses":Address* }
data type SocialInsuranceNumber { "sin":D<string> }
data type Address { "street":D<string>, "postalCode":D<int>, "city":D<string> }
data type AddressId P // placeholder, AddressId not specified in detail
data type createAddressParameter { "customer":Customer, "address":Address }

endpoint type CustomersAggregate
  exposes
    operation createAddress
      expecting
        payload createAddressParameter
      delivering
        payload AddressId
    operation changeAddress
      expecting
        payload Address
      delivering
        payload D<bool>

API provider CustomerCoreProvider
  offers CustomersAggregate
  at endpoint location "http://localhost:8000"
    via protocol "RESTful HTTP"

API client CustomerSelfServiceClient
  consumes CustomersAggregate
API client CustomerManagementClient
  consumes CustomersAggregate
API client PolicyManagementClient
  consumes CustomersAggregate
```

The first block of the contract describes the data types that are used by the operations. The middle part lists the API endpoints with its operations. Each operation declares the data types that it expects and delivers. The last part of the contract declares the API providers and clients, derived from the upstream and downstream Bounded Contexts.

DDD and Context Mapper promote SOA and cloud principles such as isolated state, distribution and loose coupling.

Our contract generator contributes a mapping to derive candidate service architectures from DDD Context Maps. Further automation is possible, for instance microservice project stubs (i.e., client and server code) can also be generated, as well as elastic infrastructure code.

4   Validation

We hypothesized that DDD adopters and service designers can benefit from Context Mapper as a modeling tool providing architectural/model refactorings in Sect. 2.2. The main objective of our ongoing validation activities is to show that the tool is indeed useful and beneficial for the target user group. We validate the tool according to the recommendations of Shaw [29] to demonstrate *correctness*, *usefulness* and *effectiveness*. Hence, we apply empirical validation strategies such as prototyping, action research [1] and case study.

Our Context Mapper implementation prototype uses the Xtext DSL framework in version 2.20.0 and is offered as plugin in the Eclipse marketplace[15] (it is compatible with Eclipse 4.8 and newer). The tool is developed iteratively using CI/CD pipelines[16]; at the time of writing, 55 releases have been made. Context Mapper is listed in our Design Practice Repository[17].

Context Mapper implements the Architectural Refactorings (ARs) from Sect. 3 (and several more) as code refactorings for the Context Mapping DSL (CML). These ARs have to be validated w.r.t. their usefulness and effectiveness. During their implementation, we conducted action research to improve the concepts iteratively in short feedback cycles. We modeled larger, realistic sample projects such as *Lakeside Mutual*[18] with CML; an examples repository[19] is available. We also conducted a case study on a real-world project in the healthcare sector [11]. Another real-world use (case study, action research) of Context Mapper is an ongoing research collaboration with a fintech startup; requirements and technical designs of the startup and its clients are modelled in CML with the objective to be able to rapidly respond to business model changes on the API design level. We further used the tool as part of an exercise accompanying the DDD lesson of the software architecture course at our institution and collected the feedback of more than 20 exercise participants. We were able to evaluate the simplicity of the tool usage and could improve it according to the feedback.

Using a DSL also has its weaknesses. For example: members of the agile community might argue that it does conform with agile practices ("working software over comprehensive documentation"). The "model-code" gap [9] is a weakness of most DSL tools and generators.

The validation results so far support our hypothesis that the target user group can indeed benefit from refactorings implemented as model transformations to ease the creation, evolution and usage of DDD in general and Context Maps in particular; we have to further validate the ARs and their systematic application.

5   Related Work

Domain-Driven Design (DDD) Tools. DDD has not only been adopted by practitioner communities, but is picked up in academia as well [7,12,19,21, 23,25,28]. However, very few tools specific to DDD exist; agile modeling on whiteboards is commonly practiced. UML tools can be profiled to support DDD as well. None of the existing tools uses a hub-and-spoke architecture.

---

[15] https://marketplace.eclipse.org/content/context-mapper/.
[16] https://travis-ci.com/github/ContextMapper/.
[17] https://github.com/socadk/design-practice-repository/.
[18] https://github.com/Microservice-API-Patterns/LakesideMutual/.
[19] https://github.com/ContextMapper/context-mapper-examples/.

Architectural Refactorings. The Architectural Refactorings (ARs) [34] proposed in this paper are derived from criteria that are known to be used to decompose software systems. Many of the criteria used to do this are mentioned by the coupling criteria catalog[20] of Service Cutter [10]. The first research paper regarding this topic was published by Parnas [24]. His approach separates parts that change often from other parts of the system. Tune and Millet [32] mention use cases and other domain heuristics such as language, domain expert boundaries, business process steps, data flow, or ownership as criteria that have to be considered. They also mention the importance of co-evolving organizational and technical boundaries which is known as "Conway's Law" [6].

A similar list of criteria has been proposed by Tigges [31]. Linguistic and model differences are the primary drivers for Bounded Context identification according to Plöd [27]. He emphasizes that microservice characteristics such as the organization around business capabilities[21], decentralized governance, and evolutionary design suit the idea behind Bounded Contexts. Brandolini [4] explains how Context Maps can evolve in iterative steps. He recommends *event storming* [5], a workshop technique to analyze domains and derive Bounded Contexts.

These and many other DDD experts propose criteria and practices for decomposing a software system. However, none of them propose concrete systematic or algorithmic solutions for the decomposition process. Our ARs aim at formalizing this process and offer concrete procedures and steps that can be realized as code refactorings for DDD-based modeling languages such as CML.

To the best of our knowledge, comparable architecture modeling tools that are based on strategic DDD patterns do not exist. As Mens and Tourwé [22] mention, there has been a trend towards refactorings on design level. For example Boger et al. [2] discuss refactorings on the level of UML diagrams. Although no similar DSLs with refactorings exist, the technical concept behind them is not new. The ARs are implemented as model transformations [15] that are applied to the Eclipse Modeling Framework (EMF) models [30] behind our Xtext-based DSL [18]. Ivkovic and Kontogiannis [13] introduce another approach to refactor software architecture artifacts using model transformations.

Microservice Contract Generation. With our Microservices Domain-Specific Language (MDSL) contract generator we provide a tool that supports architects regarding the question how DDD-based architecture models can be implemented as microservices. The OpenAPI initiative[22] formerly known as Swagger[23] is a popular notation for HTTP resource API contracts; many tools exist, including editors, test tools and server stub and client proxy code gererators.

---

[20] https://github.com/ServiceCutter/ServiceCutter/wiki/Coupling-Criteria/.
[21] https://searchapparchitecture.techtarget.com/definition/business-capability/.
[22] https://www.openapis.org/.
[23] https://swagger.io/.

6 Summary and Outlook

In this paper we presented the concepts of Context Mapper and its open source tools. Context Mapper provides an architecture modeling language supporting strategic and tactic Domain-driven Design (DDD). As our research contributions, we proposed a) a modular and extensible framework architecture for DDD-based modeling tools, b) a tool-supported refactoring catalog and method for decomposing systems step by step from DDD Context Maps, and c) a mapping from DDD to the domain model of the Microservice API patterns (MAP) language that specifies how DDD models can be realized as microservice contracts, expressed in the emerging Microservice Domain-Specific Language (MDSL). The provided tool capabilities support DDD adopters in formalizing DDD Context Maps and evolving them in an iterative manner.

Our validation via implementation (prototyping), action research, and case studies already support our hypothesis that the modeling language and the transformation tools can support architects when modeling domain-driven designs and decomposing software systems. Additional validation activities are required to find out whether the proposed ARs are sufficient or will have to be extended.

In our future work we plan to evolve and enhance Context Mapper by extending its framework components. The tool shall evolve into a modeling framework that not only allows describing models and generating contracts from them, but also supports software maintainers that reverse engineer models from source code. The AR-based decomposition method will be validated and matured further. In addition, we could support additional analysis and design transformations and let the service contract generator create microservice project stubs. Using the JDL of JHipster[24], a popular rapid application development platform (generating JavaScript frontends and Java/Spring backends from architectural input) is another direction towards generating client and server code. Last but not least, providing support for multiple IDEs (for instance, Visual Studio Code) can (and already has) increased our user group.

Acknowledgements. This work was supported by the Hasler Foundation (https://haslerstiftung.ch/) in the project "Domain-Driven Digital Service Engineering".

A Appendix: Introduction to MDSL

Microservice Domain-Specific Language (MDSL)[25] abstracts from technology-specific interface description languages such as OpenAPI/Swagger, WSDL, and Protocol Buffers. MDSL design principles are a) promote platform and protocol independence with a modular language structure separating abstract contracts from provider bindings, b) support agile modeling practices with partial specifications and c) promote readability over parsing efficiency.

---

[24] https://www.jhipster.tech/jdl/.

[25] https://microservice-api-patterns.github.io/MDSL-Specification/index.

The abstract syntax of MDSL is inspired and driven by the domain model and concepts of Microservice API Patterns (MAP), featuring endpoints, operations, and data representation elements [20]. The concrete syntax of *service endpoint contracts* is elaborate; the concrete syntax of *data contracts* is compact yet simple. It generalizes data exchange formats such as JSON and type systems in service-centric programming languages such as Ballerina and Jolie. Endpoint, operation, and one representation element can be decorated with patterns from MAP[20]; these decorator annotations are first-class language concepts that can be processed by tools later. For instance, API linters may validate them, and they could influence the output of cloud deployment scripts.

Most programming languages declare variables by name and type; MDSL uses a *name-role-type* triple (e.g., `"customerName": ID<String>`) to specify *Atomic Parameters*. The role can be any *element stereotype* from MAP (i.e., ID(entifier), Link, Data, or Metadata). A generic, unspecified placeholder P can replace role and type; the parameter name is optional if the role is defined. Implementing the *Parameter Tree* pattern from MAP, simple (yet powerful) nesting is supported in an object- and block-like curly brace syntax `{{...},
{...}}` known from data representation languages such as JSON. Cardinalities such as `?`, `*`, `+` can be specified as well. Listing A.1 gives an example:

Listing A.1. MDSL Example: Data Contract and Endpoint Contract

```
API description HelloWorldAPI // a.k.a. service contract
data type SampleDTO {ID, D<int>} // partially specified tree (two leaves)

endpoint type HelloWorldEndpoint serves as PROCESSING_RESOURCE // MAP decorator
exposes
  operation sayHello with responsibility  COMPUTATION_FUNCTION // MAP decorator
    expecting payload "greeting": D<string>+ // one or more greetings
    delivering payload <<error_report>> SampleDTO // MAP decorator (<<pattern>>)

API provider HelloWorldAPIProvider1
  offers HelloWorldEndpoint
  at endpoint location "https://..." via protocol HTTP
API client HelloWorldAPIClient1
  consumes HelloWorldEndpoint
  from HelloWorldAPIProvider1 via protocol HTTP
```

`sayHello` accepts a scalar string value `D<string>` as input. This operation returns a Data Transfer Object (DTO) called `SampleDTO`, which is modeled explicitly so that its specification can be used elsewhere too. `SampleDTO` is specified incompletely: it pairs two atomic parameters, in ID and (D)ata roles, whose names and types have not been specified. This partial yet expressive specification supports early use and continuous refinement. For instance, MDSL specifications can be drafted in workshops with non-technical stakeholders and then completed iteratively and incrementally (e.g, adding data type information).

References

1. Avison, D.E., Lau, F., Myers, M.D., Nielsen, P.A.: Action research. Commun. ACM **42**(1), 94–97 (1999). https://doi.org/10.1145/291469.291479
2. Boger, M., Sturm, T., Fragemann, P.: Refactoring browser for UML. In: Aksit, M., Mezini, M., Unland, R. (eds.) NODe 2002. LNCS, vol. 2591, pp. 366–377. Springer, Heidelberg (2003). https://doi.org/10.1007/3-540-36557-5_26
3. Brandner, M., Craes, M., Oellermann, F., Zimmermann, O.: Web services-oriented architecture in production in the finance industry. Informatik Spektrum **27**(2), 136–145 (2004). https://doi.org/10.1007/s00287-004-0380-2
4. Brandolini, A.: Strategic domain driven design with context mapping (2009). https://www.infoq.com/articles/ddd-contextmapping
5. Brandolini, A.: Introducing EventStorming: An Act of Deliberate Collective Learning. Leanpub (2018)
6. Conway, M.: Conway's law (1968)
7. Di Francesco, P., Lago, P., Malavolta, I.: Migrating towards microservice architectures: an industrial survey. In: 2018 IEEE International Conference on Software Architecture (ICSA), pp. 29–2909, April 2018. https://doi.org/10.1109/ICSA.2018.00012
8. Evans, E.: Domain-Driven Design: Tackling Complexity in the Heart of Software. Addison-Wesley, Boston (2003)
9. Fairbanks, G.: Just Enough Software Architecture: A Risk-driven Approach. Marshall & Brainerd (2010)
10. Gysel, M., Kölbener, L., Giersche, W., Zimmermann, O.: Service cutter: a systematic approach to service decomposition. In: Aiello, M., Johnsen, E.B., Dustdar, S., Georgievski, I. (eds.) ESOCC 2016. LNCS, vol. 9846, pp. 185–200. Springer, Cham (2016). https://doi.org/10.1007/978-3-319-44482-6_12
11. Habegger, M., Schena, M.: Cloud-native refactoring in einem mHealth Szenario. Bachelor thesis, University of Applied Sciences of Eastern Switzerland (HSR FHO) (2019). https://eprints.hsr.ch/806/
12. Hippchen, B., Giessler, P., Steinegger, R., Schneider, M., Abeck, S.: Designing microservice-based applications by using a domain-driven design approach. Int. J. Adv. Softw. **1942–2628**(10), 432–445 (2017)
13. Ivkovic, I., Kontogiannis, K.: A framework for software architecture refactoring using model transformations and semantic annotations. In: Conference on Software Maintenance and Reengineering (CSMR 2006), pp. 10–144, March 2006. https://doi.org/10.1109/CSMR.2006.3
14. Johnson, R., Gamma, E., Vlissides, J., Helm, R.: Design Patterns: Elements of Reusable Object-Oriented Software. Addison-Wesley, Boston (1995)
15. Kapferer, S.: Model transformations for DSL processing. Term project, University of Applied Sciences of Eastern Switzerland (HSR FHO) (2019). https://eprints.hsr.ch/819/
16. Kapferer, S.: Service decomposition as a series of architectural refactorings. Term project, University of Applied Sciences of Eastern Switzerland (HSR FHO) (2019). https://eprints.hsr.ch/784/
17. Kapferer, S., Jost, S.: Attributbasierte Autorisierung in einer Branchenlösung für das Versicherungswesen. Bachelor thesis, University of Applied Sciences of Eastern Switzerland (HSR FHO) (2017). https://eprints.hsr.ch/602/

18. Kapferer, S., Zimmermann, O.: Domain-specific language and tools for strategic domain-driven design, context mapping and bounded context modeling. In: Proceedings of the 8th International Conference on MODELSWARD, pp. 299–306. INSTICC, SciTePress (2020). https://doi.org/10.5220/0008910502990306

19. Landre, E., Wesenberg, H., Rønneberg, H.: Architectural improvement by use of strategic level domain-driven design. In: Companion to the 21st ACM SIGPLAN OOPSLA, pp. 809–814. ACM, New York (2006). https://doi.org/10.1145/1176617.1176728

20. Lübke, D., Zimmermann, O., Pautasso, C., Zdun, U., Stocker, M.: Interface evolution patterns: balancing compatibility and extensibility across service life cycles. In: Proceedings of the 24th European Conference on Pattern Languages of Programs. ACM, New York (2019). https://doi.org/10.1145/3361149.3361164

21. Mazlami, G., Cito, J., Leitner, P.: Extraction of microservices from monolithic software architectures. In: 2017 IEEE International Conference on Web Services (ICWS), pp. 524–531, June 2017. https://doi.org/10.1109/ICWS.2017.61

22. Mens, T., Tourwe, T.: A survey of software refactoring. IEEE Trans. Softw. Eng. **30**(2), 126–139 (2004). https://doi.org/10.1109/TSE.2004.1265817

23. Munezero, I.J., Mukasa, D., Kanagwa, B., Balikuddembe, J.: Partitioning microservices: a domain engineering approach. In: 2018 IEEE/ACM Symposium on Software Engineering in Africa (SEiA), pp. 43–49, May 2018

24. Parnas, D.L.: On the criteria to be used in decomposing systems into modules. Commun. ACM **15**(12), 1053–1058 (1972). https://doi.org/10.1145/361598.361623

25. Pautasso, C., Zimmermann, O., Amundsen, M., Lewis, J., Josuttis, N.: Microservices in practice, part 1: reality check and service design. IEEE Softw. **34**(1), 91–98 (2017). https://doi.org/10.1109/MS.2017.24

26. Plöd, M.: DDD context maps - an enhanced view (2018). https://speakerdeck.com/mploed/context-maps-an-enhanced-view

27. Plöd, M.: Hands-On Domain-Driven Design - By Example. Leanpub (2019)

28. Rademacher, F., Sorgalla, J., Sachweh, S.: Challenges of domain-driven microservice design: a model-driven perspective. IEEE Softw. **35**(3), 36–43 (2018). https://doi.org/10.1109/MS.2018.2141028

29. Shaw, M.: Writing good software engineering research papers: minitutorial. In: Proceedings of the 25th International Conference on Software Engineering, ICSE 2003, pp. 726–736. IEEE Computer Society, Washington, DC (2003). http://dl.acm.org/citation.cfm?id=776816.776925

30. Steinberg, D., Budinsky, F., Merks, E., Paternostro, M.: EMF: Eclipse Modeling Framework. Eclipse Series. Pearson Education, London (2008)

31. Tigges, O.: How to break down a domain to bounded contexts? https://speakerdeck.com/otigges/how-to-break-down-a-domain-to-bounded-contexts. Accessed 14 Feb 2020

32. Tune, N., Millett, S.: Designing Autonomous Teams and Services: Deliver Continuous Business Value Through Organizational Alignment. O'Reilly Media, Newton (2017)

33. Vernon, V.: Implementing Domain-Driven Design. Addison-Wesley, Boston (2013)

34. Zimmermann, O.: Architectural refactoring for the cloud: decision-centric view on cloud migration. Computing **99**(2), 129–145 (2017). https://doi.org/10.1007/s00607-016-0520-y, http://rdcu.be/lFW6

Author Index

Arvaniti-Bofili, Margianna 3

Barzen, Johanna 66, 86
Böhm, Sebastian 127
Breitenbücher, Uwe 66, 86

Chaldeakis, Ilias 3

Decker, Christian 169

Falkenthal, Michael 86

Gkouskos, Stelios 3
Gogolos, Georgios 3

Kalampokis, Konstantinos 3
Kapferer, Stefan 189
Képes, Kálmán 12
Kotstein, Sebastian 169
Kruse, Felix 151

Leymann, Frank 12, 66, 86
Lichtenthäler, Robin 107

Magoutis, Kostas 3
Marx Gómez, Jorge 151
Mitschang, Bernhard 45

Papaioannou, Gerasimos 3
Petridis, Konstantinos 3
Prechtl, Mike 107

Reimann, Peter 45

Salm, Marie 66
Sangiovanni, Mirella 33
Schouten, Gerard 33
Schreier, Ulf 45
Schröer, Christoph 151
van den Heuvel, Willem-Jan 33

Weder, Benjamin 66
Weigold, Manuela 86
Wild, Karoline 66, 86
Wilhelm, Yannick 45
Wirtz, Guido 107, 127

Ziekow, Holger 45
Zimmermann, Michael 12
Zimmermann, Olaf 189

Printed in the United States
By Bookmasters